Singing and Dancing Wherever She Goes

Singing and Dancing Wherever She Goes
A Life of Maud Karpeles

by
Simona Pakenham

London
English Folk Dance and Song Society
2011

Published by EFDSS 2011

Copyright © Simona Pakenham

Simona Pakenham has asserted her right under the Copyright, Designs and Patents Act 1988 to be identified as the author of this work.

This book is sold subject to the condition that it shall not, by way of trade or otherwise, be lent, resold, hired out, or otherwise circulated without the publisher's prior consent in any form of binding or cover other than that in which it is published and without a similar condition, including this condition, being imposed on the subsequent purchaser.

First published in Great Britain in 2011 by the English Folk Dance and Song Society, Cecil Sharp House, 2 Regent's Park Road, London NW1 7AY.

ISBN 978-0-85418-216-9

Text edited by David Atkinson and Malcolm Taylor
Photographs selected and annotated by Rebecca Hughes and Nick Wall
Designed and typeset by Bryan Ledgard
Printed and bound by Henry Ling & Co. Ltd

Contents

Introduction by Malcolm Taylor	vii
Preface	x
Singing and Dancing Wherever She Goes	1
Notes	259
Select Bibliography	265
Select Discography	267
Note on the Author	268
Acknowledgements	269
Index	270

Introduction
by Malcolm Taylor

In the history of fieldwork in folklore, Maud Karpeles ranks very highly, although you could perhaps be forgiven for not realizing this. The publication of this book is consequently important for a number of reasons – not least that part of its own history that is not covered in Simona Pakenham's charming preface. For Maud's unpublished autobiography proved something of a 'hot potato' when it emerged following her death in 1976. In part, this was a consequence of the sheer lack of substance in it about its principal subject, Maud herself. But rumour has it that the typescript was offered for publication to the English Folk Dance and Song Society (EFDSS), only for it to be turned down as 'not shedding any further light on the life of Cecil Sharp'. This is not just inaccurate – if only on account of its insight into Sharp's state of health – but to dismiss Maud's invaluable contribution to the development of the folk revival, fieldwork, the evolution of the English Folk Dance Society (EFDS), and, actually, the life and work of Cecil Sharp, displays an astounding insensitivity and lack of vision on the part of the EFDSS. Why a treatment of her autobiography of the type undertaken here by Simona Pakenham was not attempted at that time is perhaps now beyond our knowing. With this publication, however, the EFDSS can finally put the situation to rights and allow Maud's story be told, mostly in her own words.

This is not a critical biography of Maud, nor is it an attempt at an academic analysis of the context in which she moved and viewed the world. For that you should consult the select bibliography on pp. 265–6, and in particular the work of Georgina Boyes. There you will not find the somewhat rose-tinted glow provided in Maud's very personal account of events, but rather the wider significance of her role in the post-Sharp era. For Maud was undeniably the major force behind the foundation of the International Folk Music Council in the aftermath of the Second World War, at a time when her work with the EFDSS was seemingly done; and it was also Maud who continued Sharp's work in exploring the British song traditions to be found in Newfoundland – another impressive feat.

There is no doubt from reading her Appalachian diaries and the corresponding parts of her autobiography that her time in America with Cecil Sharp was the most important passage of her life, and that Sharp was her inspiration. What does not stand out from the pages is that Maud's own presence was a key ingredient in the endeavour. Contrary to much that has been written about that critical period of collecting, Mike Yates, arguably England's greatest folk music collector of the modern era, has often told me of the warm and generous comments he heard about both Cecil and Maud from singers and musicians he met in Appalachia during his own visits there. These were people whose own families had met, played, and sung for them during the First World War years, and again in the 1950s when Maud returned to the region. Indeed, there is a lovely recording of Emma Shelton in the BBC archives from one of Maud's later visits in which she recounts how Sharp had actually paid for her to attend school, only for her to run away back home on the third day. Mike also recalls with great affection his afternoon teas with Maud at her London flat in the 1960s when he, too, was won over by her charm and presence.

Put yourself, if you can, in the place of Maud in the Webb Hotel in Manchester, Clay County, Kentucky (see the photograph on p. 103): a young woman from the English middle class, genteel and of slight stature, educated in the finer things, transplanted to what can only be described as a totally alien environment, where, as she often comments in her diaries, the sanitation left much to be desired and some of the people were notably wild and unruly. Fear and discomfort are not far from the surface in those diaries, but so too – and in good measure – are an obvious courage, determination, and underlying humanity – and a love of hats! As Ursula Vaughan Williams observed so well in her obituary of Maud in *English Dance and Song*: 'Like most girls [of her background] she felt obliged to undertake some social work, and through this she came in contact with the other London, a world of poverty, deprivation and the lively toughness of the Cockney. She was drawn into situations where she inevitably had to inspect new babies and recently laid-out corpses, and to hear stories of love and death that she would, later, find in the songs and ballads made by the forebears of her clients.'

The Maud Karpeles manuscripts are in the archive of her beloved Cecil Sharp House in London – as, now, are the materials from Peter Kennedy's collections relating to his aunt Maud, which include the never previously seen photographs from her Newfoundland trips. Perhaps the time is ripe, using these primary sources, for a serious look at Maud's contribution to folk music and dance – brought out from the shadows of Cecil Sharp's towering frame and seen in her own modest, yet constantly glowing, light. I hope this book in some way serves that purpose.

Malcolm Taylor, OBE
EFDSS Library Director
July 2011

Preface

In her ninetieth year, Dr Maud Karpeles took time off from editing Cecil Sharp's folk song collection and from organizing, almost single-handedly, all the folk music festivals of the world, to write her autobiography. With her usual efficiency, she had it finished before dying a few weeks short of her ninety-second birthday. She delivered it for safe keeping to her long-time friend Ursula Vaughan Williams. For years, people had been urging Maud to put her life on paper, but the subject had no great appeal to her. She did it in the end for two purposes: to add more to the record of Cecil Sharp's life and work; and to tell the story of the International Folk Music Council (IFMC), which, from its foundation after the second World War, had occupied almost every moment of her time. In the intimate details of her personal life she seemed to have had very little interest at all.

Maud did, however, express anxiety that use should be made of these memoirs for the reasons stated above, so, after her death, Ursula was at pains to have them put into a state in which they would stand a chance of publication. She passed them on to Marie Slocombe, Maud's colleague in the work of the IFMC and travelling companion to many festivals. After long thought and attempted revision, Miss Slocombe admitted herself defeated and returned the manuscript. From time to time, Ursula had heard me say that I would like to work on a biography, so she gave the book to me. I had known Maud Karpeles since 1957, the year in which I had met Ralph Vaughan Williams and Ursula. From the moment they entered my life, I found myself involved in endless parties and concert-going, and at many of these events Maud would be one of my fellow guests. We must have taken to each other on sight because I do not remember any time when she did not seem to be an old friend. Though small, distinctly plump by this time, and witch-like in appearance, she was immensely attractive. My husband, Noel Iliff, though normally more apt to seek the company of pretty girls, was similarly drawn to her. He did not care for parties, but if an invitation came would ask, 'Will Maud be there?', and if the reply was 'yes' would

Preface

instantly accept. He would then endeavour to pin her in a corner and monopolize her for the duration. In this, he had many competitors, a lot of them young, male, and attractive. The last time we saw Maud was at her splendid ninetieth birthday party, at which she was surrounded by friends of every generation.

I was therefore delighted to have a look at her manuscript to see if I could find a way to make it a viable proposition, but, like Ursula and Marie, had to admit defeat. Good as she was at making propaganda for folk music, Maud had little talent – or little desire, it would seem – for making herself come alive on the page. The only chapters that conveyed her sparkle were the episodes about childhood (as so often happens with autobiographers) and some vivid recollections of the London Blitz, where she seemed to shake off her discretion and let her hair down. There was, moreover, one great defect. I had been expecting to find a fuller and more personal account of her four years in the Appalachian Mountains. On the track of English songs, she and Cecil Sharp had existed, as if in a bubble, almost totally insulated from the world and the 1914–18 war which raged around them. Yet what she had written of this amazing episode added nothing to the sparse account she had made for Sharp's biography, with hardly a comment from her own point of view.

When, with the help of Malcolm Taylor of the Vaughan Williams Memorial Library, I discovered that diaries, kept by both Cecil and Maud, existed for those years, as well as a goodly collection of letters, it became obvious that Maud's reticent script would have to be abandoned in favour of a biography. With Ursula's encouragement, I set out to write the following account of Maud's life, using the letters and diaries, supplemented with copious quotations from her own book and the reminiscences of many of her friends.

None of this could have been done without the help of three people in particular: Ursula Vaughan Williams, for the initial suggestion and many helpful pointers; Malcolm Taylor, for the hospitality of his library and for his enthusiastic searching in the archives of Cecil Sharp House; and Marie Slocombe, for her reminiscences and for her own written account of the history of the IFMC. I have, besides, had conversations with Maud's relatives and friends, and would especially thank her niece Katie Kacser, her nephew Peter Kennedy and his wife Beryl, and Gwen Ffrangcon-Davies, Rosamund Strode, Jane van Boschan, and Mike Yates.

Joseph Karpeles
EFDSS Photograph Collection

Chapter 1

Joseph Nicolaus Karpeles was a tea merchant with a business in Mincing Lane. He moved with his wife, Emily, and two small daughters into 33 Lancaster Gate in 1883. It was here, two years later, on 12 November, that Maud was born. Lucy was then three and a half and Florence a year younger. The tea business was not particularly profitable, but the family lived in what, even as a small child, Maud recognized to be luxury. This was largely due to a marriage settlement made for Emily by her father, Henry Lewis Raphael, banker and senior partner of R. Raphael & Sons. It was of her maternal grandparents that Maud was thinking when she told her friends that, as a small child, she thought the word 'grandparent' meant a rich person.

Joseph Karpeles had been born in Hamburg but had come to settle and work in England. He had been naturalized some time before he met and married Emily Raphael and had dropped the 'u' from his second name. Both families were of Jewish ancestry but neither practised their forebears' religion. They had a prejudice against Christianity too, and did not have their children baptized. By the time the family was complete, Maud was the middle child and third daughter. Her younger sister, Helen, was also born in Lancaster Gate, two and a half years after her. The fifth child, Arthur, ten years younger and something of an afterthought, was born when they had moved to a slightly smaller house in Kensington.

No. 33 Lancaster Gate was 'one of those imposing and somewhat sombre-looking mansions' that faced on to Christ Church, the Anglican church with the graceful spire which still shows as a landmark from the middle of Hyde Park, though the bombed nave and chancel have been replaced by a group of hideous flats.[1] Decorated with pairs of lions' heads above the first-floor windows, the house faced west and formed part of the north-east corner of the little square that embraced the church. Like so many in Bayswater, it consisted of six floors above a basement, involving daily climbs up and down many flights of stairs to reach the nursery floor. The domestic staff – eight in number, apart from nannies and nursemaids – included a cook, a kitchen maid, two each of parlourmaids, housemaids, and ladies' maids, and a coachman, who was later to be transformed into a chauffeur. The housemaids in particular must have needed excellent constitutions, having to carry coals to all the rooms in winter, as well as brooms and buckets of water up and down all those floors.

Maud did not remember a great deal about that particular house, which they left when she was six, except the eternal climbing of stairs and a general impression of gloom. She pinned down her earliest recollection to a time when she was under three. It was of daily excursions across Bayswater Road to walk in Kensington Gardens, with the nurse carrying Helen in her arms. The long robes that were the correct wear for babies at the time helped Maud to give a date to this memory. She saw little of Lucy and Florence. The older girls were in the care of different nannies and governesses. Indeed, the family seems to have fallen, from the beginning, into two groups – Maud and Helen being boon companions, with little Arthur coming as a later, somewhat detached, appendage.

Their first move, in 1891, was to 3 Durham Villas, now called Phillimore Place, a solid, south-facing house in an attractive little street on the hill between Kensington and Bayswater. There was one storey less than in the previous house and the first floor was set high above the front garden, reached by a flight of steps, giving a brighter basement for the kitchen regions. It was here, in 1895, that Arthur was born. Helen and Maud were sent away for their mother's confinement, which took place at home. Mrs Karpeles also underwent a number of operations at home and Maud noted that on these occasions 'the kitchen-table used to be brought up from the basement to the bedroom and the operation was performed upon it'.[2] She did not explain how cook managed in its absence. For such a crisis, as for the

Emily Karpeles
EFDSS Photograph Collection

Maud Karpeles (centre) with sisters Lucy and Florence, 1888
EFDSS Photograph Collection

confinement, it was the custom to have straw strewn over the road in front of the house to deaden the sound of horses' hooves and the clatter of metal wheels in the days before tyres were general. Maud wondered, but never managed to find out, how much payment was expected for this amenity and to whom it was made.

Maud retained one vivid recollection from what must have been the Lancaster Gate days. It was the custom to draw all the curtains facing the street when somebody had died in a house. 'The death of an aunt by marriage occurred when I was very young. I felt I should have been upset by the news, but it left me unmoved until I happened to walk into the night-nursery and found unexpectedly that it was in darkness. Whereupon I burst into tears, to my self-gratification.'[3]

The house to which they moved after Arthur's birth was 87 Westbourne Terrace, where they remained until the death of Emily Karpeles in 1914. Here they were back to six floors above the basement in a tall house, somewhat plainer and even more substantial than the one in Lancaster Gate, in that long, wide, slightly forbidding avenue of Victorian family residences. The house faced west and was quite a step from Kensington Gardens.

Life in all three houses, with a staff of eight to ten to look after two adults and four children, was comfortable and Maud was aware from a very early age of the fact that this was not so for everybody. Shopping expeditions, especially to Marshall & Snelgrove, were a weekly pleasure. The two youngest girls, with their mother, would be taken in their carriage to Oxford Street, where the coachman would draw up at the door for them to be assisted down by a concierge. He then withdrew to the middle of the street and waited until he was summoned to pick them up again. When they went on holiday a private bus would take them to the station, and this was the occasion for Maud's earliest twinges of conscience at being better off than the majority. 'A particularly painful experience occurred at the end of each summer holiday when one or two men used invariably to run behind our horse-driven private bus all the way from the station to our home in order that they might earn a shilling or two helping to unload the luggage.'[4]

This lively concern for other people's needs and feelings manifested itself early in Maud's life and became the chief motive in her plans for living – indeed, had she never seen a folk dance or heard a folk song, there is little doubt that she would have dedicated her time to good works. Not that this pressing concern for the welfare of the less fortunate caused her to enjoy her own comforts any the less. She was appreciative of excellence wherever she found it, relished the good things that came her way, and did not see how mortifying her own flesh would benefit the poor.

Lowestoft was the setting for most of the children's summer holidays. They went as a bunch in the charge of nurses, giving their parents a respite from family life. The chilly seas off the Suffolk coast do not seem to have detracted from the pleasure, indeed the ecstasy, of bathing and may have helped toughen Maud for the rigours of life to come. But then, she was in love. The object of her passion was one Frank, a bathing-machine attendant. In those days, 'undressing was performed in bathing-machines which were drawn down to the water's edge. Ordinarily one would descend the steps which were attached to the machine and plunge into the sea.'[5] But Maud was taken into Frank's arms and gently dipped into the water. It was an overwhelming romance, the earliest of many.

Lowestoft was also the place where Maud underwent her first 'conversion' to Christianity, though the fervour induced by the preacher who conducted a mission to children on the beach did not survive long after her introduction to school. At home, there was little talk of religion and it was presumably through their nannies, and not by way of her atheist parents, that the children heard stories from the Old Testament. Maud, always impressionable, took these extremely seriously and one day announced that she wished to offer one of her toys as a sacrifice to the Lord. Her parents were deeply shocked and decided the children were too young for such inflammatory literature. It must have been this that decided them to censor some of the nursery picture books. Maud quickly discovered that pages had been glued together here and there and managed to unstick some of them without damaging the paper. On one page she discovered a picture of the Good Shepherd. 'Oh, if only I were allowed to believe in Him, how easy life would be!' she decided, her eyes full of tears.[6]

Though it was not until considerably later that she embraced religion formally, feelings about it came and went throughout her childhood and schooldays. Whenever she looked out of the house where she was born she was, of course, confronted with a view of the north-east corner of the chancel of Christ Church, and when she returned from her daily excursions to Kensington Gardens she must have wondered at that beautiful spire. But it was a long time before she seriously suspected that she would end her days as an Anglican.

About those Lancaster Gate days, presumably even before the Lowestoft 'conversion', she wrote: 'As a very small child I was once lying in bed and playing with a blue ribbon which I eventually tied round my head. Then I got out of bed and looked in a mirror to see the effect. I was delighted and said to myself: "Oh Maudie, how beautiful you are." But then, overcome with remorse, I added: "But what a pity you are not better inside."'[7] This last remark was apropos of a recurring conviction that she had 'marred the beauty and fitness of things' by her own imperfections, and that she was 'out of tune'.[8]

Despite the comfort and security of home, Maud was troubled from a very early age with 'immortal longings' and found life did not give her the satisfaction she expected of it. She wrote that, despite a considerable affection for both her mother and her father, the many-servanted life of a Victorian child resulted in 'a lack of intimacy between parents and children, and I often felt the need of an understanding and sympathetic friend on whom I could unload my pent-up emotions and with whom I could share my flights of imagination'.[9]

Though her father was capable of strumming on the piano and enjoyed it, her parents had, in general, little interest in any branch of the arts. This is Maud's description of her early discovery that music gave her the answer to most of what she was looking for:

> '[Music] gave me a glimpse of the ideal in which there were no contradictions or jarring notes. I believe that my first musical experience was through some kind of musical box, the name of which I do not know. It was a square box on which was placed a perforated cardboard disc. It was played, not by clockwork, but by turning a handle, whereby the disc was made to pass under a metal comb. I had about a dozen discs, each with a different piece of music . . . I could not read at that time, but I was able to distinguish the discs by the pattern of the perforations.
> I do not know at what age I started taking piano lessons, but I cannot remember a time when I was not constantly at the piano. Always when I was playing or music was in my mind I felt that beauty and goodness were the natural state of affairs and that it was impossible for me ever to be naughty again. Alas, a very transitory emotion! The only times when my enjoyment of music was at all disturbed was when one of my piano teachers used to insist upon my not putting expression into the piece until I had learned to play it correctly. Bach was always my favourite composer. This greatly astonished an early teacher, who, when I told her, exclaimed: 'Then you must be really musical!'[10]

There were few public concerts at the end of the nineteenth century and those, like Maud, who wanted to hear and discover music were forced to make it themselves. But she insisted always that she had very little natural talent or facility for the piano. As for the rest of her education, she declared it to have been 'decidedly skimpy'. After the usual succession of private governesses, she was sent for a few years to the Kensington High School, run by the Public Day School Trust. She spoke admiringly of its curriculum. Meanwhile, Lucy and Florence were boarders at Hamilton House, Tunbridge

Wells, but they had left school by the time fifteen-year-old Maud and twelve-year-old Helen were sent there. The place was not, however, altogether unfamiliar:

> I was not entering unexplored territory and I felt immediately at home. The headmistress and owner of the school was Miss Goldie and the second in command was Miss Hake who was of German origin. For her I conceived an absorbing passion, 'adoring' her, to use the schoolgirl expression. This adoration lasted throughout my schooldays and beyond and brought me much happiness, though some misery due to frustration owing to my not being able to give full expression to my devotion or to receive a reciprocal return. On the whole my five years at Hamilton House were very happy ones. Whereas most of my school-fellows counted the days to the holidays, I reversed the process and during the holidays looked forward in joyful anticipation to my return to school.[11]

Hamilton House had about a hundred boarders and Maud was to make many friends among them and, especially, among members of the staff. At first, a small clique sought to adopt her but she quickly became bored with their main interest, which was to explore the Old Testament for the juicy bits, with the object of learning the facts of life. 'It seems extraordinary', she wrote, 'that in those days the young, and even not so young, should have been so shielded from the knowledge of matters pertaining to sex. On one occasion I was asked confidentially and innocently by one of the school-mistresses in her late twenties if I could give her any information as to how children came into the world.'[12] Unfortunately, Maud did not reveal whether she was able to oblige, but it seems likely that the Karpeles girls had been brought up with some idea as to how these things were brought about.

It was at boarding school that Maud had some lessons on the violin as well as the piano. She did not pursue these for long because her acute musical ear could not endure the horrible noise that a learner must invariably produce, though she got some pleasure from playing 'third violin' on the open strings in the school orchestra. Nevertheless, she retained what she learned well enough to play Joseph Raff's *Cavatina* in 'supposed unison' with Ralph Vaughan Williams at a social gathering at Stratford-upon-Avon, 'much to the entertainment of all present, for his playing . . . was little better than mine'.[13] This was evidently the great man's favourite party piece. He had played it at school at Rottingdean and 'Fifty years later, at one of the Three

Choirs Festivals . . . was suddenly moved to seize W. H. Reed's violin and play through Raff's *Cavatina* by heart, double stops and all, while Reed vamped an accompaniment, before a discerning and enthusiastic audience.'[14]

Though abandoning the violin, Maud pressed on with the piano. It was while she was at boarding school that she was taken, with a select collection of musical pupils, to hear a recital by Vladimir de Pachmann. 'It was a revelation. His phrasing of works by Chopin which I had stumbled through made them almost unrecognizable to me. Coming away from the concert, I said to my friends: "But he made the notes disappear."'[15]

Indeed, the very best thing about her days in Tunbridge Wells for Maud was the amount of time given up to music, especially to piano playing. She described how she had instruction from a piano teacher, Ernest Kiver, who came once a week from London:

> I shall always be grateful to him for his imaginative teaching and for the new worlds of music he opened up for me. In my last term he presented me with Hubert Parry's *The Evolution of the Art of Music*, which was the first history of music that I had read, though I was familiar with some of Dent's Master Musician series. Incidentally, my bedroom walls at home were lined with portraits of the great composers, whom the housemaid referred to as 'Miss Maud's uncles', for she did not think I should have displayed them on account of their good looks.[16]

The Lowestoft 'conversion', which had happened in the summer of Maud's fourteenth year, just before she went to school, was wiped out quickly in the excitement of music. 'I found myself thinking more of Bach and Beethoven than of Jesus Christ. But I did not allow myself to be shocked. Always I felt I needed a focus for the non-material things of life and I knew instinctively that some day my thoughts would right themselves.'[17]

The *Schwärmerei* for Miss Hake had the excellent effect of making Maud work hard at her German, in which she became fluent. Another mistress, Nellie Kendall, gave her private lessons in English literature and ended up a close friend owing to their shared love of the classics. Maud had discovered the pleasures of literature shortly before going to Hamilton House through reading *Sesame and Lilies*. The passage 'Will you gossip with your housemaid, or your stable-boy, when you may talk with queens and kings?' made her realize what she was missing through her devotion to fourpenny *Heartsease* novels and Horner's *Penny Stories*, which had been her sole literary diet up until then – not that she would have put it in quite the same words as Ruskin did! Apart from these subjects, she did not think highly of the education she received at school – 'somewhat haphazard and decidedly unacademic'[18] – and regretted what she regarded as a lack of mental discipline all her life. Nevertheless, she must have acquitted herself well enough, since during her last year she was appointed Head Girl, a responsibility she took very seriously indeed.

Chapter 2

Maud was getting on for twenty when she left Hamilton House, which she did with a great and sorrowful wrench and a feeling of loss. University, which would have suited her, was then for the bluestocking only. Unsure what she was to do with her life, she did what many musical people were doing at that time and went to Germany to continue her study of the piano. This was not a difficult move because her father had relations in Berlin and, thanks to her passion for Miss Hake, she was to have no trouble with the language. Maud was by now a charming, if not extraordinarily pretty, slim young lady, considerably smaller than her sisters and quite dwarfed by Helen, who had shot up and become very tall. Her hair was smooth and raven black, her eyes the darkest brown. She was received with kindness and hospitality into the house of Julius Stern, director of the Nationalbank, her uncle by marriage to Aunt Gonni, Joseph Karpeles's sister. There she found all the luxuries to which she was accustomed, in 'a large and beautiful flat in the Bellevuestrasse . . . and also a house at Potsdam'.[1]

At their lavish receptions she met people who were to become important to her when she discovered her real interests, notably Gordon Craig, stage designer and son of Ellen Terry, and Isadora Duncan, the dancer, who came to the house with him. Among the musicians was Ferruccio Busoni, 'whose scintillating personality invariably raised the spirits of any company in which he found himself'.[2] Of her musical life, she wrote:

> I took private lessons with a professor from the Hochschule für Musik. He was not very interested in me since he knew I should never become a professional pianist, but I had compensations in the amount of concert-going I was able to indulge in. Every Monday morning I sallied forth to Bote und Bock, the concert agent[,] and supplied myself with tickets for the week. For a recital I could get an excellent seat for the price of one mark . . . Orchestral concerts cost rather more – three marks fifty, as far as I remember. It would be tedious to give a list of all the great artists I heard,

which included Busoni, d'Albert, Carreno, Joachim, etc. My chief hero was Felix Weingartner, the conductor. Then there was the opera, generally conducted by Richard Strauss. My main diet was Wagner and Mozart.[3]

Her introduction to the last composer, not quite so generally admired in the period before the 1914 war as he is today, came by way of friendship with the art critic Emil Heilbut. Heilbut was to become her brother-in-law through marriage to her eldest sister, Lucy. When, a year or two later, Lucy set off to begin her life with him in Berlin, Maud revealed that her growing interest in the underprivileged had still not altered her attitude to luxury in great houses. 'Lucy ... announced that for economy's sake she would employ only one maid. Whereupon I exclaimed in horror: "But, Lucy, on her day out that means you will have to answer the front door yourself!"'[4]

After six months in Berlin, sometime towards the end of 1906, Maud had decided that she was not the stuff of which concert pianists were made and that music could be no more than a hobby to her. She returned to Westbourne Terrace, debating what she was going to do with her life. To stay at home and indulge in sociabilities until the right husband came along was the expected fate of girls in her circumstances, but she had known since she had been a small child that such an existence would bore her to distraction. She did not trouble her mind a great deal, though, having already discovered that one thing led to another and that, if she allowed herself to wait, some fascinating opportunity would present itself unsought. This conscious 'policy of drift' was adopted early and proved unfailing to the end of her days. 'Looking back,' she wrote, 'it would seem that my path in life was initially determined in my schooldays by a talk I heard on the work of Dr. Barnardo. It registered in my mind the idea that I might one day be of use to those that were less fortunate than myself. The means of fulfilling this wish soon turned up.

'I heard through a friend of the Mansfield House Settlement at Canning Town, and I offered my services, which were readily accepted. At that time no special qualifications were required for social work and it was mostly undertaken in a voluntary capacity. I worked three or four days a week in the districts of East Ham and Barking for the Invalid Children's Aid Association, visiting the homes of afflicted children, conducting them to hospital, advising the parents and so on.'[5] In this work she picked up experience that was to stand her in good stead for the rest of her life, even preparing her for the London Blitz. In her social work it often happened that she was dragged to see corpses of newly laid-out loved ones: fathers, for instance, of her invalid children. 'Oh, Miss Maud, you must come and see him, he does look so Beautiful!'

Maud's experience with children, up until that time, was not extensive. Her reminiscences never mention her young brother, Arthur, as a child. By now he would have been ten years old. In Berlin, however, she spent time in the company of her cousin, the musically talented small son of Uncle Julius and Aunt Gonni – 'a delightful little boy who was slightly retarded mentally'[6] – and this friendship may have shown her that she had a talent with children. She persuaded Helen to join in the weekly meetings of a club for children called the Guild of Play, which took place in the hall of Mansfield House. 'The standard programme consisted of songs (mostly action songs) and made-up dances, such as the maypole dance. The quality of the material was probably somewhat mediocre, but it was the best I knew at that time; the children enjoyed themselves and so did I.'[7] She little realized at the time that she was on the brink of discovering her vocation.

It was an exciting period in Maud's life and many new interests began to present themselves. She frequently went to stay with her uncle, Sir Herbert Raphael (son of those munificent grandparents), at his country house, Allestree Hall, in Derbyshire. Herbert Henry Raphael, created baronet in 1911, was, from 1906 to 1918, Liberal MP for South Derbyshire. He had

Children from the Guild of Play, Mansfield House
The Guild of Play Book of Festival and Dance, part 1, by G. T. Kimmins

been educated chiefly in Hanover. Then he went to Cambridge, where he took a degree in law. Among other things, he was a governor of Guy's Hospital and a Trustee of the National Portrait Gallery. He had married an English wife, Rosalie (Aunt Rosie) Coster, but they had no children. Their London house was in Cavendish Square. It was in these two houses that Maud, after her return from Germany, began to meet politicians and to develop an interest in politics, as well as hearing more about the world of art than she had ever done in her parents' home. As a result of encounters there, she became a member of the Fabian Society, whose meetings she attended for a number of years:

> I delighted especially in the skirmishes between Bernard Shaw and H. G. Wells, in which the latter always got the worst of it. G.B.S. was noted for his uncompromising attitude. I once went to a public meeting in aid of the founding of the National Theatre. The speeches were for the most part lengthy and boring, and the audience waited impatiently for Bernard Shaw, the last speaker. When at last he stood up, he pulled out his watch and said: 'Ladies and gentlemen, it is now ten minutes past five. The subject is not exhausted, but we are.' He then sat down and nothing would persuade him to say another word.[8]

At the same time, Maud was flirting with something of a very different nature from Shaw, Wells, and the Fabians. She does not make it clear in her autobiography exactly when she returned to her pursuit of religious enlightenment, but it must have been a short time after she left Hamilton House that she began to seek out preachers who could satisfy this thirst. She was not particular about denomination and went around London sermon-tasting at a number of different churches. She wrote: 'it was not until I came under Archdeacon Wilberforce's influence with his gospel of Divine Immanence that I felt completely satisfied. For many years I used to make a morning and evening pilgrimage every Sunday to St. John's, Smith Square, Westminster, to hear him preach.'[9] Even so, she did not feel moved to make any formal commitment, and though she continued to be a sporadic churchgoer it was not until almost thirty years had passed that she decided to be baptized.

Theatre had been an interest for some years. Maud and Helen were in the habit of going to Stratford-upon-Avon to take part in the yearly celebrations of Shakespeare's birthday on 23 April. This was the start of the season of his plays at the Memorial Theatre under the direction of Frank R. Benson. She wrote that the productions 'were sometimes criticized as being amateurish. Perhaps they were, but only in the best sense of the word. The actors were in love with their work and there was a feeling of intimacy between them and their audiences which led to a deeper understanding and a greater appreciation of the plays than I have received from almost any other stage performances.'[10]

The Shakespeare Festival was of shorter duration in those days, but long enough for Maud and Helen to make a number of visits each year. In May 1909, they were in Stratford to see plays and heard that a folk song and dance competition was being held in a local hall. Out of curiosity they decided to go and have a look. For both of them, it was the most fateful decision of their lives, as Maud described:

> Immediately we were spell-bound. We stayed all day witnessing team after team of children and young people giving performances of dances and songs which were entirely unfamiliar to us and yet somehow seemed to arouse a sense of recognition. Cecil Sharp was there. He was the sole adjudicator for the singing and one of the panel, including Miss Mary Neal, for the dancing. This consisted entirely of Morris Dances. They were not very well performed, but we got an inkling of what they should be,

EFDSS Photograph Collection

and the accompanying music of both dances and songs thrilled and enchanted us.[11]

This was the first time that Cecil Sharp had assisted at such a gathering in Stratford, but Maud does not make it clear whether, on this fateful occasion, when the whole of her life changed direction, she actually met and talked to the man who was to become its guiding spirit. Cecil Sharp was in his fiftieth year at the time Maud first set eyes on him, she being nearly twenty-four. The many photographs, and a small number of busts, that exist show him as glum-looking: a long-faced, beaky-nosed, solemn man, with mousy hair receding further and further back over a domed forehead. Smiling photographs were rare in those days, when poses had to be held much longer for the camera, but even allowing for this the impression is uninviting. He was, besides, a martyr to chronic asthma as well as a number of other ailments – mostly genuine, some undoubtedly imagined. Yet it is clear that this impression, which is reinforced by the occasionally querulous tone of his diaries, is far from accurate. Nearly everybody who met him was bowled over by a charm that does not come over from the pictures and he was beloved by many, notably by the 'peasants', as they were still often called, from whom he had spent the past six years collecting songs and dances. To extract a tune or a caper from a total stranger of a different class and background requires a considerable degree of charm, mixed with guile, and it is a well-attested fact that Sharp possessed this in full measure. Though he often inveighed against the pitfalls of uninformed enthusiasm, he was himself an enthusiast capable of infecting almost anyone who came in contact with him.

Maud was to become Sharp's biographer and she published her life of him in 1967. Later, in her autobiography, she made this précis of his career and aims: 'Cecil Sharp had an arresting personality. His clearness of vision and intensity of purpose made him a dynamic leader. But with all his earnestness he had a tremendous sense of fun and humour. He had an immediate attraction for those who came into contact with him. I was no exception, and my admiration and love for him grew as I came to know him more intimately.'[12] Sharp's whole life, she wrote, was dedicated to music:

'It was perhaps prophetic that he was born on St. Cecilia's Day (in the year 1859). During the early part of his life . . . he followed a conventional musical career, teaching, lecturing, conducting and composing, first in

Cecil Sharp
EFDSS Photograph Collection (James Bacon & Sons, Leeds)

Australia ... and then in England. It was his educational work that led him indirectly to folk music. He deplored the fact that the musical upbringing of young people should be based almost entirely on German music, and he looked around for something that would provide a national medium of expression. He turned to old English songs and among them he found a few that had been taken from traditional sources. He recognized the distinctive flavour of these songs, but he did not realize the full significance of traditional music until he came upon it in its living form.

His first discovery ... was the Morris Dance, led by William Kimber, which he witnessed by accident or by Divine Providence, on Boxing Day, 1899, when spending his Christmas holidays with his mother-in-law at Headington, near Oxford ... it was a turning point in his life. On that occasion he noted the tunes from William Kimber, but strange as it now seems he did not note the dance-movements until some years later ... But it had fired his imagination and it led him to seek for further treasures.

His next great find was when staying ... at the village of Hambridge in Somerset he heard John England, the vicarage gardener, singing ... 'The Seeds of Love'. From that moment his course was set and he never deviated from it. [He] knew that he had found what he was looking for

John England (seated bottom left) with the Rev. Charles Marson and others, 1896
EFDSS Photograph Collection

William Kimber
EFDSS Photograph Collection

– the natural musical expression of the English people – and he felt that no sacrifice would be too great to save this heritage from oblivion ... He laid aside all his other musical ambitions, though he had to continue his teaching for a number of years in order to support his family. Every available moment, week-ends and holidays, would see him starting off on a collecting trip.[13]

Maud chanced to come into Cecil Sharp's life at one of its turning points. Four years earlier he had met one of his fellow adjudicators at that Stratford competition, Mary Neal. Her work came to his notice when he was puzzling over how to make his discoveries more widely known and wishing that schoolchildren, in particular, should be brought up with a knowledge of their precious heritage of song and dance. He had no intention, at the time, of teaching dance himself. So, 'he was delighted when Miss Mary Neal came to seek his advice concerning material that would be suitable for her working-girls' club, later called the Esperance Girls' Club. He introduced her first to the songs and then to the dances. On his advice she sought out William Kimber and got him to come to London to teach the Morris Dances to the girls. From this beginning interest in the dance spread rapidly and the members of the Club became actively engaged in performing and teaching dances both in London and in the provinces. Cecil Sharp cooperated with the Club whenever the opportunity offered and he frequently lectured at its performances.

However, he soon became critical of the standards adopted ... There was a fundamental difference of outlook between him and Miss Neal. The artistic aspect was all-important to Cecil Sharp, whereas Miss Neal regarded the dances primarily as a means of social recreation. Gradually he came to the conclusion that if the dances were to be disseminated in their true traditional forms, he must himself take direct control over their teaching ... Many attempts were made to reconcile the two schools of thought, but in vain, and Cecil Sharp and Miss Neal continued to work independently. Her activities came to a standstill on the outbreak of war in 1914 and were not resumed.'[14]

Eventually, in September of 1909, Sharp found the opportunity he wanted, at the South Western Polytechnic Institute. The Board of Education had now revised its syllabus so as to include morris dancing as a subject and Sharp was approached to help found and direct a school to teach it at the Chelsea Physical Training College. He embraced the idea enthusiastically, and it was in this way that Maud heard of accessible classes in London where she could pursue the dancing that had so fascinated her in Stratford that spring. She dragged Helen along with her and they attended weekly. Her first motive was to learn dances that could be taught to her children at the club in Canning Town. 'This we did,' she wrote, 'but our action had more far-reaching consequences than we could have imagined. From the very first step I took I knew that I was "involved" and that I had come across

Mary Neal
EFDSS Photograph Collection

something that was to play a big part in my life. This premonition proved to be correct, for from that time onward folk music – dance and song – occupied almost continuously a central position in my interests and activities. The thrill of those early days is something never to be forgotten, especially when week by week we were introduced by Cecil Sharp to dances that he had recently collected.'[15]

In her account of her childhood and schooldays Maud makes no mention of dancing classes, yet these must surely have figured in the prospectus of her Kensington school and of Hamilton House, such lessons being indispensable to the education of a well-bred young lady at that date. Yet the dance seems to have taken her by surprise and the skills she developed became the only thing about herself that tempted her towards boasting: 'It was the only thing that has ever come easily to me and in which I feel I have excelled. It seemed that every time I performed a dance I discovered in it fresh beauties and a deeper significance ... Sometimes when performing the half-capers in the morris jig, *Princess Royal*, I used conceitedly to imagine that my movements were like those of Nijinsky and that in leaping into the air I had only just to go up and then pause a while before coming down.'[16]

There exists, in the Vaughan Williams Memorial Library at Cecil Sharp House, a short film of Maud, Helen, and Sharp himself, with the composer George Butterworth making up the four, performing a country dance. Their movements are skilled, neat, and precise – indeed professional – and the diminutive Maud is shown to possess an elfin quality. Many of the photographs kept in the library show her leaping or being tossed up by her partners and seeming, indeed, to pause in the air, just as Nijinsky is described as having done. Until she discovered folk dance, the only dancer who had impressed her was Ruth St Denis. Later, she was to be overwhelmed by the Diaghilev ballet, but in this case she was to come into opposition with Sharp, who detested what he called 'aesthetic' dancing.

Of her own skill, she recorded one incident with pride: 'Dancing has been described by someone as music made visible ... But, contradictory as it may seem, I consider that one of the highest compliments I was ever paid came from a traditional Morris dancer who was blind ... I danced a Morris jig for him and when I had finished he said, "Of course, I can't see, but I know you are a very pretty dancer by the jingling of your bells."'[17]

Caught up in the middle of a dance, she became as if possessed, as at a Manchester demonstration described by Helen: 'Miss Karpeles, who generally danced in the middle place in the Morris side was transferred to

Maud and Helen Karpeles
EFDSS Photograph Collection

Cecil Sharp, Maud and Helen Karpeles, and George Butterworth, still from Kinora film. EFDSS *Photograph Collection*

an end place on this occasion. She was feeling particularly jubilant and free. "Blue-Eyed Stranger" was being danced, and in the second half of the "up-and-back-twice" Miss Karpeles, with tremendous energy and violent waving of handkerchiefs, went full tilt down the room all by herself, disappearing away from the rest of the set into the vast hall.'[18] Vaughan Williams, remembering her, said that Maud's dancing was so beautiful that it made him cry.

The Chelsea school taught morris, sword, and country dancing. Cecil Sharp extended this last category by introducing dances from John Playford's *Dancing Master* of 1651. These were not considered pure 'folk', having been danced at court and furbished up by dancing masters, and he was criticized for allowing them in. Genuine country dances, however, were in short supply and, in addition, Sharp always had more women recruits than men. He thought the beauty of the tunes justified their inclusion and, as far as style was concerned, was guided by performances he had watched of traditional dancers. As for the morris and sword dances, these were properly performed only by men and only, as far as the purists were concerned, at specific times of the year. However, in allowing them to be danced, occasionally, by women,

Sharp was to ensure their preservation, especially when, in the near future, the 1914 war would remove nearly all men of dancing age. Thus the tradition, which he was helping to rescue in the nick of time, was saved.

Maud and Helen's excitement at the discovery of this new form of expression was so great that the weekly meeting in Chelsea was too little to satisfy them. They managed to infect a few girl friends with their enthusiasm and, once a week, held extra parties at home. This departure demonstrates the extraordinary generosity of the Karpeles parents. In their drawing room at Westbourne Terrace the girls not only threw out all the furniture and pulled up the rugs but – without, it seems, the slightest protest from Emily or Joseph – they were allowed to go down on their knees and ruin the highly polished parquet floors by applying a liberal quantity of Vim so as to give a secure, non-slip surface for the dancers. The girls then managed to recruit a few men and together they founded a folk dance club. Helen wrote:

> We began to feel so pleased with our Morris side that we thought we would give a Drawing-room performance for our friends. However, on counting the number of people we all wished to invite, we thought it more practicable to hire the Small Portman Rooms and give a public performance . . . the tickets quickly sold out and we had hastily to cancel the Small Portman Rooms and book the large Hall . . . we eventually had an audience of about five hundred . . . The performance did not run without a hitch. Mr Sharp had kindly promised to lecture and play for us, but before he was able to play, he had to extricate various hooks and keys from the inside of the piano . . . all went well until the capers, when one of our dancers made a large hole in the middle of the temporary platform. This naturally added a little to our anxiety during the remainder of the performance. We were not, however, unduly depressed . . . because we had secured real men to take part in the Country dances, and such a thing had never been done before. I use the word 'secured' advisedly, as the men were friends who had been dragged in . . . The performance was a tremendous success and we made a profit of £60, but alas! this had rashly been promised to a charity.[19]

Cecil Sharp had brought his protégée Mattie Kay to sing folk songs and the venture was successful enough to warrant the planning of further performances. Sharp was impressed at the girls' enterprise and admiring of their style of dancing and it was soon afterwards that he wrote to Maud: 'I am very anxious to rope you and your sister into my staff of teachers because you appear to me to be both interested in the subject and skilled. We will see what we can do.'[20]

This, the first surviving letter from Sharp to Maud, was written on 19 May 1910, shortly after they had been, along with Vaughan Williams, to watch the Whitsun morris at Bampton in Oxfordshire. 'It was quite one of the pleasantest days I have ever spent,' Sharp wrote, and, after some dissertation on the then troublesome problem of Mary Neal and their conflicting ideas about the dance, he went on to issue an invitation from his wife for the sisters to come to tea.[21] It was to be the first of many such invitations, and Helen described the occasion:

> As soon as we arrived we each had an old umbrella or stick thrust into our hands. We then were taken out into the garden and asked if we would mind going through some evolutions of a wonderful sword dance, which Mr. Sharp had just collected. He said that with the charwoman we would be just six in number, and he would be free to conduct operations and note down the results ... We ... were constantly arrested in the middle of an evolution and kept standing, generally in a rather uncomfortable position, while Mr. Sharp noted down our different positions ... I remember that Joan and Susannah Sharp, dressed in attractive blue overalls, witnessed, along with the cat, this curious exhibition from the roof of the summer house.[22]

Out of these meetings came the germ for the foundation of the English Folk Dance Society (EFDS). Though the idea of forming a public body came from Sharp, the real beginning of the movement that was to grow and flourish was in those joyful gatherings on the scrubbed parquet of the Karpeles's home. Neither Maud nor Helen had the slightest idea, in the beginning, of what running a public society would involve. They relied on Sharp for guidance and were both flattered and alarmed at the degree of confidence he placed in them, as well as daunted by the technicalities of quorums and of having to draw up a table of rules.

In the summer of 1911, just before the EFDS had been officially established, Sharp was invited by the Governors of the Shakespeare Memorial Theatre to take charge of a four-week vacation school to teach the dances performed at Chelsea and also singing games. The latter became Maud's speciality, though she always protested that she had not much of a voice. Both

Singing and Dancing Wherever She Goes *A Life of Maud Karpeles*

Children from the Mansfield House Settlement Guild of Play at Stratford-upon-Avon, 1911. EFDSS, Peter Kennedy Collection, Maud Karpeles Materials

Chapter 2

sisters were enchanted to be officially placed on the teaching staff and departed to their beloved Stratford in a state of euphoria. Helen, however, was so intimidated at the thought of teaching in front of an audience that she spent the whole morning before they left practising on one of the housemaids by instructing her in the 'Headington Hey'. Stratford rewarded them with an excellent attendance. They had 'a daily period for the singing of folk songs. It could hardly be called instruction', wrote Maud, 'for we just sang, inspired by Cecil Sharp's piano accompaniment. And the members of the staff gave a daily dance-demonstration. In addition, there was a weekly Country Dance party and a weekly performance on the banks of the river Avon. Visiting groups were invited to take part in these performances, and among them was a group of children from my Canning Town Club, who had hitherto travelled no further from home than Epping Forest.'[23]

This was to be the first of many such meetings. As soon as it was over, Maud was invited to undertake her first solo teaching engagement. This was at Hamble, in Hampshire, where she was deputed to teach morris and sword dances to the boys of the training ship *Mercury*. Cecil Sharp sent down a consignment of swords and Maud was received by the head of the school – none other than C. B. Fry, the famous cricketer. Of him, Maud wrote: 'He became greatly interested and even attempted to dance a Morris Jig. He was not very successful, for he found it difficult to perform a caper without a preliminary run.'[24]

Chapter 3

So it was that the club formed by Maud and Helen Karpeles grew into something much bigger. A meeting was held on 6 December 1911, chaired by T. Lennox Gilmour, private secretary to Lord Rosebery, who was also a barrister and a leader writer for the *Morning Post*, then one of London's principal daily papers. He had written at length on the urgency of preserving folk culture. A surprising number of people attended and the principal resolution of the day was 'That a Society, to be called the English Folk Dance Society, be established, having its headquarters in London, with the object of preserving and promoting the practice of English Folk Dances in their true traditional forms'.[1] The objectives of the society were summarized and were to include the training of teachers, the granting of certificates, the publication of literature, the setting up of local branches, and the 'technical and artistic supervision of the Vacation Schools of Folk Song and Dance at Stratford-on-Avon, organized by the Governors of the Shakespeare Memorial Theatre'.[2]

The committee appointed included, of course, Cecil Sharp. Others were Perceval Lucas, brother of the writer E.V. Lucas and a keen folk dancer; Lady Gomme, expert on children's singing games; and Dr R. Vaughan Williams. The latter had started collecting songs independently only three months later than Sharp in 1903. Though the two men had known each other for some time, they did not immediately get together on the subject, for the astonishing reason that RVW was afraid of boring Sharp! Now, however, they were often to compare their discoveries and RVW, though not designed by nature as a dancer, became a fairly regular member of the morris team, where he performed 'with great zest'. Another member of the committee was Sir Archibald Flower, the brewer, a member of the governing body of the Shakespeare Festival and, according to Cecil Sharp, one of the nicest men he had ever come across.

Maud, of course, was on the committee and Helen was appointed Honorary Secretary. Another secretary was Peggy Walsh, a dancer from the

Karpeles's drawing-room group. The Honorary Treasurer was Captain W. Kettlewell. Not long after this, Peggy and the captain became man and wife, making a couple who remained her friends until the end of Maud's life. Peggy had a bright, red face, a downright manner, and said, very directly, whatever came into her head, regardless of her listeners. Her husband, on the other hand, was a gentle, amiable man, with a soothing manner. Maud became immediately immersed in committee work, to the exclusion of a good deal else, including her political and Fabian interests, which were relegated to the background. Folk dance and song were to occupy her almost exclusively for the rest of her long life.

After a pre-Christmas meeting at Stratford-upon-Avon, the next important occasion for the EFDS was an at-home on 27 February 1912 in the Kensington Town Hall. Sharp lectured, Steuart Wilson, a handsome young tenor at the beginning of a distinguished career, sang, and the highlight of the meeting was the appearance of complete male teams of morris and sword dancers. The experiment was repeated a month later with equal success when Maud brought her Mansfield House children to demonstrate singing games. Maud had also recruited Elsie Avril, a violinist she had discovered playing in a small ensemble at a Cliftonville hotel where she had been on holiday with her parents.

The movement, by this time, was attracting a considerable amount of publicity, and the small band of regular performers began to spread their wings and travel up and down the country and even abroad. On 2 December 1912 they gave a matinee at the Savoy Theatre, which had been offered to them by the actor/producer/playwright Harley Granville-Barker. The acquaintanceship with Granville-Barker was to have far-reaching effects on Sharp's future, as well as that of Maud.

Granville-Barker's company was then in the middle of a run of *Twelfth Night* – a notable production, designed entirely in black and white. The white-painted scenery served as an excellent background for the dancers. Sharp was still in the process of devising a costume suitable for demonstrations, one that belonged to no archaic period and would help to persuade spectators that the dances were alive and for all times. To this end, he banned the wearing of sun bonnets by the women, though most of them protested that it was hard, without headgear, to keep their long hair tidy. Norman Wilkinson designed flowing blue dresses for them, while the men wore white flannels, white shirts, and cross-baldrics, the costume worn at Headington by William Kimber and his morris men. Sharp was insistent on

The EFDS women's team dancing, 1912
EFDSS Photograph Collection

stressing, in a programme note, that he did not consider the theatre to be the proper setting. Folk dancing was for doing, not for watching. The aim of the EFDS was to exhibit it, performed to the highest technical standard, not in order to entertain but to encourage the spectators to learn and practise it themselves. Within a few years, he hoped, dances like these would become so widespread that they would no more need demonstration than did the polkas and waltzes that were danced in private drawing rooms.

The next two years were full of activity for the young EFDS and Sharp's vision began almost to look capable of being fulfilled. Maud particularly enjoyed what they called 'the quartet show', when a smaller group got together to take the gospel of folk dance to villages. It was generally performed by Cecil Sharp and Douglas Kennedy, with Maud and Helen Karpeles. Douglas was an excellent dancer, of Scottish origin, related to the folk song collector Marjory Kennedy-Fraser. Sharp would lecture, some of the four sang, three of them would perform jigs to Sharp's accompaniment, and then all of them would join in country dances to the accompaniment of a pianist recruited locally. In this set-up, and in a mood of blissful enjoyment, Maud travelled to small towns and villages, especially in Cornwall, Devon, and Somerset. While thus providing entertainment, they added, incidentally, to their store of knowledge, being introduced to local customs – the Hobby Horse ceremonies at Minehead and Padstow, and the Furry Dance at Helston.

Maud took pleasure in teaching as well as dancing. In London, during the week, she held regular classes, as well as continuing to instruct her Canning Town children. Excursions to teach in different localities came at weekends. Of these, the most colourful was a visit to Lewtrenchard, in Devon, where Maud and Helen had been asked to coach the villagers for a pageant to be performed at Plymouth. They stayed nearby at Lydford, but were fetched in a pony trap each evening to the home of the rector, the Rev. Sabine Baring-Gould. This remarkable cleric was a folk song collector of some fame and an old friend of Cecil Sharp, with whom he had collaborated in 1905 on the publication of a book of 121 songs from the West Country.

Sabine Baring-Gould was tall, handsome, and courteous, Maud remembered, 'a figure that might have stepped straight out of the mid-Victorian era'.[3] Besides books of folklore, he had published lives of the more obscure saints, biographies, and a

Rev. Sabine Baring-Gould
EFDSS Photograph Collection

Chapter 3

quantity of novels, though nowadays he is chiefly remembered as the author of the words to 'Onward, Christian Soldiers' and 'Now the Day Is Over'. With his black cloak, his silver-buckled shoes, and the rectory which, Maud said, would be better described as a mansion, he was a flamboyant figure and nobody, least of all himself, seems to have been able to count his children. All that is agreed is that there were upwards of twenty of them, of whom only two were boys. It was perhaps not surprising that he was apt to forget their names and that they, in return, though 'wrapt up in "Papa" . . . did not always trouble to learn the names of his books'.[4]

A number of these children must have been born when he was getting on in years, for though he was rising eighty when Maud and Helen went to the rectory, there were plenty of girls young enough to turn the head of seventeen-year-old Arthur Karpeles, who had been taken along by his sisters. 'Most of the daughters were at home on that occasion', Maud remembered. 'Each one was prettier than the other, and Arthur fell in love with all of them in turn.'[5]

Their host took them tramping across Dartmoor and regaled them with the history of local antiquities. Another Devon clergyman, the Rev. Francis Etherington, vicar of Minehead, also sent for Maud and Helen to give classes in his parish hall and was to become, later, one of Maud's closest friends. Cecil Sharp, who had gone collecting gypsy songs with him in 1907,

The EFDS women's team dancing at Kelmscott, 1912
EFDSS Photograph Collection

described him as being 'as delightful a companion as man could have, witty and serious and most sympathetic'.[6]

But amongst all this London activity and travelling far and wide, as well as visits to Paris and Belgium, it was the Stratford-upon-Avon vacation schools that provided the best opportunity for pooling and passing on the EFDS's increasing knowledge and expertise. Maud and Helen went there to dance and teach for a four-week period in the summer and for a further week at Christmas every year, and Maud was to find it difficult in later years to attempt to convey the rapture and enchantment of those meetings. She had indeed discovered her vocation and, in Cecil Sharp, the person who was to occupy her thoughts and dominate her actions for the rest of her life.

Apart from the members of the EFDS, visitors from all walks of life, 'with a good sprinkling of professional people including musicians and university dons',[7] turned up to swell the numbers, attracted by the mixture of serious study with light-hearted fun. Most of the new recruits were inexperienced

EFDS dancers at Stratford, 1913
EFDSS Photograph Collection

in the dance but threw themselves into it with such wholehearted enthusiasm that, as Helen wrote, 'the local chemist . . . complained that he was sold out of Elliman's Embrocation on the second day of the school'.[8]

Since the venue was Stratford, it is not surprising that a number of Americans were drawn in as spectators. One of these was W. D. Howells, who left a description in his book *Seen and Unseen in Stratford-on-Avon* (1914) which conveys some of what Maud was seeking to put into words:

> I should not be able to say indeed just how or why we found our favored way, one of the first mornings, to the Parish Parlour where we somehow knew that there was to be folk-singing and folk-dancing, and a lecture about both. Two years earlier we had formed the taste for these joys at a whole day of them in the Memorial Theater, and had vowed ourselves never to miss a chance at them. The songs then were sung and the dances danced by young people and children from the neighboring factories and farms, but now the intending teachers of those gay sciences were being taught by one deeply learned in them and of an impassioned devotion to them. One of the ballads was so modern as to be in celebration of the *Shannon*'s victory over the *Chesapeake* in the War of 1812, when the American ship went out from Boston to fight the British, and somehow got beaten. It has a derisive refrain of 'Yankee Doodle Dandy O', and whether or not the lecturer divined our presence, and imagined our pain from this gibe, it is certain that the next time he gave the ballad to be sung he adventurously excused it on the ground that it possibly celebrated the only British victory of the war. Nothing could have been handsomer than that, and it was in the true Shakespearean spirit of Stratford where fourteen thousand Americans come every year, to claim our half of Shakespeare's glory.
>
> Three days of the week the lecturer taught the teachers by precept and example; he talked a little, very simply and unaffectedly, from a full knowledge of his theme, and then he called upon the students to sing and dance. He was not above giving them the pitch from his pipe, and then playing the tune on the piano with the accompaniment of a girl violinist; and we could not choose whether we liked the singing or the dancing better. They sang old country ballads and they danced old country ballets, telling stories, and reverting to the primitive earth-worship in the lilting and the stamping and the bell-clashing of the morris dances. The pictures which the learners made in illustration of the

Maud Karpeles raised up dancing 'Brighton Camp'
EFDSS Photograph Collection

Chapter 3

lecturer's theme were our unfailing joy, but the first morning we had our soul's content absolute beyond any other fortune when the whole glad school issued from the place, and formed in the middle of the street, where, men and maids together, they took the light of the open day with the witchery of their art, as they wove its patterns with their intercircling shapes and their flying feet and their kerchiefs tossing in the air above their heads. This wild joyance was called a Processional, and it was likewise called Tideswell, after the village where it was first imagined. One morning the lecturer joined in it, and became a part of its warp and woof.

It was a vision of Merry England which the heart could give itself to more trustingly than to any dream of the olden time when, with whatever will, England had far less reason to be merry than now.[9] . . .

Twice a week, in the gardens of the theater, there were Morris Dances and Country Dances by the pupil-teachers, whom we could see every morning at the lectures in the Parish Parlor. These joyous events were called by the severe and self-reproachful name of Demonstrations, but by any name they would have been enchanting . . . For a contrast to the lusty blonde English girls, there were two lithe Greek maidens come from their far shores to fly like M[ae]nads on a Grecian urn in the wild figures of those northern dances.[10]

Maud Karpeles with EFDS dancers including George Butterworth
EFDSS Photograph Collection

Cecil Sharp leading dancers in the Tideswell Processional, Stratford-upon-Avon, 1913
EFDSS Photograph Collection

Chapter 3

This last reference was to the black-haired Karpeles girls. Indeed, their surname did frequently result in their being asked if their origins were in Greece. A few years later Maud met W. D. Howells in Boston and disabused him of the idea. At the same time, she enquired of him what a Maenad could be. His reply pleased her: 'Well, I don't exactly know, but I rather think it's something naughty.'[11]

Cecil Sharp was, of course, the lecturer heard by Howells and the

EFDS men's team dancing at Burford, 1913
EFDSS Photograph Collection

demonstrations in the theatre gardens were danced by his team of six men: Perceval Lucas, George Butterworth, and Douglas Kennedy, along with Claude Wright, A. J. Paterson, and George Wilkinson. The last had succeeded Sharp in 1910 as music master at Ludgrove, a preparatory school for Eton, and was 'a beautiful dancer – neat and finished in his movements'.[12] The seventh, or spare man, was Reginald Tiddy, an Oxford don and an Oxfordshire man, who was fluent in the dialect of the villages around

Woodstock, where he went on expeditions with Sharp to teach or to learn from the inhabitants. Among the women, along with Maud and Helen, and Mattie Kay to teach the singers, was Douglas Kennedy's sister. Confusingly, as Helen Karpeles was shortly to become Helen Kennedy, her name was also Helen.

In the summer of 1912 the vacation school was enlivened by the presence in Stratford of Ralph Vaughan Williams, who came to join the dances whenever he was free. RVW was in his fortieth year and, as a somewhat late developer, was just now making his name as a composer. His *Sea Symphony* and *Tallis Fantasia* were behind him; the *London Symphony* was in the process of composition. That season, he was resident composer at the Memorial Theatre – not altogether happily placed because he did not see eye to eye with the producer, Frank Benson, on the incidental music to the plays. Vaughan Williams had the ambition to shake up the theatre's tired repertoire and contribute something fresh, whereas Benson wanted more of what they had always had. The two men may also have failed to hit it off because, while Benson liked to cast his plays and appoint his staff with a view to making up an excellent hockey or cricket team – advertising, for instance, for 'a good fast bowler capable of Laertes' – RVW was notably allergic to games.

The vacation schools introduced a system of examinations for those

Maud Karpeles, George Wilkinson, Helen Karpeles, and Douglas Kennedy, Burford, 1913. EFDSS Photograph Collection

students who came for serious study and granted certificates to the successful. Maud fast became an excellent adjudicator and began to find herself perfectly at ease in such a situation, giving impromptu critical analyses in front of large audiences. In this she astonished herself since, up to that time and on any other topic, she had found extempore speaking impossible. The subject took hold of her and enabled her to abandon all self-consciousness in her eagerness to impart knowledge. This enthusiasm led her to insert into her autobiography many pages of dissertation on the art of the adjudicator and on the detailed aims of the EFDS, along with other subjects that can be found in the archives of the EFDS, to the regrettable exclusion of her personal thoughts and feelings.

Ever since that first Stratford meeting of 1909, Maud and Helen had been in constant touch with Cecil Sharp and their friendship, particularly in the case of Maud, had blossomed. Cecil Sharp was then living at 183 Adelaide Road, Hampstead. His family, which was to become a second family to Maud, consisted of his wife Constance (née Birch) and their four children. The eldest, Dorothea, was eleven years younger than Maud; then came Charles, followed by two more daughters, Joan and Susannah. Joan was the daughter most interested in her father's work and the one who became Maud's particular friend. The Sharps had always been short of money, Constance having brought to the marriage only about £100 a year, a sum less useful in 1910 than it had been in 1893, the year of their marriage. However, they had never permitted the question of finance to worry them and, according to Maud, it was Constance who had persuaded her husband to give up his post as a teacher at Ludgrove School in order to follow his inclination and devote himself almost entirely to the pursuit of folk music, though she cannot have expected him to make a living at it. This represented a considerable sacrifice on her part, as Maud described: 'Constance's lot was not an easy one. Poverty, the ill-health of herself and her family, and the depressions and enthusiasms of her husband – she bore whatever came her way without complaint, and if at times she was worried she did not let Cecil see it. It was a great disappointment to her when he gave up composing for the sake of folk music, but she accepted his judgement as to its greater value, and she willingly shared the sacrifices which it demanded. Indeed, she was always ready to persuade him to give up remunerative work for the uncertain or negative financial return of folk music.'[13]

Between her first visit to the Sharps in Hampstead and 1913, Maud was to become more and more involved with the family. Quickly rising to be

EFDS dancers: (top l-r) Reginald Tiddy, George Jerrard Wilkinson, James Paterson, Perceval Lucas, George Butterworth; (middle l-r) May Stubbs, Maggie Muller, Cecil Sharp, Joan Sharp, Helen Karpeles; (bottom l-r) Maud Karpeles, Douglas Kennedy. EFDSS Photograph Collection (Percy Simms, Chipping Norton)

one of Sharp's most valued teachers, she plunged into regular correspondence with him. In those days, when the telephone was a rarity and you could post a letter in the morning and get a reply by the evening delivery, people were in the habit of writing letters daily. Each night on his folk song excursions Sharp would sit down in the bedroom of his lodgings and write a regular letter to Constance, followed by half a dozen to friends, frequently including Maud. By the middle of 1911, 'Dear Miss Karpeles' had given way to 'My Dear Maud', with the valediction 'yours affectionately'. With the difference in their ages and the more formal manners of that period, Maud's replies were always to be to 'Dear Mr Sharp'.

Though the EFDS was expanding and seeming to flourish, things were not easy for the Sharp family, deprived of the regular salary from Ludgrove, and Cecil, in a mood of depression, talked at one time of throwing up everything and returning to Australia where he had worked, first in a bank and then as a music teacher, for the ten years before his marriage. His eldest daughter, Dorothea, now fell seriously ill, though Maud does not make clear the exact nature of her malady. It was principally on her account that the family decided to leave Hampstead and move to Uxbridge, little more than a village at that time. In May 1911, they moved to a house called Dragonfield, where there was a large airy study for Sharp's work and he was able to enjoy a new pleasure, gardening. Journeys to town, however, proved tiring. Dorothea's health responded and she got well. It was in this year that a bunch of musicians got together and put their names to a petition which they presented to the government, as a result of which Cecil Sharp was awarded a yearly pension of £100 from the Civil List. This brought the family's total income up to about £500 a year.

Not long after the move to Uxbridge, Sharp developed the neuritis in his arm which was to lead to Maud becoming much more to him and the family than an acquaintance and a demonstrator of folk dances. Though it did not curtail his work as a lecturer or prevent him from dancing, it put an end to his piano playing for the time being and made the process of writing words or music agonizingly painful. Peggy Kettlewell took over as accompanist whenever she was free, and when she was absent Butterworth and Maud took turns to play. In 1913 Maud, somewhat tentatively, offered herself as his amanuensis and secretary – tentatively, because she had not yet learned to type. She made this offer in a letter and was delighted to receive an enthusiastic acceptance. She started by taking letters down in longhand but soon managed to learn to use a typewriter, although, to the end of her days, she never became an accurate typist. She also took the trouble to learn shorthand, but found that Sharp preferred to dictate to her typing. Later, however, this rudimentary skill was to prove useful for taking down the words of songs.

She started by doing odd secretarial jobs on the occasions when their activities found them in the same place. Then, over a period of six months, she went almost daily from Bayswater to Uxbridge, getting up at dawn to be at Dragonfield by 8.30 a.m. Sharp's letters, in which he had begun to refer to himself as 'your adopted father', urge her not to overwork or to become too spartan, especially in the matter of the early breakfast hour.

In September, she went on holiday with her parents, taking the typewriter along for practice. Sharp, who was clearly in the habit of teasing her about her size, wrote, 'My dear *little* Maudie! . . . we shall have heaps of work to do when you come back and I hope you will by then have learned to type at railway speed . . . You are a good little soul to help as you do.'[14] It was in this

Stratford-upon-Avon (c. 1912):
(top row l-r) George Jerrald Wilkinson, George Butterworth, Marjorie Sinclair, Douglas Kennedy, Helen Kennedy North, Peggy Walsh, Helen Karpeles, W. Cox;

Chapter 3

(bottom l-r) Winifred Holloway, Maud Karpeles, Cecil Sharp, May Hobbs, Elsie Avril
EFDSS Photograph Collection (F. D. Spencer, Stratford-upon-Avon)

month that they decided it would be best for Maud to live for most of the time with the Sharps. He wrote again: 'My dear small Maudie . . . I expect I shall fag you disgracefully – but you say you like it – and I believe you do – so I shan't spare you. I often see you in my mind's eye sitting by my side writing away patiently & uncomplainingly! I wonder what I should have done without you during the last six months . . . I have got so used to your being in the room when I am working now that so far from hindering you help me! Good-bye. Get as well as you can in the sea air. You were looking very tired like all of us when you said Good bye in that drenching rain on Monday.'[15]

To have an extra daughter in the house was by no means unusual for Constance Sharp. She had, for example, given a home to Mattie Kay, the singer her husband had discovered in Lancashire in 1899 and persuaded to come south for proper training. Mattie was now launched on her professional career, and no doubt there had been others who had shared the Sharp home. Maud was to take her place at Dragonfield and experience a new sort of living, with one maid instead of ten assorted servants, and Constance Sharp providing, according to Douglas Kennedy, 'ample, substantial, but not very interesting food' – the sort of food that drove Cecil Sharp to experiment with vegetarianism. It was a spartan life after the Karpeles's luxurious homes,

Cecil Sharp and dancers on a cross-Channel ferry
EFDSS *Photograph Collection*

but Maud embraced it with the fervour of a young nun taking the veil.

In June of that year, 1913, the 'team' went to Paris to give, for the second time, performances on the stage of a theatre. The trip was a success and was given rapturous notices in the newspapers, French and English alike. For Helen, it was a memorable occasion. She went through the last performance in a blissful dream – mixing up the steps of 'Black Nag' with 'Blue-Eyed Stranger' – having, ten minutes before curtain up, accepted a proposal of marriage from Douglas Kennedy.

Chapter 4

Maud wrote in her autobiography: '1914 was an eventful year.'[1] But the events to which she referred were not the ones that were shaking the world. She was speaking, firstly, of the death of her mother early in the year and the consequent abandonment of the big house in Westbourne Terrace. Though living chiefly in Uxbridge, Maud needed a *pied à terre* in London, and Helen, who was to marry in September, was glad of someone to share a flat with her in Gloucester Road.

The second important event was the fabulous, indeed notorious, production of *A Midsummer Night's Dream* at the Savoy Theatre. With sets and costumes by Norman Wilkinson, this was to gain a place in theatre history on account of the golden fairies. To make a distinction between mortals and supernatural beings, Granville-Barker had the idea of painting gold over every part of their bodies that showed. As the costumes, particularly for the children attendant on Titania, were of the absolute minimum, this virtually meant from head to foot. The legend got about that one unfortunate child literally expired as a result of having all the pores of his skin sealed up. According to Granville-Barker, the most remarkable things about this venture were not 'those d—d gilt fairies', as he called them afterwards, but his superhuman efforts to teach the actors to speak lyric verse, and 'the pushing of Mendelssohn'.[2]

The seeds for the unusual production had been sown two years earlier when the EFDS had danced at the Savoy Theatre. Granville-Barker had watched folk dance, and Sharp had taken an interest in Granville-Barker's Shakespeare presentations, which were more lavish and much more sophisticated than Benson's shows at Stratford. In September 1912, Sharp had been to a performance of *The Winter's Tale* and was moved to write the producer a letter. He described the production as 'one of the most lovely things I have ever witnessed – with, however, one serious qualification – the so-called folk-dancing scene'.[3] This sentence revealed Sharp's fear that the dances staged in the sheep-shearing scene (act 4, scene 4) to music by Felix

Mendelssohn might positively do harm to the folk dance movement.

The reprimand had struck home and had planted an idea in Granville-Barker's mind. Eighteen months later, he enlisted Sharp's active cooperation, contracting him to supply music and arrange dances for *A Midsummer Night's Dream*. £100 was offered, to be paid two weeks after opening, and £5 a week after the first six weeks of the run. Articles were published in the press defending Granville-Barker's decision, for the first time in many years, to scrap the popular Mendelssohn music in favour of something that would be more appropriate to Shakespeare's time and that would not hold up the action to the extent that the Mendelssohn did, however beautiful it might be. Maud attended rehearsals and helped train the dancers, and was even fitted with a pair of gold tights in case she was called upon to understudy – something that, to her regret, never came to pass. She was fascinated to watch, for the first time, a professional director at work. To his letter of thanks to the composer for having brought off 'something real and genuine and beautiful for us', Barker added a PS: 'I have sent a line to Miss Karpeles.'[4] He sent with it a copy of the acting edition of the play, inscribed:

> To Miss Karpeles
> A very small keepsake
> In much gratitude
> H. Granville Barker
> May 1914.

It was this production that was to transport Cecil Sharp across the Atlantic and to lead indirectly to his four years' adventure with Maud in the Appalachians.

The happenings that were to make 1914 an eventful year for the rest of the world caught up with Maud and her colleagues at Stratford-upon-Avon. She wrote: 'Though we had felt uneasy for some time, war came as a thunderbolt to many of us (certainly to me). It was the end of an epoch. No one who has not experienced the pre-war days can have any idea of what they were like. We felt we were on the eve of some Utopia. We believed in progress . . . I found it difficult to realize its implications. The only war I had previously known was the Boer War and that was far off and had not affected me personally.'[5]

The vacation school, her third, was well under way when war was

Scene from Harley Granville-Barker's production of A Midsummer Night's Dream, Savoy Theatre, 1914
EFDSS Photograph Collection (Daily Mirror)

Chapter 4

declared and, though a few subscribers cancelled, was allowed to run its normal course until the end of August. The men's demonstration team remained intact up to the last day, then dispersed, never to dance together again. The next four months remained hazy in Maud's mind. Douglas Kennedy was already enlisted in the London Scottish Regiment when he and Helen married on 28 September. Up until then he had been studying botany at the Imperial College of Science and Joseph Karpeles was not best pleased to be giving his daughter away to what he called 'an impecunious student'. In the end, though, he was persuaded to give his blessing to the match.

At fifty-four, Cecil Sharp was too old for active service, but his son, Charles, went off, without consulting his parents, added three months to his age, and eventually broke through the barrier imposed by his imperfect eyesight to become a private in the Middlesex Regiment. All the members of the folk dance team managed to get into uniform. Ralph Vaughan Williams, edging towards being too old at the age of forty-two, got himself into the Special Constables as a sergeant and thence into the Royal Army Medical Corps. Butterworth immediately joined the Duke of Cornwall's

EFDS men's team, 1912, with Elsie Avril on fiddle
EFDSS Photograph Collection

Chapter 4

Arthur Karpeles and friend
EFDSS Photograph Collection (Moore's Studio, Camberwell)

Light Infantry and was commissioned in November. Tiddy went into the 24th Oxfordshire Regiment. Young Arthur Karpeles joined up. But Cecil Sharp could find no job of national importance, though his need to earn a living was acute.

Then, on 15 December 1914, ten months after the London production of *A Midsummer Night's Dream*, Granville-Barker sent a telegram to Dragonfield from New York. It read: 'Almost certain produce *Dream* January advise you travel *Lusitania* anyway glad pay expenses.'[6] In the circumstances, with nothing he could usefully contribute to the war at home, Sharp decided to act on Granville-Barker's proposition, the more so as he had been in correspondence with one or two people in America on the subject of folk song and dance and was confident that a programme of lectures could be arranged.

On that particular occasion, the ill-fated *Lusitania*'s journey was uneventful, apart from horrible weather. Sharp wrote to Maud on 21 December that he was, for him, exceptionally well, not being subject to seasickness, but was suffering from depression, homesickness, and the dread of arriving in a country where he knew nobody apart from the Granville-Barkers. He was upset, moreover, at having had Maud's parting present – a new umbrella – stolen on the ship. 'I expect you too, little woman, are feeling rather slack with no one to bully you and make you work for him!'[7] Indeed, she wrote later: 'I felt bereft by his absence. I dealt with his correspondence as best I could and kept the ball rolling by doing some folk-dance teaching and other work in connection with the EFDS.'[8] The rest of the time she spent improving her shorthand.

On his arrival in New York, Sharp went straight to the Algonquin Hotel. The hotel, which was later to become the somewhat notorious mecca of American writers, was then comparatively unknown, and he described it as 'fairly comfortable but distinctly 2nd-class'.[9] This judgement was later revised, for it became, in fact, his and Maud's 'American home' for four years, where they left superfluous luggage and had their correspondence addressed, and where the welcome, each time they returned, was effusive from management and staff alike.

Two days after his arrival, Sharp spent Christmas with the Granville-Barkers. As well as *A Midsummer Night's Dream*, Granville-Barker was planning a repertory to include Shaw's *Androcles and the Lion* and *The Doctor's Dilemma* and Anatole France's *The Man Who Married a Dumb Wife*. Lonely and out of sorts, Sharp wrote copious letters, in spite of the pain in his arm, describing to Maud all that he disliked in New York: the 'steam-heated rooms' and cold air outside,[10] as well as the insincere effusiveness of many Americans, combined with an unashamed dedication to personal advantage.[11]

The weather was icy and, prompted by Granville-Barker, he spent ten dollars on a fur coat because an ulster was 'not the correct thing' in New York.[12] He also bought a new umbrella, but this he promptly left behind at the Granville-Barkers' hotel. Rehearsals and auditions for dancers were soon under way, and he was able to arrange for a number of lectures on folk song. Elated by this success, he cabled for Mattie Kay to come over to sing the illustrations for him.

The great event of the beginning of 1915 was his meeting with Mrs Storrow, one of his correspondents. She owned a beautiful house at Lincoln, Massachusetts, and on the first occasion that he was her weekend guest he wrote enthusiastically to Maud: 'Mrs Storrow is quite charming. She is 50 years of age as she told me ... she is mainly intellectual ... like all Unitarians, especially of the Boston type – although she has an emotional side and great kindliness more or less atrophied or at any rate reformed. I fancy we shall quarrel a bit – we have already differed – but we shall get on all right.'[13] He was delighted with the 'Gorgeous suite of rooms' in which she had installed him,[14] and enjoyed joining the family in tobogganing in the all-too-plentiful snow. He was also enchanted with the superior quality of the American trains, finding his trip to Boston 'not a journey so much as a ceremonial'.[15]

Mattie Kay arrived, bearing messages from Maud and a box of slides to help illustrate the lectures, but Sharp was soon to discover that bringing the singer across the Atlantic had been a costly mistake. New York audiences were unimpressed by the songs, their interest being solely in folk dancing. They had no conception of the style of singing folk song required, and Mattie's soft, pure contralto had a lady enquiring why he did not employ a good trained opera singer.

The *Midsummer Night's Dream* rehearsals went badly, the dancers being inexperienced and hard to teach. The only bright spot Sharp noted was the casting of Bottom the Weaver. He thought Ernest Cossart, brother of Gustav Holst, 'much better than [Nigel] Playfair'.[16] *Androcles* and *The Dumb Wife* opened, and went better than anybody had expected, and Granville-Barker, much to Sharp's relief, agreed to postpone the opening of the *Dream*. The altered arrangements, however, cut into an agreement to lecture in Boston and made Mrs Storrow understandably angry. Distress at offending his new friend and patron, and a disagreement with his agent, upset Sharp to the extent that he resolved to leave the USA as soon as the play was over. He wrote Maud an anti-feminist letter, which he knew would provoke her wrath, stating that his agent, Jean Wick, was *non compos mentis* because she was pregnant, and never again would he employ a woman.

Changed habits – cigarettes instead of a pipe, no afternoon nap, bed as late as 4 a.m. after rehearsals – put him out of sorts. He was angry that Granville-Barker would not pay for his work on *The Dumb Wife* and that the American dancers were awful. However, in the event, the first night of

Helen Storrow and Maud Karpeles, Amherst, 1928
University of New Hampshire Library, Milne Special Collections, CDSS Archives (MC 140)

A Midsummer Night's Dream went surprisingly well and he wrote to Maud: 'The more I hear the music and see the dances the more I like them. But this does not make me feel at all conceited. I simply feel that it is a triumph for folk dance and folk song, and all the credit that I can gather is that I have had the sense to use folk stuff for the purpose. I think Shakespeare ... would thoroughly approve of our way of handling it!'[17]

Meanwhile, a visit to a demonstration by Isadora Duncan and her pupils provoked a letter that must have diverted Maud. The dark room, the drab curtains, left a nasty taste in his mouth, and Isadora herself 'presented a gruesome spectacle ... very fat & rather coarse'.[18] The dancing, rather than rhythmical movements, he described as 'mere posing', concluding, 'if I were to prescribe I should recommend ... at least six men of the Butterworth type!', George Butterworth being solidly masculine, with a gruff voice and a bushy black moustache. Sharp was invited to tea with the dancer next day but regrettably did not describe the occasion.

About this time he met Mrs Dawson Callery, the beautiful young wife of a Pittsburgh steel magnate. She was to become, like Mrs Storrow, a pillar of strength, and it was her prompt organization of vacation courses, lectures, and demonstrations that caused Sharp to change his mind about shaking the dust of America off his feet. He wrote: 'Both [Mrs Storrow and Mrs Callery] are well-off. They are the only two women I have met here whom I should call *ladies* ... *you* know what I mean by that.'[19]

He also made friends also with Charles Rabold, a practising musician who danced well, and Susan Gilman, principal of a fashionable New York dance studio, who at once fell in with his ideas and ideals. The two were to become his best friends across the Atlantic and did much to propagate the dances in future years. Thanks to the help and commissions from these people, Sharp was able to settle his rather embarrassing account with Mattie Kay and despatch her back to England.

With plans for a return visit to hold classes in Boston and Pittsburgh in June – plans that were to include Maud – and with his practical work at the theatre finished, he busied himself with the formation of an American branch of the EFDS, with centres in New York, Boston, Chicago, and Pittsburgh. This was later to be named the Country Dance and Song Society of America.

But Sharp was getting impatient to be at home with his family, the more so as the future seemed securely mapped. Three days of classes at Pittsburgh, followed by a week in Chicago, proved tiring, and he did not yield to his

American friends' advice to cancel his passage on the *Adriatic* on 21 April in favour of the *Lusitania* a week later. They argued that he could rest and that the ship would be familiar to him. Sharp, however, hated changing his plans – and, as Maud pointed out, on this occasion his obstinacy probably saved his life. Before he left New York he bought presents for his wife, the children, and Maud, and gave a farewell dinner at the Algonquin for the Granville-Barkers, after which they went to see Isadora Duncan play *Oedipus*. Again, regrettably, he wrote no description of the event.

Chapter 5

Maud was at Euston when Cecil returned home. Constance had journeyed to Liverpool to meet him, and all three proceeded to Uxbridge. Maud had been looking forward to his arrival with 'joyful anticipation . . . I had come to picture him', she wrote, 'almost as a knight in shining armour. This vision was dispelled when I caught sight of him walking along the platform with weary, dragging step and a careworn expression on his face.'[1]

He recovered strength and spirits after a short time spent peacefully at home, but most of his four weeks' stay in England was a bustle of activity. Maud went with him to judge an eisteddfod in Bristol. They discussed the future of the Stratford Festival, and met friends such as A. H. Fox Strangways and Gustav Holst. The latter, unfit for army service, was employed on military music and he and Cecil discussed the possible use of folk songs for marching tunes. Maud and Cecil also went on endless walks, making plans for a pageant at Wellesley College, Massachusetts, and taking time off to search for a tea service as a belated wedding present for Helen and Douglas Kennedy.

Nine days after Sharp's return they read of the sinking of the *Lusitania*, but undaunted by this narrow escape they went on enquiring for a suitable ship, not only for themselves but for Lily Roberts, a dancing colleague who had been persuaded to go ahead of them to Wellesley as a paid teacher. On a more personal level, the Sharp family was again involved in moving house, with the intention of returning once more to Hampstead, and on 3 May Sharp signed the lease on 93 Fitzjohn's Avenue. This, clearly, came second in his scale of values to the American project, for his diaries make no mention of his ever going to look at the house. Then, just as all plans had been completed, disaster struck. Along with Constance and other members of the Sharp household, Maud developed scarlet fever and Cecil had to sail from Liverpool alone, on 29 May. He reported to his diary that his cabin companions were extremely apprehensive of submarines as they steamed through the danger zone, but that he himself slept soundly. Rabold and Miss

Gilman welcomed him to New York and he went straight to the Callerys in Pittsburgh, where he conducted classes.

Maud was not far behind. She sailed a week later on the American ship *St Louis* and arrived to be overcome with wonder at her first sight of Manhattan. She had to restrain an impulse to fall flat in worship: 'It resembled grand mountain scenery, but it seemed all the more impressive for being man-made.'[2] Sharp was on his way from Pittsburgh to Boston, but Mrs Storrow sent a young man from her staff to drive Maud around New York to see the sights before putting her on a train. She arrived overcome with embarrassment: 'In my ignorance of American travel customs I did not realize that checked luggage was not necessarily . . . put on the same train as the passenger, and I felt rather foolish when . . . I finally arrived at Boston with only a portable typewriter.'[3]

Cecil met her and they drove to the luxurious house in Lincoln where, no doubt, a nightdress and toothbrush were lavishly supplied. The missing cases turned up the next day and enabled Maud, correctly dressed, to dance in the Wellesley College pageant. Lily Roberts had successfully taught the students their dances, so that it only remained for Cecil to add the finishing touches. This proved a great mercy as he was suddenly stricken with acute lumbago, an attack that was to last ten days. Mrs Storrow's doctor strapped him up in adhesive plaster, to the extent that he could hardly get in and out of bed. In the end, he was seen by three doctors and an osteopath, quarrelled with them all, and dismissed the entire medical profession as a bunch of quacks. Maud, Lily, and Mrs Storrow's kind attentions were of greater solace, but a plan to visit Philadelphia to make gramophone records had to be abandoned.

It was during this period of enforced leisure that the most important encounter Sharp was to have in the States took place. Immobilized in Mrs Storrow's house, 'sitting very straight in an imposing high-backed chair',[4] he received a visit from Mrs Olive Dame Campbell. This lady had long known of his fame and, hearing he was back in America, had made the journey from Asheville, North Carolina, to consult him about folk songs. Her husband was a director of the Russell Sage Foundation, an organization that assisted educational projects in the Southern mountains, and she brought with her a collection of words and music that she had noted on expeditions in the Appalachians with him. Sharp apologized for not being able to rise to greet her, explaining that his disability was gout – 'a rich man's malady ... but that he owed it to his ancestors rather than to any luxuries permitted by his own income'.[5]

They quickly got down to business, Mrs Campbell explaining that she was not a trained musician. Sharp spent a long time perusing her bundle of papers, while she waited in trepidation. Then he questioned her closely on her method of recording and pronounced it to be 'very unscientific'. While she was recovering from this blow, he 'finally laid the pile of manuscripts on the table ... as he explained how many people had brought "ballads" to him before, but that this was the first time that he had come on any really original and valuable material'.[6]

'I am told', she wrote later, 'that he improved from that day.'[7]

Certainly, it was not long afterwards that he noted in his diary that he was now 'only half a cripple', and the next day was instructing Maud and Lily on the lawn. The day after, he danced himself before a luncheon gathering of forty-five people. Mrs Campbell's hoard had opened up a marvellous prospect for the future and was a tonic as well as a potential treasure house. The songs she had brought were none other than variants of English ones, some of them of extreme antiquity, which had made their way across the Atlantic with the early settlers and which might well exist in the Appalachians in forms more ancient and authentic than any Sharp had collected at home. He resolved that he would visit and explore the mountains himself.

Olive Dame Campbell manuscript
EFDSS, Cecil Sharp Manuscripts, Miscellaneous Materials

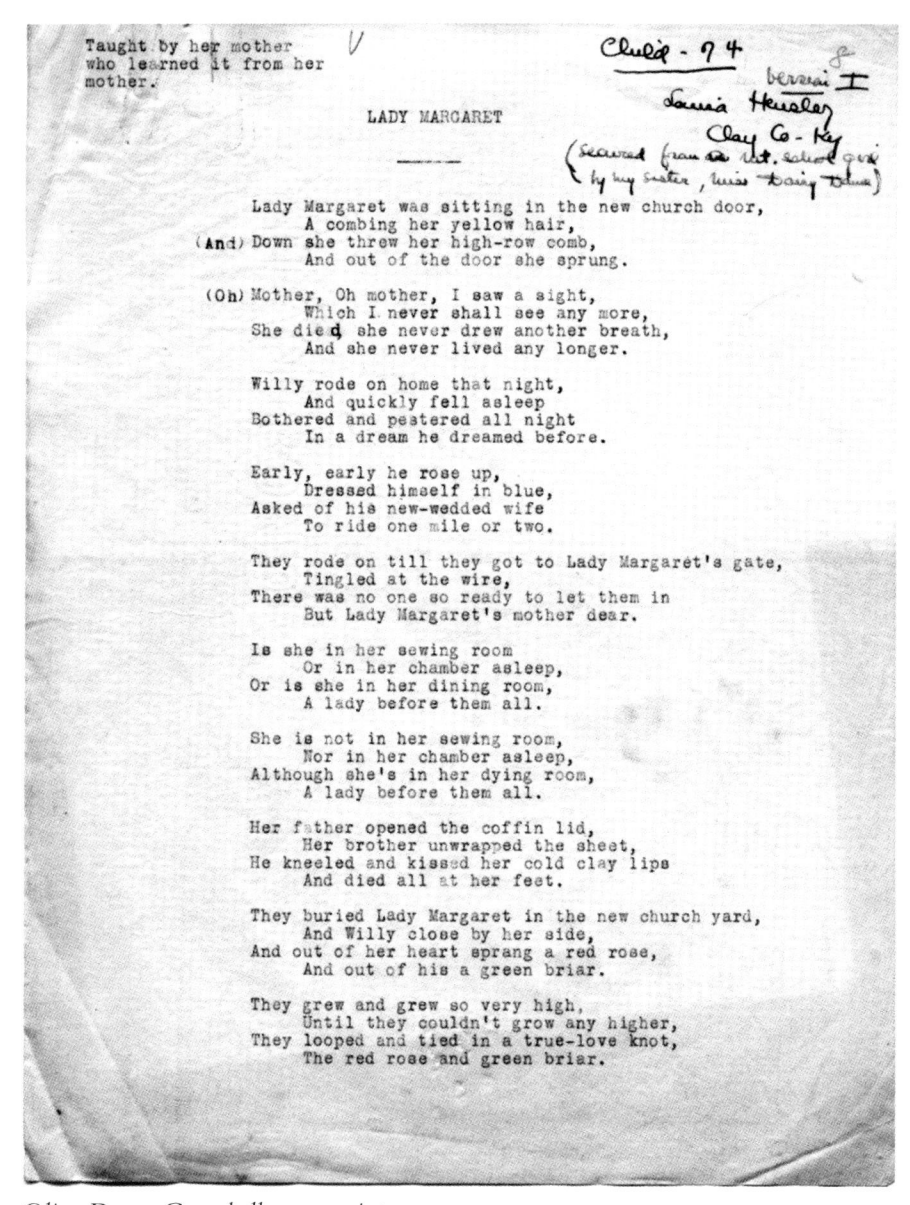

> Taught by her mother who learned it from her mother.
>
> Child - 74
> bersai I
> Laura Hensler
> Clay Co - Ky
> (secured from a dist. school girl by my sister, Miss Daisy Dame)
>
> ### LADY MARGARET
>
> Lady Margaret was sitting in the new church door,
>   A combing her yellow hair,
> (And) Down she threw her high-row comb,
>   And out of the door she sprung.
>
> (Oh) Mother, Oh mother, I saw a sight,
>   Which I never shall see any more,
> She died she never drew another breath,
>   And she never lived any longer.
>
> Willy rode on home that night,
>   And quickly fell asleep
> Bothered and pestered all night
>   In a dream he dreamed before.
>
> Early, early he rose up,
>   Dressed himself in blue,
> Asked of his new-wedded wife
>   To ride one mile or two.
>
> They rode on till they got to Lady Margaret's gate,
>   Tingled at the wire,
> There was no one so ready to let them in
>   But Lady Margaret's mother dear.
>
> Is she in her sewing room
>   Or in her chamber asleep,
> Or is she in her dining room,
>   A lady before them all.
>
> She is not in her sewing room,
>   Nor in her chamber asleep,
> Although she's in her dying room,
>   A lady before them all.
>
> Her father opened the coffin lid,
>   Her brother unwrapped the sheet,
> He kneeled and kissed her cold clay lips
>   And died all at her feet.
>
> They buried Lady Margaret in the new church yard,
>   And Willy close by her side,
> And out of her heart sprang a red rose,
>   And out of his a green briar.
>
> They grew and grew so very high,
>   Until they couldn't grow any higher,
> They looped and tied in a true-love knot,
>   The red rose and green briar.

Olive Dame Campbell manuscript
EFDSS, Cecil Sharp Manuscripts, Miscellaneous Materials

On 25 June, Maud and Cecil took the train to Eliot, Maine, a beautiful spot overlooking the Piscataqua River which divides that state from New Hampshire. There, beside an old barn, two canvas pavilions with wooden floors for dancing had been erected for the vacation school. If Maud did keep a diary of that first visit to the USA, it has been lost or destroyed. Her

Chapter 5

journals for 1917 and 1918 managed to survive even her own written injunction on the title page: 'Destroy'. Consequently, for 1915 and 1916 only Sharp's diaries provide a day-to-day record. In her unpublished autobiography Maud recalled the pleasure she felt in meeting, for the first time, a bunch of young Americans, whose 'boundless enthusiasm and eagerness to learn' produced some 'first-rate dancers'.[8]

It was more difficult to persuade them to sing, but by the time they had reached the third week most of them had shed their self-consciousness. If the school was lucky in its students, however, it was extremely unfortunate in its weather.

All began in glorious sunshine, with Cecil noting that the place seemed to agree with him. The teachers were comfortably lodged in a farmhouse,

Cecil Sharp and Maud Karpeles at Eliot, Maine, 1915
EFDSS Photograph Collection

A typical home of Appalachian singers where Cecil and Maud stayed
EFDSS, *Cecil Sharp Photograph Collection*

Chapter 5

while the students were boarded in temporary wooden shacks. The heat was tempered by a pleasant breeze. But on the fifth day this changed to an easterly gale which brought torrents of rain, so that the first demonstration had to be held in the barn. The sixth day produced 5.33 inches –'*some* rain', as Cecil wrote. It cleared for the 4 July celebrations, a day marked from midnight onwards by continual 'explosives and crackers', but two days later saw the return of the gale, which blew down the marquees, and the rain, which flooded the students' huts. Mrs Storrow made hasty arrangements to transfer the whole enterprise to a nearby hotel with a conference centre. There, examinations were held, public demonstrations given, and the whole thing ended up with a farewell 'jollification'. Though the rooms proved adequate, the food was so bad that Maud and Cecil had to go into nearby Portsmouth to buy cheese and marmalade to supplement the meagre diet. This was the beginning of a three-year battle with American food which upset Cecil and, as he had now persuaded her to join him as a vegetarian, did no good to Maud.

She looked back, however, on those three weeks as a 'happy gathering',[9] and one in which they made many good friends. They had no time to linger over farewells, though, for the Stratford-upon-Avon vacation school was looming on the horizon, so they returned promptly to New York. There, they had just time for Cecil to take Maud for a walk to show her Broadway before they set sail for England aboard the *St Paul*.

In the absence of a diary, it is only possible to speculate on Maud's feelings at the start of that eight-day voyage. Could her adoration of Cecil have been a little dampened by his intolerably cheerful well-being? His notes reveal him to have been one of those excellent sailors whose demeanour would grate horribly on the seasick. Conceit was perhaps forgivable in one who, on land, was so remorselessly subject to every illness, ache, and pain in the medical dictionary. Maud, as he noted on various crossings of the Atlantic, was inclined to keep to her cabin for the first few days at sea. This time, she was in a tiny one, while Cecil's was commodious.

She was able, however, to emerge after a few days to enjoy, and help record on paper, the fruits of Cecil's latest discovery. This was Mr Harry Perrey, a crew member and a first-rate singer of sea shanties. Every day, in his off-duty period, he would appear at Sharp's cabin door 'equipped with a sheet of newspaper which he solicitously spread on the bed before taking his seat upon it',[10] and sing to them. The travellers reached home after their less than three weeks' absence with an unexpectedly rich harvest, Harry Perrey's

Chapter 5

Harry Perrey
EFDSS, Cecil Sharp Photograph Collection

shanties adding to the store of songs that had been unearthed by Mrs Campbell.

The homecoming was not to be a happy one. There was no Constance to meet the boat at Liverpool and the news that greeted their arrival at Euston was that she was confined to bed. Serious heart trouble had succeeded the bout of scarlet fever, but this she had tactfully kept out of her letters. The move to Hampstead had fallen through and it was to Uxbridge that Maud and Cecil hastened, to discover Constance in her bed, but looking, Cecil's diary noted, very well. She was to remain a semi-invalid for the rest of her life.

Fortunately, Cecil's daughters were well and presumably ready to look after their mother, for the returned husband did not linger long at home. Indeed, Constance's frequent illnesses seemed never to have held him back from any planned project, for she always put herself second to his interests and his work. Assisted by his daughter Joan, Maud and Cecil plunged into a whirl of activity with preparations for Stratford and meetings of the EFDS, in the intervals of which they hastily copied out the new collection of sea shanties.

Joan Sharp went with them to Stratford, where rooms had been booked at Rosemary, a house with a fine garden in the Shottery Road. It was not surprising, in the middle of a world war, that the number of participants in the vacation school was down on earlier years. The celebrations, classes, lectures, demonstrations, and examinations went on for the first twenty-one days of August, with Maud working unusually hard to make up for Cecil's several trips to London to visit Constance and to go house-hunting. Maud's sister Helen came with her husband Douglas Kennedy, and his sister, the other Helen Kennedy, came too. Thus, with Cecil, they were able to make up a team to demonstrate 'fours' as they had done in the summers of peace. Occasionally they found time for a bicycle ride along what were then unmetalled, dusty roads beside the Avon.

After a final party and a dinner with Sir Archibald Flower, they packed up to return to London. Here they went to look at 27 Church Row, Hampstead, and Cecil settled upon making an offer for it. Negotiations took most of September and the family finally moved into 'a panelled house of the late seventeenth century, described by Cecil as "about the time of the sixth edition of Playford"'.[11] There seem to have been fewer rooms than at Dragonfield, for Maud took lodgings for herself and her typewriter nearby.

Chapter 6

The Stratford 'jollifications' were to be the last happy days for a long time. The rest of 1915 and the winter months that began 1916 were the most miserable Maud had ever known. After the excitement of the American visit and the busyness of Stratford all was suddenly grey and hopeless, both for her and for the family, newly settled in Hampstead, which had come to be more to her than her own.

Cecil was restive and despondent. The men of his folk dance team – Wilkinson, Tiddy, and Butterworth – were at the front; Douglas was on war work in the north; Vaughan Williams was in France; and even the semi-invalid Holst (who had, for expediency's sake, dropped the 'von' from his family name of von Holst) was in uniform, purveying music to the troops on the battlefield. There seemed nothing for Cecil to do but to continue editing his collection of songs, but the gloomy war situation made it increasingly obvious that the great English folk revival he had been hoping for was not going to come about. Everybody had more serious things on their minds. Only across the Atlantic, in a country still at peace, did there seem to be any prospects. Money was increasingly short, not only for travel and research, but for the upkeep of an invalid wife and a new house. Maud experienced the full brunt of Cecil's depression. She was herself feeling a pressing duty to go into war work, but held back because he had such obvious need of her, both as a confidante for his hopes and fears, and as his helper, secretary, and maid-of-all-work. While he had been alone in the USA, she had practised hard at her typing and now her proficiency made her indispensable.

In the intervals of preparing *One Hundred English Folk-Songs* for a Boston publisher, with revised texts and rewritten accompaniments, the two of them sent out feelers to the USA in the hope of attracting enough lecture engagements to pay for a further visit. Mrs Storrow was approached for the names of people who might help finance a collecting trip to the Appalachians. She came up with Richard Aldrich, music critic on the *New York Times*, who, she thought, might approach the Carnegie Corporation.

Correspondence with Mrs Campbell made Sharp eager to get to the mountains, but he was hesitant to rush in and gather a rich harvest where she had done the spadework, or to take to himself credit that ought to have been hers. At the same time, he was anxious that her unprofessional methods should be supplemented by some technical expertise. His approach was tactful and tentative, but he need not have worried. Olive Campbell was an exceptional character, totally disinterested and without a trace of envy or desire for personal gain or recognition. She wrote to Sharp, 'I in no way have a special right in collecting material in this region', and continued:

> I want you to understand that I would not for a moment think of your plan as interfering with anything that I may have done in the past, even supposing that some time in the future I might want to do some more collecting; indeed, it would be a distinct advantage to me to work with you. In collecting the songs, I was not considering any possible financial gain nor literary prestige. I liked [the songs], knew they were valuable from a scientific point of view, and I hoped that if I could get them published they would be a real contribution to folk lore . . .
>
> I want the collecting done and done by the person most competent to do it, and if I could have wished for a definite result from my work, it would have been to attract to this region just such a person as yourself.[1]

No help was forthcoming from Carnegie, but there was little to do at home and Mrs Storrow was urging Sharp to take the risk and sail for the USA. By the beginning of February, he had resolved to do so, confident that she, at least, would come to his rescue in dire emergency. He found it more difficult to leave Maud behind than to abandon Constance, and the parting caused them much pain for there was, at the time, no prospect of her joining him in America. Neither was it a moment when a voyage across the Atlantic was to be undertaken lightly.

A little parting festivity was organized by Maud, though, which in the event seems to have caused more distress than if Cecil had said goodbye in London. She and Joan took the train with him to Falmouth and stayed in a hotel until he was able to board the *Nieuw Amsterdam*. They had all of two days to explore the port before he was allowed on board, but they spent their time in a mood of such despondency that it was a relief when the parting came. But even when the ship stood out to sea it did not vanish out of sight of the two women on the quayside. Rumours of submarine activity kept it close to land for several hours. Eventually, in mid-Atlantic, Cecil wrote: 'How good it was of you to engineer it! . . . And partings are such horrible things . . . I carry two pictures in my mind . . . which I see when I am in my bunk trying to go to sleep. One is a picture of you & Joany standing at the end of the pier gradually fading away . . . and the other is Con's sad old face at the window seeing the taxi go off to Paddington . . . I fancy it will not be long before I shall have to send for you! You have made me feel quite dependent you little wretch!'[2]

When Maud got back to London she was able to salve her conscience by at last taking up some recognized war work. She became a clerk in the London office of the Women's Land Army and was kept fully occupied. The toil she had put in learning to be secretary to Cecil paid off handsomely and she had the added satisfaction of keeping her typing in good practice. Long letters arrived by every possible post. She shook her head in wry amusement to read that when Sharp landed in New York it was to find again that his umbrella had been stolen between the ship and the customs. But the rest of the news was good. Once on US soil and among friends engagements came pouring in for lectures, demonstrations, and vacation courses. He wrote to his friend Paul Oppé from Kalamazoo: 'I am selling myself for a week at a time to different cities – Asheville, St. Louis, Cincinnati and now here, and after this for a month at Pittsburgh. I charge a pretty high figure – high, that is, to English notions – and then let them get what they can out of me.'[3]

He was even able to send money home to keep the family going, and rejoiced that he was attracting classes of as many as seventy or eighty students. It was not long, however, before the strain of the work began to tell and it was on one of his stints at Pittsburgh that Mrs Callery begged him to send for Maud. This was, of course, exactly what he longed to do, as every letter he wrote to her bore witness. Besides, Maud had an allowance from her father and could afford to pay her own passage.

Maud had a brief struggle with her conscience at abandoning, so quickly, her war work and sailing away from beleaguered England, but she argued that the little she could do for the war effort was not comparable with the assistance she could give to Cecil; besides, she, too, was itching to get at the store of riches hidden in the Appalachians. Cecil's relief to hear that she was really starting out was enormous: 'It seemed too good to be true. I was in a horrid grubby hotel at the time and feeling very overtired & overworked and the thought that you were coming out to help me was something more than I can write about . . . I cannot meet you at New York – this seems to be my fate! . . . I have asked Rabold to meet you . . . It looks today as though there were going to be war with America but one never knows. Good bye my dear little woman.'[4]

This letter, written on 18 April, greeted Maud on her arrival five days later. She left no description of her voyage across the perilous sea, but Sharp's diary for 24 April, when she arrived in Pittsburgh, noted: 'Maud looks very well & delighted to be at the end of her journey. She brought a whiff of home with her and made me feel a bit homesick especially about Joan because she will miss Maud the most.'[5] Cecil took her straight off to see the office Mrs Callery had reserved for them and then to call on Mrs Callery herself. It is a pity Maud left no description of this lady, whom Cecil had described in a letter as 'young – not quite such a kiddy as you – beautiful and the wife of a millionaire much older than herself'.[6] Maud had been accommodated in the Country Club, to save her the expense of a hotel. In the evening, they returned to Mrs Callery's house for Cecil's favourite nightcap of milk and biscuits after a 'long & exciting day'.[7]

The Pittsburgh school continued for three weeks, with Maud taking daily 'Playground' classes for children, demonstrating morris dances, and filling every spare moment seeing the country in their hostess's car. They met a number of interesting people, including the pianist Solomon, the theatre director Ben Iden Payne, and the great William Poel who had founded the Elizabethan Stage Society. The year 1916 was the tercentenary of the death of Shakespeare, and Pittsburgh's contribution to the festivities was a production of *The Winter's Tale*, for which Sharp provided the dances for the sheep-shearing scene. The school ended with a meeting of the EFDS and a country dance party for over nine hundred people. Mrs Callery saw them off to New York the next day and they arrived at their old home, the Algonquin, after a pleasant ride through beautiful country.

New York's contribution to the Shakespeare festivities was an elaborate pageant, *The Masque of Caliban*. Sharp disliked most forms of pageantry, but he was sensible enough to see this as an opportunity to push his creed of English folk dance and song correctly performed, so he accepted a request to contribute an 'Interlude'. With five hundred dancers he staged a May Day festival on a village green with processions, morris dances, maypole, and hobby horse. 'It was like a puff of fresh country air laden with the smell of hedgerows,' he wrote.[8] 'And the spirit of the tunes and dances was such that all participants became infected by it and for the moment they became English, every Jew, German, French, Italian, Slav one of them.' Sitting among the crowd on the first night, Maud 'felt a justifiable pride in being English'.⁹ The audience, estimated at twenty thousand, in the New York Stadium, was enchanted. The Interlude was repeated at St Louis and Cincinnati, with equal success.

The now familiar round of lectures, demonstrations, and dances was staged next at Susan Gilman's New York school and culminated in the award of a Gold Medal to Sharp at the local EFDS centre. Then, from 23 June, came the engagement they most looked forward to: Mrs Storrow's summer school, this time held at Amherst College, Massachusetts. Lily Roberts and many of their dancing friends turned up and the three weeks followed the pattern that had been set at Eliot, Maine, without, however, the spectacular weather and general discomfort.

Independence Day was again marked by a celebration, 'much quieter and less boisterous than last year'. The exams were an extraordinary success since everybody passed – 'a very unusual result'.¹⁰

Lily Roberts, Cecil Sharp, Maud Karpeles, and Nora Parkes Jervis at Amherst, 1916. EFDSS Photograph Collection (C. B. Fuller)

At the end of it all, Maud was delighted to receive this note from Aunt Helen, as Mrs Storrow had now become: 'I was ever so sorry not to see you again, nor to dance again under your discerning eye ... As we learn more little by little about the dances we appreciate better the quality of your teaching, it is certainly a revelation to some of us! Please take great care of yourself and of the sacred person of Mr. Sharp.'[11] This was a reference to their impending departure for the Appalachians.

Some time before Maud's arrival, Cecil had made a brief visit to Mr and Mrs Campbell at their home in Asheville, North Carolina, and had had his first taste of life in the mountains. The Campbells' house stood on the edge of a pine wood overlooking a beautiful valley and he had spent four days going through ballads, consulting maps, and making tentative plans for the collecting expedition. Now, at last, in the second half of July, they were ready to set off on the great adventure of their lives.

Chapter 7

With over four months of lecturing behind him, Cecil Sharp had managed to get himself on a better financial footing, but most of the money was being sent across the ocean to his family. The cost of a lengthy trip to the Appalachians, without official backing, was daunting. However, Mrs Storrow came to the rescue with a donation, and Maud was only too anxious to cover her own expenses. A final week was spent in New York seeing friends (they ate an extravagant dinner at the Beaux Arts Club with Charles Rabold), making records, and fitting themselves out with sturdy shoes and practical garments for the mountains.

On Sunday, 23 July 1916, Cecil and Maud left for Asheville in tropical heat. 'The train journey', Maud recalled, 'was ordinarily an easy one taking less than twenty-four hours, but owing to recent floods portions of the main-line had been washed away and we were forced to make a big detour. This meant spending forty-eight hours in the train, the last part of the journey being made on a small branch mountain railway, and staying one night in a small mining-town hotel, which was so dirty that I did not venture to undress.'[1] It would have been a futile gesture had she done so, as her suitcase with her nightclothes had gone missing somewhere between Knoxville and Copper Hill. So, for the second time, poor Maud was to arrive to stay with American hosts minus her luggage. She was less fortunate here than in Boston, for the case had been stolen. Nothing, however, could extinguish Cecil's joy at having got to the mountains: 'despite the heat, the dust, the lack of food, the swarms of flies, hay fever, asthma, etc., it was a wonderful trip'.[2]

The next few days were spent in the comfort of the Campbell house, Maud making expeditions into Asheville to repair her losses. To Cecil's disappointment, Olive Campbell would not go along with them, pleading pressure of work. It is more likely that she felt they had better plunge in on their own. Her husband accompanied them on the first stage of their journey to deliver them to their next hosts, the Packhards of White Rock. Had it not

Olive and John C. Campbell
John C. Campbell Folk School

been for his company, the inexperienced mountain travellers might well have given up after that first day. 'We were able to motor a short distance', Maud wrote, 'and then we transferred ourselves into what was locally known as a Surry, a very primitive four-wheeled dog-cart . . . drawn by a couple of horses. The "roads" were either a morass or a dry creek-bed strewn with boulders; and over and over again we had to negotiate sharp hair-pin curves while driving along a narrow ledge on the edge of a precipice. The journey of forty miles took us ten hours, and I was scared stiff the whole time.'[3] Sharp, too, was frightened out of his wits, but found the scenery an extraordinary compensation: 'the most magnificent I have ever seen . . . The mountains go from six thousand feet, and the valley two or a little over. The weather has been very hot indeed, and I go about in a shirt and a pair of flannel trousers, and keep as cool as I can.'[4] Maud wore a light linen skirt, to her ankles in the fashion of the moment, a jacket of the same material, a shady panama hat, and good sensible boots.

Dr Packhard's small house was comfortable, and the first area for exploration was the region of North Carolina known as Laurel County, from the abundance of rhododendrons, which the mountain people called laurels. Their hosts were helpful with introductions, the first being to Miss Edith Fish. 'She looks a very grim old maid', Sharp confided to his diary, 'but I dare say she isn't.'[5]

Indeed, forbidding-looking females were the subjects of a large number of his Appalachian photographs, and most of them turned out to have hearts of gold. It became clear to Maud that Miss Fish had been laid on as a spy, to shepherd them and to report their effect upon the singers. Writing to England the year before, Mrs Campbell had exhibited a certain nervousness about the possible impact of a professional musician from across the Atlantic on her beloved mountain peasants. She had warned about the country: 'very rough, distances are great and living conditions often hard',[6] and this proved no exaggeration. She was more anxious about the people: 'The mountain people are sensitive, proud and shy but will do things for you if they like you and feel you like them . . . you would have to feel your way very carefully.'

She need have had no fears. The singers were all that appealed most to Cecil Sharp. 'The people', he wrote home, 'are just English of the late eighteenth or early nineteenth century. They speak English, look English, and their manners are old-fashioned English.'[7] It was quickly established that there was to be no problem. 'As in England, the mountain people were quick to recognize [Cecil's] friendliness and understanding, and his obvious love

EFDSS, Cecil Sharp Photograph Collection

of the songs . . . They were only too ready to sing to him.'[8]

Their first encounter, at White Rock, produced three or four songs. The second day had them walking to Allegheny, a gruelling trip and one where they found themselves too cowardly to emulate Miss Fish and ride on horseback. But they tramped back at the end of the day, beaming with pleasure and with nine good songs in their notebooks.

They had, however, run, here and there, into what was to prove a major frustration: groups of people who clearly had a store of tunes but would not give them out because they had been 'got at' by missionaries. These reformers damned the folk songs as 'love songs' and forbade the singing of them. The very term 'missionary' became the dirtiest word in Maud's and Cecil's diaries. The grim-faced Miss Fish was herself, in fact, one of the tribe, but her settlement at Allanstand seemed chiefly to look after the material rather than the spiritual welfare of the people, and Sharp had to admit that she turned out 'really not at all old-maidish or prim but on the contrary a very hard & generous minded woman'.[9]

She was their hostess for a week, lodging Maud in her own house and Cecil and John Campbell in a cabin on the other side of the road, 'a curiously built shanty but mighty comfortable'.[10] They enjoyed delicious suppers on her verandah in the long, hot evenings. In return, they gave their lecture-demonstrations, Maud dancing and Cecil talking informally in an attempt to explain the nature of their quest to Miss Fish's flock, their object being to convince the audience that they had not come into the county to make notes on the ignorance of its inhabitants!

In Allanstand they continued to discover marvellous songs, but the pleasure of the moment was horribly dampened when Cecil made an excursion to White Rock to get Maud's typewriter and came back with mail forwarded from the Algonquin. This brought the news that Perceval Lucas had been killed in action. It was the beginning of August and this was the first of the dire messages they were to receive of the carnage of the Battle of the Somme.

The next few weeks set the pattern for their collecting in the three wartime summers. It was clear they had hit on a gold mine and that their gamble in getting to the Appalachians was to be rewarded with success. But at what a cost! The ten-hour trip to White Rock was only one of many equally uncomfortable journeys. The next, from Allanstand back to the Packhards', was accomplished in a '"jolt-wagon", a cart without springs,

A jolt-wagon
EFDSS, Cecil Sharp Photograph Collection

which could be heard rattling over the boulders miles away and in which we were shaken to bits'.[11] They were shaken to pieces. They quickly discovered that their own feet provided a more tolerable conveyance, even for a journey of fifteen miles or more. If they were moving to a new base with all their luggage, they took to employing a boy with a mule, which they walked alongside. 'Cecil', wrote Maud, 'always maintained a steady trudge, but my method of progression was to alternate a sprint with a full stop.'[12] Some days, she was hardly able to get up again after resting on a stone.

Occasionally they 'missed the footpath and had to stumble our way through the thick undergrowth of a virgin forest for several miles',[13] nervous all the time about breaking a leg or being bitten by a snake. Maud's particular horror was having to cross the many creeks that they explored on bridges improvised from unshaped tree trunks. She inched her way over, terrified that the log would roll sideways and precipitate her into the water. The sight of a log cabin was always welcome, even when the owner might fire off a gun to warn neighbours of approaching strangers.

The cabin dwellers were often welcoming, but a problem arose with the food. For Cecil, determined to maintain a vegetarian diet, the fact that everything was swimming in the grease from the little black pigs that ran half-wild in the forest was hard to stomach. Even apples were cooked in hog's fat, frying being the only method of cooking the mountain people seemed to know. Standards of cleanliness were not what the travellers were used to either, and the resultant swarms of flies did not stimulate their appetites: 'Many was the time we thanked Providence for having placed eggs inside shells.'[14] When they were in reach of shops, they laid in stores of biscuits, cheese, chocolate, and raisins, not only for their own sakes but to avoid being a burden on their hosts who, often, grew barely enough to support themselves. The hospitality of the cabin folk moved and amazed them. Often, when they rose to say goodbye after a singing session, their hosts would protest: 'But surely you will tarry with us for the night.'[15]

It was during their time at White Rock that they made friends with the Hensley family, the people who gave Maud the greatest pleasure and with whom she kept in touch all her life. It was typical of Cecil's fortune that, when he and Maud got lost on the way to the Hensleys' cabin, they 'happened' on a lady who not only put them on the right road but, for good measure, 'sang a version of Outlandish Knight very sweetly'.[16]

The Hensleys comprised Reuben (a fiddler), Rosie, and their 'full grown' twelve-year-old daughter, Emma. Maud and Cecil, on this first occasion, spent three days, from breakfast till 5 p.m., 'on the verandah of their little home amongst the mountains, surrounded by huge trees and small clearings covered chiefly with corn (maize) and tobacco', where they had 'an awfully jolly time' and collected about thirty songs.[17]

Newspapers being unobtainable luxuries, the Hensleys were ignorant of world affairs and between songs Cecil was questioned as to who was fighting whom in this war in Europe and what, exactly, was a Dardanelle. More generally, he and Maud were begged to explain the Pyramids and the operation of the locks on the Panama Canal. Emma, who was a bright and beautiful blonde, was crazy to go to school, something her parents could not afford, though her mother approved of the idea in the hope that it might prevent her from getting married too young (her sister had wedded at the age of fifteen) and might cure her of her unladylike habit of chewing tobacco. Cecil was doubtful whether school was the proper place for so intelligent a girl, but Maud, with happy memories of her own schooling, was enthusiastic. They gave her parents the fare to get her to Hot Springs and Maud, when she returned there, persuaded the headmistress to accept Emma, herself paying the thirty-five dollar fee.

Richer by a great many songs, they made their way back from Laurel County to Asheville and spent a happy few days playing them to Olive Campbell. Maud shopped for skirts, boots, and writing paper, and was glad, after so long, to have a hot bath. The only blot on her happiness was worry about Cecil's health. His chronic asthma was going from bad to worse in the abnormal heat and humidity, and he was suffering dreadful neuralgic headaches.

Their return to the Packhards' at White Rock provided another adventure when their Pullman ran off the railway track and they had to resort to a 'crazy motor' driven by an even crazier driver. Three teachers with German names, the Misses Held, Lieb, and Bolch, had invited them to stay at Rocky Fork, and John Campbell accompanied them there, riding with their luggage while Maud and Cecil trudged, the latter with an acute headache. The day after their arrival brought news of George Butterworth's death in battle, which almost extinguished any pleasure in the rich harvest of the day, seventeen excellent ballads from a fine male singer. Just days later they learned of Tiddy's death: 'Now that he, Butterworth, Lucas & Wilkinson have gone', Sharp wrote in his diary, 'I seem to have lost all my pillars except one – V. Williams and any day something may befall him.'[18] He added, 'I feel too sad to set to work to do anything.' Maud's diary, if she kept one, is missing, and she made only the briefest reference to this tragedy in her autobiography, but she must have been shattered at the news. In later years, she confided to friends that Butterworth had been one of the objects of her romantic yearnings, one of those to whom, 'had he but raised his little finger', she would have gone running.

Because of tiredness and depression the travellers opted for comfort rather than adventure for their next expedition and chose to go to Hot Springs where 'decent rooms' were to be had. There they happened at once on a Mrs Gentry 'who at once fired off' 'The Two Sisters' and, on further enquiry, sang the first verse of 'The Golden Vanity' to a modal tune.[19] She promised more for the next day and the collectors had to be content to wait, parting from her with an injunction 'not to die in the night or catch cold'.[20] She quite tired Cecil out the following day with fifteen new songs. But their good luck did not last, for the next of their recommended sources for folk songs would deliver nothing but hymns, having been got at by 'these infernal Methodists'.[21]

By now Emma, in a new outfit paid for by Maud, had got herself into the Hot Springs school, and Maud and Cecil were able to invite her to dinner. She behaved 'very nicely indeed', but the school had proved quite other than she had expected and she was horribly homesick. They took her back at the end of the evening, confident that they had 'bucked her up'. They had miscalculated. Next morning they ran into her at the ferry, with all her belongings in a suitcase, running away back home with another girl. Instead of being annoyed at the waste of money, Sharp was filled with admiration at her enterprise, and they did nothing further to dissuade her. Maud reflected that she would, at least, be able to enjoy her new clothes at home. As well as comfort, the week at Hot Springs had produced seventy songs, including five Child ballads, so they returned to Asheville with a goodly score to run over with Olive Campbell.

Their next destination, Black Mountain, produced a hotel with unclean bedrooms, but a further thirty-eight songs, including a good version of 'Little Sir Hugh'. Their final assignment for this first summer was a week spent at the University of Virginia in Charlottesville to consult with Professor Alphonso Smith, founder of the Virginia Folklore Society and a famous collector of ballads. To their relief, he turned out to be 'a very nice, courteous & kindly man'.[22] They had been nervous of meeting this renowned professor because Sharp had a horror of being thought to be poaching on other people's preserves. But Smith, as they had suspected might be the case, was interested only in the words of the ballads and paid no attention to the tunes, so it was amicably agreed that they could each pursue their own researches. Sharp addressed the faculty at Charlottesville at a private meeting of their club.

This was the end of the first Appalachian adventure and on 28 September they packed their mountain gear and their vast collection of manuscripts and returned to the world of organized lectures and demonstrations, going first to Cincinnati and then to Chicago. They felt extremely satisfied, having noted close on four hundred songs. But at the Elms Hotel bad news, of an even more personal nature, was awaiting them. Three telegrams from Constance announced that Charlie, Cecil's son, had been wounded in France. No further information was forthcoming for a week, but when it came it was reassuring and included a letter from the young man himself, written in hospital at the front.

In the meantime, life had changed from the informality of mountain trekking, the alteration underlined by a note in Sharp's diary that he had gone out to buy a bowler hat. The weather was cold but bright and they enjoyed walks by the lakeside. Preoccupation with Charlie's health kept Sharp's diary brief, but life continued to follow the pattern of the vacation

EFDSS, Cecil Sharp Photograph Collection

schools, with lectures, classes, demonstrations in the park beside the water, and a final examination, which seven out of eleven students passed. After a ball given by the EFDS, they packed again and returned 'home' to the Algonquin on 14 October.

Chapter 8

The news about Charles, coming so soon after the deaths of four of Cecil's folk dance team, cast him and Maud into such a depth of gloom that they seriously considered throwing up their bookings and returning home at once. But the need to earn money was pressing. There was still no hope of work in England, but plenty of American offers for the autumn, so they decided to fulfil these engagements until November. Better news of Charles enabled them to give their minds more wholeheartedly to their students, and after the Chicago school they were claimed by similar organizations in New York, Pittsburgh, Philadelphia, and Boston.

The most rewarding week's work was at Mount Holyoke College in Massachusetts, where the trees were beginning to shed their leaves. This autumnal beauty unfortunately made Cecil's asthma worse. However, the number of students – about three hundred – was gratifying and Maud was enchanted to hear the sound of their voices all over the campus, singing 'All Along the Ludeney' and other songs recently collected in the mountains. At this time, Cecil was in fine fettle as a dancer, in spite of his age and breathlessness. 'He was lissom in his movements and he had an outstanding sense of rhythm', wrote Maud.[1] If no local group of dancers was available, the two of them provided illustrations to his lectures and they sang the tunes unaccompanied, as solos or duets. 'Neither of us had good voices but as Cecil said, it was not the voice that mattered but the song you sing with it.'[2]

By the time they arrived in Pittsburgh, they found matters had taken a turn for the better. A telegram from Constance was waiting with the news that Charlie was nearly out of the woods and was soon to be sent back to England. On 12 October, they took a train across the border to Canada, where they arrived in summer clothing to the sight of snow. 'It is nice to be under the Union Jack again', wrote Cecil, '& to see so much soldiering.'[3] Maud, however, felt 'seedy' and retired to bed for two days, a reaction, no doubt, to many weeks of discomfort combined with anxiety about Cecil's health.

They were back in New York for a Peace Celebration. In response to a presidential proclamation, everybody was giving thanks (a) for having kept out of the war, and (b) for the amount of money that, in consequence, was floating about. They shopped for Christmas presents and enjoyed evening sociabilities, generally ending up with a drink of ginger ale or milk and soda with Charles Rabold and Ben Iden Payne. On 8 December, they set sail for home on the Dutch liner *Ryndam*. Maud shared a cabin with 'a nice cabin mate', an American woman bound for Rotterdam.[4]

As usual, she started the journey 'far from well', though the weather was calm and foggy, leaving her companion to make acquaintance with the polyglot community: 'Dutch, German, French, Americans, Canadians, English and one Turk!'[5] On the third day she emerged from her self-imposed purdah, had lunch, returned to her cabin until 4 p.m., when she reappeared for tea. She dressed for dinner at 6 o'clock, but retired to bed again at 8.30 p.m. 'That is the way she lives on board', wrote Cecil. 'Says it is the effect of the sea but really she is just as sleepy on land.'[6] The improvement did not last, for the wind got up, causing Maud to vanish again, declaring herself seasick, 'but not really very bad'. The weather, however, must have been severe, for the ship's doctor had to go to the rescue of a boat seen flying a distress signal. One man had been killed on board, two had drowned, while a fourth had to have a broken leg amputated.

It is clear from Cecil Sharp's diary that Maud got the date of their return to London wrong both in her biography of him and in her unpublished autobiography. She gives the month as December, but actually they were in England from 17 November 1916 to 23 February 1917. After giving up the Westbourne Terrace house, Joseph Karpeles, with Arthur, had gone to live in Langham Street, Portland Place, in a house later demolished to make room for the BBC. Arthur was now on active service. Maud, however, lodged with the Sharp family in Hampstead, making only brief visits to her relations. Often she accompanied Constance and Cecil across Hampstead Heath to the Highgate hospital where Charles was now installed. His father made the expedition every day.

They arranged their return to America so as to get in a number of teaching engagements before a spring visit to the Appalachians. This was to be followed by the usual summer schools and then by a more prolonged sojourn in the mountains. They had, when they set out, no idea that they would remain in the USA for nearly two more years.

For this journey, Maud invested in a small but solid diary before starting out and set about chronicling her third American visit in her legible, upright, if not particularly decorative, handwriting. The first entry was made on 21 February on board the *Baltic* in Liverpool docks. The intention had been to travel, once again, on a Dutch liner, but a few days before departure its voyage was cancelled as a result of Germany's fateful and historic declaration that in future submarines would be used against neutral shipping – the declaration that was to bring America into the war. Cecil and Maud managed to obtain berths on the next British ship to leave the country. From the 21st to the 25th, rumours of submarine activity kept them moored in the Mersey, the monotony broken at intervals by the five blasts on the foghorn that summoned them to lifeboat drill. They were invited to sit at the captain's table and made the acquaintance of some of the sixty first-class passengers. Maud had equipped herself with a suitable pile of literature to cover this tiresome delay and spent most of her time reading in her 'magnificent' cabin. She noted the titles and authors: Kipling's *Kim*, Stevenson's *The Master of Ballantrae*, novels by Ian Hay, H. A. Vachell, E. Phillips Oppenheim, and Arnold Bennett. Between these diversions, she kept her mind stretched with Stanford and Forsyth's *History of Music*. As well as her reading, Maud's diary chronicles the recipients of all the letters she wrote and the occasions when she washed her hair.

The *Baltic* was a sister ship of Cecil's old friend the *Adriatic*. Maud described his mood at the start of the voyage as 'strained and nervous . . . alive to physical danger', insisting that he did not disguise his fear.[7] His own diary gives little hint of nerves and shows him interested and diverted by all aspects of life on board. The passage was the roughest he had experienced, but this was something of a relief to him, if not to his seasick companion, making the danger a good deal less because 'it would be impossible for submarines to live in such a sea except below the surface.'[8]

It proved to be a record slow passage, for they went further north than usual, running into icebergs and snowstorms. By 3 March, Maud was acclimatized and began to sit, muffled up to the eyes, in a deckchair. In the evenings, one of the male passengers entertained them on the saloon piano with Chopin, 'in a very neat accurate but unemotional way'.[9] A 'millpond' lull for two days enabled Maud to swallow a number of meals, but this was followed by the roughest sea Cecil had witnessed, with waves thirty feet high. He wrote of the five lady passengers: 'their chief anxiety was how to dress for the life-boat. They were not so much concerned with the matter of comfort and warmth as with the look of the thing. O these women!'[10]

Sharp's diary makes frequent mention of Maud on the voyage. Hers, after the first day, reads as if she had been totally on her own and it was not until several days after they had landed that she so much as alludes to her constant companion. When she does bring in his name, in connection with a dinner with Richard Aldrich, she refers to him as C#, and throughout her American diaries that is how he appears, or, on occasions, even more formally, as 'Mr Sharp'. Maud's most lasting impression of the voyage was of her wonderful cabin, for which she paid only twelve dollars!

They were welcomed at the Algonquin by Charles Rabold and Susan Gilman, but the news they had to deliver was depressing. A week's engagement in St Louis had been cancelled and there was no substitute in view. However, an offer came in from Illinois and Mrs Callery was expecting them in Pittsburgh. So they settled back into their New York routine, met old friends, lunched or dined at their favourite Peg Woffington's or Old England restaurants. The most interesting evening was spent with Aldrich and included the Paderewskis. The conversation, unusual for America, centred on the war, and, not surprisingly, on the condition of Poland. After an EFDS meeting they went for a brief visit to Boston, where Cecil stayed in the Storrows' comfortable house and Maud was as a guest of Lily Roberts.

After week-long sessions in Illinois, Champaign, and Pittsburgh, they set out, on 10 April, for a spring visit to the mountains. This time they went to Knoxville, Tennessee, where John Campbell met them and installed them in a hotel with a number of friends, teachers from Asheville, who were there for a conference. Their pleasure was dampened by a Mr Claxton, who opened the proceedings with 'an unedifying discourse concerning the industrialization of the mountains', in which he mentioned 'dollars – usually in billions – in every sentence, a most egregious & depressing performance'.[11] Maud was fortunate to have arrived with a splitting headache which gave her an excuse to slip out and go to bed.

The next few days were spent in giving and listening to lectures, the highlight, for both of them, being a contest of mountain fiddlers. They went on to Sevierville through country of surpassing beauty and Maud, after a stroll around the town, felt she had at last arrived in the 'real America'.[12] A less pleasing aspect was the primitive condition of the Central Hotel, far from clean and with uneatable food, though run by 'a nice old widow woman'.[13] The entertainment on the first evening consisted, appropriately, of a lecture on sanitation given by a Dr Johnson who had travelled with them. They were heartened the next day, however, by getting some good songs, including the best version to date of 'Edward'.

But their greatest pleasure at that moment was in the beauty of the fresh spring landscape, with flowering dogwoods making the slopes of the mountains white, huge magnolias, and drifts under the trees of purple iris and violets. They missed the singing of birds, for the Tennessee woods were strangely silent. Here they fell back into their familiar pattern of collecting: long walks and bumpy drives; lodgings in small hotels, mission houses, or log cabins of variable comfort. Their hope that in the spring they would at least be comfortably cool was doomed to disappointment. Both diaries were soon recording unpleasantly close weather, unnaturally hot, humid, and thundery for the time of year.

Their first hosts were a couple called Storey, who became the missionaries Cecil liked best, in spite of the fact that they had a twelve-year-old daughter, Lualle, who drove him out of his mind. She stayed up late, ate what they ate, and showed off: 'It is as bad as having a dog in the house!'[14] Storey himself was, however, 'a very humble, extraordinarily simple and nice man'.[15]

The house, church, school, and dormitory were 2800 feet up in the hills, with mountains all around, and they preferred it to any missionary settlement they had found, in spite of the poor and meagre food and a distinct taste of iron in the water. Also, in spite of the fact that after arriving at the end of a gruelling seven and a half mile climb, Cecil found he was expected to share a bed with Dr Johnson. Much as he liked him, Sharp drew the line at this. 'So I sat in a chair', he wrote, '& he went to bed for 4 hours. Then he woke up & insisted on my getting into bed! About an hour after he was called out to a confinement case and I slept on till morning!'[16] Such was Appalachian life. But they collected many songs with the help of lifts in the Storeys' buggy, and were sorry to say goodbye at the end of their stay.

Both felt under the weather when they returned to Sevierville and concluded that they were affected by the intense, unseasonable heat, the altitude, and, in all probability, the water; but they were still replete with satisfaction at work well done. This was the beginning of the most anxious time that Maud had so far experienced. While she began to recover, Cecil got worse, with a cough and obvious fever, though they had no thermometer to check this. After a day's rest, they took the train to Cumberland Gap, where they were met and driven to Lincoln University at Harrogate, Tennessee. There they were installed in comfortable adjacent rooms and given dinner before an audition of Kentucky fiddlers. Cecil then attempted to lecture on folk song but kept having to break off with paroxysms of coughing.

The next day a doctor and a thermometer had to be sent for. The latter showed the fever to be 103°F, and the former declared, 'Well, you've swallowed it whole this time! And judging by your age you won't get over it very quickly.'[17] Maud now decided he was unfit to be left alone and moved her bedding into his room, where she slept on the floor beside him. Cecil was so depressed at this setback to their work that she went out to round up singers and brought them to his bedside. He was declared to have a sharp attack of 'grippe', as it was known locally, an infection rampant at this time in Kentucky and Tennessee.

When he felt able to leave his bed, he descended to the porch where he cheered himself up – if he did no good to his cough – with endless cigarettes. His face now became so sore that he could not touch it or brush his 'silver locks', but he managed to receive two ladies who sang to him and noted with satisfaction that he had taken down twenty-four tunes that week, some of them very fine ones, making sixty in a fortnight.

This success seems to have done him good, for they were able to move on to Pineville and enjoy the wonderful scenery on the way. The Continental Hotel was comfortable, friendly, and surrounded by tree-clad mountains. Here they did well enough, with several 'ripping songs', but they decided to move on to Harlan, Kentucky. This proved to be a mining town with a grubby hotel, so they hastily retreated to the comfort of Pineville and enjoyable warm baths, 'the last we shall see for some weeks I expect'.[18]

The next port of call was Barbourville, where the hotel was 'possible'. After walking a long way and drawing total blanks, Cecil collapsed in a state of exhausted depression, so Maud ventured out alone on the search, but returned empty-handed. On their third sortie, this time together, they suddenly hit upon 'a nest of singers of the right sort',[19] in the persons of the Sloan family. Mrs Sloan, her sister, and a little girl all sang together, about eleven songs in an hour. Maud recorded: 'We cld. not get their songs down fast enough.'[20] For several days, they returned over and again to the Sloans, but their successful harvest was gathered against a daily growing background of interested audiences and squalling children. They could hardly breathe and Cecil was feeling far from well.

This proved to be the start of another attack of the mysterious 'grippe'. His temperature was back up over 100°F and Maud again decided to take her mattress into his bedroom. This was replaced by a stretcher bed, supplied by the hotel. This led to an incident that clearly upset Maud a great deal, when an unknown young man made unpleasant and insinuating remarks to

Chapter 8

Sudie Sloan, Barbourville, Knox County, Kentucky
EFDSS, Cecil Sharp Photograph Collection

her. Cecil, however, noted in his diary: 'Maud most devoted. Camping out in my room every night and does anything she can think of to help me. The Proprietors of the Hotel . . . are most kind & helpful.'[21]

They were eventually moved into a more airy room with two beds. It had been Cecil's habit, in their different hotels and lodgings, and indeed since she had gone to live with the Sharps in London, to refer to Maud as his adopted daughter. Whether this made the situation better or worse in the eyes of the aforementioned young man is not clear.

The local doctor diagnosed Sharp's condition as possibly typhoid, but refused to come back the next day or to suggest anything to relieve the fever, 'apparently because it would interfere with his diagnosis!', causing his patient to express his contempt for the medical profession: 'Clearly the patient is made for the doctor in these as in other parts of the world.'[22] Later, he reappeared with 'another brother saw-bones, ironically named Albright'.[23]

The doctor uttered 'non-committal platitudes', but more effective medicine was provided by Mrs Knuckles, an excellent singer who cheered the patient with 'rather nice' songs; and Maud and Cecil also managed to get through a lot of proof-reading. Maud had sent a message to Campbell, who replied by wire that he would come and bring Dr Packhard with him.

When the two men arrived, and decided that the 'grippe' theory was the right one, Cecil aroused himself, dressed, and staggered to the local barber, supported by Packhard, to have eight days' worth of beard removed. The effort exhausted him and he confided to his diary that he could never remember being such a crock. It had become obvious to Maud that further journeys into the wilds were out of the question and she combined with Campbell and Packhard to persuade Cecil of this. However, he would not hear of giving up collecting. As a compromise, he agreed to settle at Berea, where there was a college for mountain students.

They made their way there in stifling weather, the train halting at every station, and were in a state of collapse when they reached their destination. Here they 'rested', while Cecil's temperature fluctuated daily between normal and 104°F, collecting over a hundred songs in two weeks. Maud, however, dismissed that particular field of study as too sophisticated: 'the singing of traditional songs was apt to be despised as belonging to a past and discarded mode of existence. We were told that the singing of love-songs was only practised by the rough, common people, and an earnest young College student was reluctant to sing a version of "The Swapping Song", as he cared only for songs which contained "great thoughts".'[24]

Most of the students came obligingly enough and sang very sweetly, but the only ones Cecil approved of were those who had just come in from the mountains. He had 'about as much strength as a mouse',[25] but did not let this prevent him from delivering lectures and attending meetings of the faculty. The doctor here was convinced his trouble was tuberculosis, which he had had unknowingly for twenty years or more, and he prepared to inject him with arsenic. This remedy was firmly refused.

It was while they were staying at Berea that Maud had a cable from Helen, reading: 'Arthur wounded satisfactorily.'[26] This meant that their young brother had received 'a blighty one', in the parlance of the day – a wound that, without being fatal, took him decisively out of the battle and home to England. In fact, Arthur Karpeles was to remain a semi-invalid all his life.

Towards the end of their stay, Maud and Cecil were prevailed upon to attend a prayer meeting at the house of some of their singers. This was something they normally avoided like the plague, but Cecil hated to offend those who had given him songs. Mrs Talithah Powell and her sister prayed first, followed by their brother, who especially commended their guests to the Almighty for the profitable work they were doing, while Cecil knelt in deadly fear that he would be called upon to pray aloud impromptu. Happily he was 'spared this ordeal and indignity'.[27]

When they left, they found that the president of the college had instructed their hostelry to remit payment of their expenses – an unexpected and welcome courtesy. They were back in their comfortable rooms in Pineville at the start of June, the comfort a little lessened when a large piece of Cecil's ceiling fell down in the thunderstorm that greeted their arrival. There they were reunited with old acquaintances who were ready to hug them with delight, the more so because news had come of a man and woman arrested as spies in nearby Middlesboro. Their friends had feared that Maud and Cecil might be that couple.

After a few days of profitable collecting, Cecil was again laid low, this time with violent toothache. They decided to return to Asheville, rising at 3 a.m. to catch a train at 4 o'clock. They had to wash from a shared bucket of cold water, for in Pineville the taps were shut off between 11 p.m. and 5 a.m. as an economy measure. After a long, hot, and uncomfortable journey, they were met and driven by the Campbells to the Grove Park Inn, 'a very wonderful and crazy sort of place',[28] according to Cecil, with marvellous views, luxurious rooms, and wholesome, well-cooked food. They settled in with the idea of rebuilding their strength.

Maud Karpeles and Cecil Sharp at Berea railway station, Kentucky
EFDSS, *Cecil Sharp Photograph Collection*

Such, however, was the perversity of Cecil's nature that four days later he was writing, 'I am getting very sick of this idle, rich sort of life, and am wondering how I am going to stick it through the present week. I suppose the rest in such healthful conditions is good for me – but I hate it none the less on that account!'[29] Maud made no such comment and it can be deduced that she was only too ready to bask in a little luxury.

The comfort, for Cecil, cannot have been so very great, as the local dentist decreed that six of his upper teeth must come out and extracted them the next day under an unsuccessful administration of gas. He was left suffering from shock. New dentures were made for him, but when they were fitted he doubted that he would ever be able to speak again. Nevertheless, three days later he was delivering a private talk and recital of mountain songs to their nice old hostess, followed, after dinner, by a two-hour lecture to the Pen and Plate Club. John Campbell, who turned up in time for the latter, was 'all agog' with the impression it made on his friends.

Chapter 9

On 16 June, they said a brief farewell to the mountains and spent a few days in New York, teaching for Susan Gilman. Cecil reported Maud as feeling seedy and she had to rush to the dentist, to be told that one of her teeth had better come out. The extraction was fitted in between teaching sessions; she went under gas after her morning class, a 'very disagreeable proceeding', and was back on the job at 5 o'clock.[1]

She felt well enough after dinner to walk along Fifth Avenue to see the golden illuminations in honour of the Italian War Commission. The next day, they enjoyed a performance of August Strindberg's *Pariah* and, after a week of work and sociabilities, went off to Boston and 'gorgeous rooms' at the Hotel Touraine.[2] It was there that they had some talk with a chambermaid from Newfoundland who told them about the songs that were sung in her country. This led them to promise themselves a collecting expedition there.

Mrs Storrow's summer school, the third at which they had assisted, was held at Amherst that year. The weather was beautiful, the lodgings comfortable, 'the delightful Misses Peabody' motored them to and from classes, and Lily Roberts and Charles Rabold were there to make a dance foursome. Maud, however, was still feeling 'seedy' and did not make a single entry in her diary. This did not prevent her taking classes, but she was glad to have Lily to take over when necessary. They were disappointed to find this year's entry was a mere twenty students, 'partly because of the war,' wrote Cecil, 'partly because Mrs. Storrow spread rumours of my illness abroad.'[3]

The twenty proved to be of the highest possible quality and their first public demonstration was so good that it attracted a further ten students for the rest of the course. If Maud was flagging, Cecil was congratulating himself on his dancing abilities, performing more often at this school than he had ever done. The session ended with a celebratory Old English dinner, after which Cecil delivered one of his 'comminations' on the subject of ballet and aesthetic dancing, and exhorted the students to teach accurately and uphold the *accurate* dissemination of the dance. It had been a success, but Maud was glad to return to the Algonquin, which felt more and more like home, at the end of the three weeks.

They were in a rush now to be back to the mountains, former discomforts pushed into the background in a frenzy of preparations: visits to publishers, to hairdressers, to shops for walking shoes. The journey back to Asheville – the start for all their Appalachian adventures – involved a night in the train in stifling heat. Next day, the Campbells saw them off on another train, which poured coal dust and cinders by the bucketful into the carriages, to Balsam.

Here there was a delightful hotel, and the place, in the heart of the mountains, appeared ideal. They went out eagerly to search for people who had been famous for songs, but either they had recently died or, when found, they could remember nothing. 'We are both coming to the conclusion', wrote Maud, 'that Balsam is not the right place.'[4] Everybody was welcoming, but they gained nothing but a few songs from a woman they chanced to hear singing as they walked by. They were too near an industrial centre and Cecil complained in a letter to Mrs Storrow that the inhabitants of the log cabins were too clean. 'It is sad that cleanliness and good music, or good taste in music, rarely go together. Dirt and good music are the usual bed-fellows, or cleanliness and rag-time!'[5]

So they moved to Sylva, where the Commercial Hotel was suspiciously clean, though it could produce little to eat but beans roasted in hog's fat, so they had to fall back on their stores of crackers and marmalade. They spotted log cabins at the top of a tremendous hill and Maud climbed up and knocked, breathless, on the door of one. 'A man said "Good evening", turned round & behold he was a negro. We had struck a negro settlement! Nothing for it but to toil back again.'[6] Folk songs of English origin were hardly to be expected from the black population and Maud was obviously alarmed at the encounter – black faces were but rarely seen at home, and so far few had been encountered in the mountains. The next day, they climbed five miles to a settlement called Almond, where the people were white but turned out to be '"advanced" too far on the down grade towards sophistication'.[7]

In the intolerable heatwave – which their diaries do not exaggerate, for the papers reported it the worst for fifty years, with scores of deaths every day in New York and Boston – they were saved by the discovery of a drugstore. Cecil downed two lemonades, while Maud swallowed three in succession. A tremendous thunderstorm transformed the dryish creeks into raging torrents the next day, with waves leaping over the bridges, and so, as Maud felt even seedier than before, they decided to return to Asheville. There she took to her bed, while Cecil settled into Campbell's office to work on proofs. After a day's rest she was well enough to go to the Campbells' for tea, and the four of them spent the evening at an amusing movie show.

Cheered by this sociable episode, they entrained once again, this time for Knoxville. They had decided to return to their profitable research in Kentucky, which had been cut short in May by Cecil's illness. The new venture did not begin well. In intolerable heat they were herded into a filthy train, 'about 150 of us like pigs in a stye [*sic*], not even with the information that we were in the right stye!'[8] They marvelled that they got through the day, suffering as they did from an assortment of headaches, asthma, hay fever, and general lassitude. Their arrival, at a 'perfectly terrible' hotel,[9] provided little relief.

Next day, they battled on to Barbourville, where they went to call on their old friends the singing Sloans, confident that, once again, they would be regaled with plenty of songs. But they were met with yet another disaster. One of the Sloan husbands had blown himself up with gunpowder and the family were too shattered to sing. The victim would not hear of hospital and they found him 'lying on a bed covered with burns and black with flies'.[10] They gave them some dollars and plenty of commiseration, but retired thwarted of the rich harvest they had expected. Cecil was so knocked up by his recent experiences that he was forced to rest. Maud went out to do the rounds, to Mrs Knuckles and Ben Henson, but came back empty-handed, for their friends, though welcoming, seemed all to have dried up. She resorted to the movies again in the evening, but this time with no pleasure.

They were, for once, at a loss as to where to go or what to do. Pineville, on which they decided for a rest in relative luxury, turned out to have no rooms, so they put it off in favour of a visit to Manchester – pronounced Man*ches*ter – in Clay County. The weather had changed with a vengeance and the journey, in a swaying carriage through wooded mountains, ended in a terrific thunderstorm. Instead of sweltering, they were suddenly so cold that Cecil's diary became a catalogue of complaints against inadequate cotton quilts and the absence of blankets. He developed a nasty cold and a sore throat. Manchester turned out to be smaller and more primitive than Maud had expected, which raised her hopes. It was certainly dirty enough. Cecil wrote to Mrs Storrow: 'Manchester . . . has no . . . system of sanitation. The hotel faces a vacant square with a dry creek running across it, covered with large boulders. Residents just throw the contents of their dust bins out upon the streets where the hogs, which are numerous, eat of it what they can!'[11]

Their first day yielded only a couple of songs, though one was a good Child ballad. On the next, with Cecil wheezing and sneezing, they went to search for a singer called Finlay, but were wrongly directed and spent the day negotiating creeks where half the bridges had been swept away. Maud got caught in barbed wire in the middle of one of the few remaining logs and feared she was going to perish. On the morrow, Cecil was 'hoarse as a crow',[12] so Maud did the prospecting. Nobody could have been more friendly than the families she called on, but all had been converted to the Holiness sect and hardly anybody would sing. The 'poor food, dirt and beastly manners of the travelling men who frequent the hostelry' drove them out of Manchester.[13]

They took a jolt-wagon to a mountain school at Oneida, where they were kindly received and given delightfully clean rooms. The food, however, was almost non-existent. One dinner, wrote Cecil, consisted of 'a few crumbs of corn bread and a baked apple & water';[14] another, according to Maud, comprised a cabbage salad. If this spartan living had resulted in a harvest of songs, they would not have complained, but it became apparent, once again, that the folk tradition had died out. The principal invited them to a corn supper party; 'very dull and stupid', was Maud's verdict, but the square meal enabled them to have a proper night's sleep.

They decided to walk the fourteen miles back to Manchester rather than endure another journey by jolt-wagon, sending their luggage by the local Mail Hack. Their reputation had evidently got abroad, for they were pursued by a posse of schoolchildren who called out 'we can sing', but they only managed to get down a couple of their songs before a bell rang and the singers scampered away. The weather, however, now became positively pleasant – 'A really lovely day with fresh air, fleecy clouds, just like an English summer's day'[15] – but Maud detected the first signs of autumn in the air. A 'crazy train' took them to Barbourville, and another back to Pineville. Though relieved to find herself in civilization and able to enjoy warm baths, Maud was not surprised to find her insides upset. An attack of dysentery persuaded her to seek out a drugstore for a dose of castor oil. This somewhat drastic remedy was successful enough to make them decide to start for Pine Mountain in the morning. In the meantime, they captured a number of songs and replenished their emergency rations.

The six-mile journey took them three hours, but nothing could have been better calculated to comfort the weary travellers than this Settlement School and their reception there. The school had been founded, four years before, by Katharine Pettit, with whom they were soon sitting under the apple trees, enjoying a picnic tea. Cecil's room was in the farm superintendent's house. Maud was lodged in a tent, shared, for company, with one of the schoolgirls. At supper, in a beautiful hall, the seventy or eighty pupils sat at round tables with neat cloths and dinner napkins. The place was superior to any mountain school they had seen. 'The feeding of the children is excellent', noted Cecil, who declared that they were 'delightful, clean, bright & intelligent and are indistinguishable from the children of gentle-folk'.[16]

After supper, the children sang to them and they replied with songs from their own collection. Evelyn Wells, a member of the staff, wrote about the occasion years afterwards: 'I can remember the twilight creeping in on us, the youngest children falling to sleep, dropping on their crossed arms at the table, as if they were being sung to at their own firesides, the voices of the singers getting more and more impersonal in the dusk as song after song was finished' – '"The Knight in the Road", "All along in the Ludeney", "Edward", "The Gypsy Laddie", and many nursery songs.'[17] Maud retired to her tent feeling far better than she had expected.

Miss Wells also recalled the first morning: 'Mr Sharp came to our six o'clock breakfast late, having lost his way to the dining-room in the thick mountain mist that filled the valley – suffering terribly from an attack of asthma … and then going off down the valley within the next hour, walking miles to get songs from singing Willie Nolan'.[18] Then Maud and he tramped up Greening Creek to Mary Ann Short, where they gathered a goodish number more.

This improvement in their circumstances was not reflected in their physical state, for Maud reported worse asthma in Cecil and Cecil recorded that Maud's dysentery had started again. He was soon to note the same symptoms in himself. Maud was moved from her tent into Miss Pettit's house, where she spent most of the next day in bed, emerging, however, for two hours at noon, when, as Miss Wells recorded, 'eight workers from the staff learned "Rufty Tufty", "The Black Nag" and "Gathering Peascods" on the porch of Laurel House to Mr. Sharp's teaching and Miss Karpeles's singing of the tune … All the work of the day stopped during these lessons – children stopped weeding the vegetable gardens, girls stopped washing the clothes, even the workmen stopped building the school-house. And this was in the days when we worked incessantly to put roofs over our heads and to can food against the winter, and every minute counted.'[19]

Chapter 9

The Webb Hotel, Manchester, Clay County, Kentucky
EFDSS, Cecil Sharp Photograph Collection

The following day, Cecil went to talk with the co-principal and wrote, 'I am greatly enamoured with the way in which things are conducted here. I expected to find Miss de Long a very precious, Arty & Crafty sort of person but she really isn't, while Miss Pettit is a really capable, energetic person of wide vision'.[20] Miss Pettit had been one of the founders, eleven years earlier, of the most celebrated of the mountain colleges, Hindman Settlement School, in Knott County, Kentucky. The aim of these schools, supported by the Russell Sage Foundation, for which John Campbell worked, was one dear to Cecil's heart: 'to revive the old culture'. A part of that culture was about to be revealed – the 'Running Set'. This was Maud and Cecil's first sight of a dance that was to interest them as much as any of the songs they brought home with them from the Appalachians.

> It was danced one evening after dark on the porch of one of the largest houses of the Pine Mountain School with only one dim lantern to light up the scene. But the moon streamed fitfully in lighting up the mountain peaks in the background and, casting its mysterious light over the proceedings, seemed to exaggerate the wildness and the break-neck speed of the dancers as they whirled through the mazes of the dance. There was no music, only the stamping and clapping of the onlookers, but when one of the emotional crises of the dance was reached . . . the air seemed literally to pulsate with the rhythm of the 'patters' and the tramp of the dancers' feet, while, over and above it all, penetrating through the din, floated the even, falsetto tones of the Caller, calmly and unexcitedly reciting his directions.[21]

On the first day of September, very reluctantly, they left Pine Mountain, promising themselves and their hosts that they would come back. The journey back to Pineville by foot, ox-cart, and, finally, train, took nearly nine hours, but they were rewarded by delicious baths. Neither felt well. The doctor pronounced them to be suffering from the effects of the local water and said, depressingly, that the symptoms usually lasted two weeks.

As soon as they recovered, they set out for Barbourville, where they were in for a week of dirt, discomfort, and near-starvation, but as these things were synonymous with good collecting they did not complain. Indeed, they could hardly have done better. Tramping along creeks and climbing mountains, they gathered songs from friendly people. One gave them their forty-second version of 'Queen Jane', another a dozen ballads in one session, and on 10

September Cecil took down his '4000th tune, and my 200th for this trip – quite a double event. I want about 150 more here to complete my 1000 tunes in the mountains'.[22]

The weather now was cold, making Cecil, whose constitution was peculiarly susceptible to change, feel liverish, 'dull, sleepy & stupid'.[23] They moved to Hazard, which Cecil dubbed 'Hap-Hazard',[24] and Maud called 'a perfectly terrible place. Regular mushroom town. Cheap, dirty & on the make.'[25] Their reputation had gone ahead of them and the first singer they went to fled at the sight of them, influenced by missionaries. The hotel proprietors, on the other hand, could not have been more friendly, pressing them to use their out-of-tune piano.

From there, they made their way to Hindman, Miss Pettit's first settlement school. Maud did not think it had the unique character of Pine Mountain, being situated in a more sophisticated region. It boasted fourteen buildings and three hundred students. Here they found themselves once more on the track of their dearest objective, a performance of the 'Running Set' which could be captured on paper. A party was arranged for their benefit, which Maud described thus in her diary: 'Had to walk 1½ miles in dark along very muddy road. Mr Sharp tumbled into mud hole and lost shoe. Dance was an interesting experience but actual dancing was no good. The girls did not know the dance and took little interest[,] the men were too fuddled with whisky to be much good, & there was no one to call . . . I danced & had to pull my partner around as his head was swimming!'[26] Cecil recorded: 'It was a queer business because in these parts a party is always a public affair and we were crowded out with loafers who didn't dance but took up the space on the floor.'[27]

They remained a week at Hindman, teaching the children and enjoying picnics and a wonderful supper with Miss Stone and the staff in their log-cabin rest house. Their initial depression was dispelled when, in the evenings, schoolgirls came in to sing to them. The entire staff turned out after 6 a.m. breakfast to see them off. 'Everybody has been so nice to us', wrote Maud.[28]

After a bumpy journey in a wagon, which lasted eleven hours, they were back to the questionable comfort of the Beaumont Hotel in Hazard, out-of-tune piano and all. They actually made use of it, harmonizing their new songs, while they rested for a few days, trying to pluck up courage to make the uncomfortable journey to Hyden, a place where they had hopes of set dancing.

Eventually they went off, after rising at 5 a.m. on a day after it had rained in torrents. The roads, and their vehicle, the local Mail Hack, were equally unpleasant: 'No springs, a crazy "Tarpoleon" [*sic*] covering it, seats without cushions and soaking wet and a young casual irresponsible Jehu to drive us.'[29] They 'got out and walked, and except where the road went down the middle of the creek – wh[ich] it did for about 5 miles of the journey – we tramped all the way'. 'Quite the worst road we have seen', it went over five mountains and they ended by wading a river. The Lewis Hotel was new but primitive, but Cecil found some comfort in Mrs Lewis's nice smile and the fact that she, too, was a martyr to asthma.

As far as songs were concerned, they drew an immediate blank, the local school being 'permeated with presbyterianism and sloppy bible religion and utterly devoid of art of any kind'.[30] Then they happened on a character who caught Cecil's fancy, Mrs Eliza Pace, who had been sentenced a number of times for the offence of retailing moonshine – illegally distilled whisky. She had some good songs. They entertained themselves by sitting in on a session of the local court: 'Plenty of melodramatic American spread-eagleism, every platitude uttered as though it were a deep & serious truth and every sentence punctuated with the use of the spi[t]toon'[31] The climate of Hyden was particularly bad for asthmatics, and Cecil declared he had never suffered so much in his life.

Eliza Pace, Hyden, Leslie County, Kentucky
EFDSS, *Cecil Sharp Photograph Collection*

At last they met a man who promised to get up a 'Running Set' for them. On 2 October, exhausted by a successful day which had involved a twelve-mile walk and getting soaked, Maud went early to bed. No sooner had she dropped asleep than Cecil was knocking at the door with the news that a 'Set' was about to be run for them. She hustled into her clothes and they were escorted to a house where four couples had assembled. Though far from expert dancers, they performed sufficiently well for notes on the figures to be taken down. This was a joy and relief to them both, as it meant they need not return to Pine Mountain. Much as they had enjoyed the school, they were in need of a complete holiday.

The next day, Cecil's temperature shot up again, with asthma and a hacking cough. He was prevailed upon to stay in bed. Maud, meanwhile, was invited to attend a 'bean stringing'. Here, about fifty people sat around in the firelight gossiping as they dealt with the beans. When they had finished, they danced, and this time Maud was able actually to take part in a 'Running Set' – 'there was not enough room to dance & the atmosphere was poisonous',[32] but it was a tremendous satisfaction to get the movements securely fixed. While Cecil languished in bed, they got it safely down on paper. 'This dance is as valuable a piece of work as anything that I have done in the mountains', he concluded.[33]

They passed through old hunting grounds on the train to Richmond, feeling melancholy as they saw the mountains recede. It was odd to see the horizon again. The country was flat, with good roads, and looked very much like England. The Campbells had booked them the same rooms in the Grove Park Inn as they had occupied in the spring, and Maud gave thanks for having reached this familiar place without further mishap and retired for a 'night's rest in a really comfortable bed with linen sheets',[34] after the first good meal they had eaten for weeks. The air was delightfully refreshing.

Cecil, however, was unable to sleep, and after less than a day of holiday was writing that he 'must be careful I do not make myself ill, eating too much & taking no exercise.'[35] New dentures were awaiting him. Maud washed her hair and went shopping in town. They remained for ten days, going for walks up Sunset Mountain, Cecil harmonizing, Maud indexing, both sad to leave the Appalachians, uncertain if they would ever return. Recovered from his asthma, Cecil developed a new symptom, pains in the eye. Anxiety caused him to admit to his diary that he had strayed from his vegetarian regime. Could soup or chicken, he wondered, account for this trouble?

On 27 October they took the overnight train to New York,

congratulating themselves that it was the last time they would have to pack their mountain gear, being thoroughly fed up with packing and unpacking after thirteen weeks on the road. There, it was all business with meetings of the EFDS. Mrs Storrow and Lily Roberts arrived from Boston; Susan Gilman was endlessly hospitable. Two new and generous patrons, Charlotte Foss and Peggy Scovill, were introduced. Even their protégée, the reluctant schoolgirl Emma Hensley, came on a visit and joined their parties. Lectures on the mountain experience were quickly organized; publishers were seen; the notation of the 'Running Set' was finalized and quickly put into practice by Charles Rabold and dancers from the Gilman school.

At the same time, Cecil went to a doctor, who, after a minute examination and an analysis of everything that could be analysed, came up with the theory that nothing was wrong with him except continual insistence on overworking, a disease in itself. They enjoyed pleasant evenings with good-humoured argument about the state of the war, something they had almost forgotten in the mountains, but they were put out by the amount of half-concealed pro-German sympathy they encountered. The Campbells came from Asheville and listened to the new songs, Olive clearly not expecting her name to appear on the book that would result from this second year's collecting. Cecil then asked permission to dedicate it to her and this gave her obvious pleasure.

Maud celebrated her thirty-second birthday in New York. Cecil bought her a handbag. Rabold arrived, bearing a sheaf of pink roses, to take her out to lunch and a picture exhibition. In the afternoon they rehearsed the 'Running Set', and they ended the day by celebrating with a dinner party. Ten days later, it was the turn of Cecil to have his, fifty-eighth, birthday. Rabold produced a hamper containing a pipe, cigarettes, an ashtray, nuts, prunes, and other luxuries. The Gilmans sent a basket of grapes and a bottle of French plums. 'Haven't had so many presents on my birthday for years!' Cecil exclaimed.[36] Maud's present was a walking-stick and a tie from Fifth Avenue, both 'very nice and very expensive of course'.[37] They dined at their favourite haunt, Peg Woffington's. Cecil's eye, however, was still causing pain. The next day he gave a lecture to the Russell Sage Foundation, feeling extremely nervous. It proved a success, and he was able to emphasize the necessity of collecting rapidly before the songs and dances vanished forever.

On 1 December they returned to the 'most gruesome business' of packing again.[38] This time it was for a social event. They were on their way to Boston to see Lily married. Summoned to America to assist, even before Maud had arrived, Lily Roberts was now a valued colleague of Mrs Storrow's and had been living in Boston for two years. She had met Richard Conant there and the engaged couple had requested Maud and Cecil to take important parts in the ceremony. Never one to be confident about dressing, Maud spent her first few days searching the Boston shops to find something that pleased her. After a 'hopeless quest',[39] she reluctantly agreed to Lily's persuasion and had a green silk evening dress she already possessed altered by a dressmaker. She bought Cecil a new tie and saw to it that he had a clean pair of spats for the occasion. She was made nervous by having to spend the evenings in the company of the engaged couple, playing reluctant gooseberry, while Cecil stayed with Mrs Storrow. They were all nearly late for the ceremony because of a heavy fall of snow. It fell to Cecil to give away a nervous Lily, resplendent in white, with veil and orange blossom, while Maud, in her green silk, was the solitary bridesmaid.

The last weeks of the year, spent in New York, included visits to concerts and the theatre. An evening recital gave Cecil the chance to record one of his choicer remarks against the over-artistic: 'Caruso is just a sentimental ordinary minded person with a natural organ wh[ich] he has done his best to spoil.'[40] Christmas was upon them, Sharp's second in New York. Maud bought him warm gloves; he gave her a pound of marshmallows – 'good ones'. This was the occasion of one of their triumphs. Low in funds, they had economized when on their own by eating out of tins and packets in their bedrooms, cooking some of their meals by means of a solidified type of fuel called Sterno. On Christmas Day they decided to 'have a real blow out and an orthodox Xmas dinner ... regardless of expense ... Turkey, with cranberry sauce, potatoes & turnips, plum pudding, coffee' and – for Cecil only – a liqueur.[41] When they asked for the bill, full of guilt and apprehension, they found that Mr Case, the Algonquin manager, had made them a present of the dinner. 'Thus is vice rewarded!' exulted Cecil. 'Had we been less greedy and more economical we should never have forgiven ourselves!'

But 1917 did not end, for Maud, on this note of euphoria. A strenuous four-day engagement at the Washington Irving High School left her angrily convinced that Cecil had been cheated. Of the 400 dollars taken, his share was only 150, and out of that he had to pay her. Money was of little consequence to her, but she felt she should maintain a professional attitude and accept her fee. There was, besides, no backing to be found for further Appalachian research and Cecil could think of no other organizations to turn to 'in this philistine country', he wrote bitterly. 'There is more money in it than any other spot on the Globe but it is only for those who are interested in money, and those who spend it spend it on something material and concrete.'[42]

Chapter 10

A 'very critical year for the whole world' is how Cecil Sharp greeted 1918 in his new, larger, and more splendid diary, a present from Maud.[1] It began with a change of scene. On 1 January, Charles Rabold saw them off to Chicago. The Elms Hotel, where they were to live for several weeks, provided rooms with a view of the lake, which they found frozen over and looking extremely beautiful with the ice piled in fantastic hummocks. Their first action was to order a piano so as to be able to work on harmonization. They had timed their arrival well, for in a couple of days snow stopped all trains and most other forms of transport.

Lecturing commitments took them to outlying places, involving icy roads and delayed, overcrowded buses. None of the schools offered any hospitality and food in restaurants was beginning to be scarce in the big freeze-up. The only consolation at the end of a gruelling day was a cheque in the pocket, more munificent here than for their previous engagements. Beautiful though it was, they did not care for Chicago. Courtesy was not its strong point: '"Sauve qui peut" should be their municipal motto', wrote Cecil.[2]

It was now Maud's turn to fall ill, her condition not helped by the coldest winter of the war and the impossibility of getting fresh air in the steam-heated rooms they both detested. She managed to drag herself to demonstrate dances, but collapsed with a bad throat and a temperature of 102°F, which prompted the summoning of 'a pompous, owlish doctor',[3] who diagnosed a septic patch in her nose. The only comfort that day was the arrival of the first mail for a long time, bringing letters from Constance and one from Vaughan Williams, who, to their inexpressible relief, was contriving to remain alive. It was decided that Maud's disease was only tonsillitis, but that she must stay in bed, Cecil spending the little time he was not at school acting as nurse, filling hot-water bottles, making pots of tea, and going out in search of comforts such as calves-foot jelly.

The shortages of food and fuel intensified Cecil's anti-American sentiments, making him wonder how a nation with such huge coal stocks and the best railway system in the world could find itself unable to cope with a few falls of snow and, if they could not, what possible help they could be to their allies in the war. He was maddened, at the same time, by effusive publicity that advertised him in the school prospectus as 'The Greatest folk dancing man in the world'.[4]

After a week Maud began to improve, sitting up in her room. Two days later she ventured out and insisted on attending a class. The result was a relapse and swollen glands. She began to have fears, imagining TB, smallpox, and meningitis in turn. Her face swelled and she developed a rash and took to her bed again.

Cecil, meanwhile, was taking three hours of evening classes on top of the day's work and was exhausted. He awoke with flu and was ordered to bed. This galvanized Maud into returning to the world. They swapped roles, she taking classes and filling bottles, he arguing with the doctor about the nature of his malady, which seemed identical with the fevers he had suffered in the mountains. The attack was mercifully short, because offers of work kept coming in. These included one from Miss Breckinridge of Hull House, 'a nice woman, and the first lady in our English sense of the word we have spoken to since we came here'.[5]

Her students were attentive and comparatively skilled dancers. This came as a relief to Maud, whose students at the University of Minnesota had been atrocious, with a hopeless accompanist, the sessions sandwiched between awful journeys in a packed bus and walks at either end during which rain poured down on her and floods rose up around her feet from the piles of thawing snow. By now, they were so busy that they worked separately, going independently to schools all over the suburbs, and, for once, they were making money. The result was that Maud exhausted herself yet again and had to go back to bed.

They had been in and around Chicago, mostly in icy weather, for the whole of January and February and ten days of March. The brief thaw gave way to cold as they returned to New York: 'This winter will never end!' wrote Cecil.[6] A huge pile of letters greeted them at the Algonquin and they were happy to be back among their friends, but they were, nevertheless, down in the dumps. 'Feel very seedy and depressed about things in general,' recorded Cecil, 'partly the weather, partly my own health, but mainly reading the newspapers which give no comfort anywhere at present.'[7]

This was, in fact, the moment in 1918 when the Germans made their last, and nearly successful, push along the front – truly the darkest hour before the dawn. The expatriates began to wonder whether they would ever get home and, if they did, whether it would be to a defeated country. Cecil became a prey to doubts as to whether any of their work over the past years had been of the slightest value. His gouty foot was troubling him again and he spent evenings talking to friends with it propped up on a pillow, 'feeling very old and fearful of the future'.[8] Maud, meanwhile, was dejected as a result of a painful course of injections against typhoid.

One bright spot in this depressing New York stay was an evening treat given them by Peggy Scovill, who swept them off to a theatre to see the first American production of *Mrs Warren's Profession*. Maud found it 'perfectly thrilling', and Cecil wrote: 'It is I think on the whole as good as anything Shaw has done [–] perhaps his most perfect play.'[9]

The whole detested business of packing began again, with a return to Boston. They longed to be quit of hotels but knew they would be moving almost weekly for the foreseeable future. Two days in Lincoln seemed like paradise, although their hope that they might be invited to rest there before the mountains was disappointed. Mrs Storrow was deep in war work and her beautiful house was filled with convalescent soldiers from Monday to Friday. But they were pleased at Lily's obvious happiness. Richard Conant appeared an ideal husband for her: 'a nice simple minded big bear of a man who suits her very well I think'.[10] The anniversary of the USA's entry into the war, on 6 March, was the occasion for Boston to stage a procession of eighty thousand people, marching with simple but effective home-made decorations. The news was that the Germans were being driven back.

All set for another expedition, funded by savings from Chicago and a cheque from Peggy Scovill, they went first for a visit to Washington. Their hotel, unkempt and none too clean, cost them twice what they were used to paying, four dollars a day – 'ye Gods!' exclaimed Cecil.[11] They went 'rubbernecking' about the streets in a manner not typical of either of them, and Maud was thrilled by a glimpse of the president coming out of the White House. There were marvellous displays of uniforms: '63 000 non-combatant officers doing civilian office work in Washington – all be-decked in khaki and strutting about with very un-military bearing'.[12]

Their friend and patron, Richard Aldrich, was resplendent in a tight-fitting, wasp-waisted captain's uniform. The Alphonso Smiths took them to see the Academy, the Senate and Congressional Chambers, the Supreme Court, and the Capitol Library. Of this last Cecil wrote, 'very imposing and the whole thing is very dignified and noble … Nothing has affected me in

America more than this'.[13] Maud, too, wrote that she was 'immensely impressed. A fine conception. It seems to embody America's finest ideals' – but then added in brackets '(What tosh!)', whether at the same moment or later on is not clear.[14]

They went on a five-hour journey south to humbler surroundings at Woodstock, where the mattresses were made of straw, but they were spending less money. It was the start of a six-month stay in Virginia. Maud worked all day on maps to prepare an itinerary for the Blue Ridge country. It poured unceasingly, so they spent their evenings watching Douglas Fairbanks movies at the local cinema.

They started their journey to the wilds in a cheerful mood because favourable news was coming in from France. The wilds, however, were not such as they had been used to. Civilization had progressed further in Virginia than in Kentucky and the Carolinas, with the pleasant result that lodgings were generally less primitive, but they had to work harder to get songs. On the other hand, many of the finest tunes of their American harvest were gathered here, which compensated for the labour. In Afton, where lovely views almost diverted them from work, they set about trying to capture a dance called the 'Square Eight', but it proved, in the end, to be a tame and sophisticated version of the 'Running Set', hardly worth taking down.

Buena Vista was another beautiful place and showed welcome symptoms of the dirt and squalor that generally meant good hunting. They put on oilskins and tramped through mud to a farmhouse. There they were rewarded by a beautiful 'Lord Randal' and 'Jack He Was a Sailor', which compensated them for getting soaked on the return journey. The next day was one to be remembered forever. They happened on a poor cabin full of countless children. In fact, there were fourteen of them, and when their mother, Mrs Wheeler, sang 'The Green Bed', 'to a first rate air',[15] first one, then another, of these dirty but delightful children joined in, singing or humming in an undertone, producing an effect that Maud and Cecil would never forget. They were able to take photographs of all the family together, discovering that while seven of them were Mrs Wheeler's own, the rest were stepchildren.

At the end of this notable day they again resorted to the movies, for there seem to have been picture palaces in even the smallest Appalachian town. In spite of the Wheelers, they concluded that too many local people were employed in factories, so, having first extracted good versions of 'The Two Crows' and 'Green Bushes', they took the train to Natural Bridge. They were well and truly back into their packing routine.

Mrs Laurel Wheeler and family, Buena Vista, Rockbridge County, Virginia
EFDSS, Cecil Sharp Photograph Collection

Natural Bridge, a beauty spot named after a feature of the landscape, provided a private bath – an almost unheard-of luxury – as well as eatable meals, but the people turned out to be 'pious & fanatical soft shell Baptists & wd. only sing hymns'.[16] They next attempted Massie's Mill, another pretty little place but another dead loss as 'one half of the population were industrials aiming at gentility',[17] and the other half black people working at the mill. 'It might be an African village', commented Maud.[18]

A friendly black man offered to drive them to Nash, where the population were said to be Scotch-Irish. It was a ten-hour journey through wonderful scenery, the country once again white with blossoming dogwoods. They found rooms in a clean little cabin with the Coffeys, whose three small children even Cecil admitted were delightful. The entire household took turns to wash in a basin on the back porch, but with the unusual luxury (for a cabin) of jugs of hot water. Mrs Coffey sang good songs and soon they were walking through woods a hundred feet above a rushing river to call on Aunt Betty Fitzgerald, 'a dear old lady of 85, wonderfully active, who fell in love with us & we with her'.[19]

She told them they had been discussed after the Sunday prayer meeting and the considered opinion of the village was that they must be German spies, because 'noting tunes etc was clearly a blind to hid[e] nefarious intentions – the fact that we eat no meat too was a clear indication that there was something wrong. Then we had asked at Mrs. Taylor's yesterday where her spring was (of course we had done no such thing) and that meant we intended to poison it! Although how killing poor Mrs. Taylor would assist the Kaiser, no one seemed to think!'[20]

Old Betty had two Mormon elders staying with her so she felt unable to sing to them. She sent them to her relative, Philander Fitzgerald, who obliged, but who also told them about their supposed spying activities. Cecil now thought it prudent to show the Coffeys their passports in case they, too, might be influenced by the rumours, but they laughed the story off and they spent an enjoyable evening joking, talking, and singing on their verandah. They regretted leaving the Coffey family: 'thoroughly nice people, with nice feelings', Cecil wrote.[21] 'They never did anything snobbish or affected or unpleasant' was Maud's comment; 'I think they enjoyed us as much as we did them.'[22] All the same, they were not displeased to find a proper bath and comfortable beds in Charlottesville.

They returned to Washington, where Richard Aldrich had arranged for Cecil to lecture in the 'large ambassadorial' house of Henry White. The

Chapter 10

Mr & Mrs Philander Fitzgerald, Nash, Nelson County, Virginia
EFDSS, Cecil Sharp Photograph Collection

audience was somewhat different from the ones in the mountain schools and included M. Jusserand, the French ambassador, Lady Reading, some Vanderbilts, a number of judges and generals, and Cecil's old friend Shane Leslie, who had been one of his pupils at Ludgrove. A number of listeners remarked that it was pleasant to hear an Englishman speak about something he had found in America! They were taken, next day, to visit the Rock Creek Cemetery, where the statues impressed Maud as much as anything she had seen in the USA. They were both unwell and exhausted but contrived to keep on their feet and be sociable, though Cecil thought he had some kind of poisoning. Maud went to the drugstore to obtain morphia for him.

They took the train back to the neighbourhood of Afton, lodging in a Queen Anne-style farmhouse. There they found a quantity of excellent singers, including an old slave woman, Aunt Maria Tombs, who sang them 'Barbara Ellen' and other ballads most beautifully in the intervals of smoking her pipe. She was the only black singer mentioned as having added to their collection. To start with, everybody was friendly, but after a few days the local papers raked up the spy scare and when they moved on they had to show their passports before accommodation could be agreed. Nevertheless, they left with a 'very respectable haul' of forty-five tunes.

Their next foray was a five-hour journey across three mountain ranges – Shenandoah, Blue Ridge, and the Alleghenies – to

Example of Maud's shorthand from Cecil Sharp's field notebooks
EFDSS, *Cecil Sharp Manuscripts, Field Notebooks*

Ronceverte, 'a beastly railroad town, very dirty and very smelly', in a hollow.[23] A nice old lady, also smoking a pipe, sang them a few songs but advised them not to linger as the population was too well-to-do. They removed themselves gratefully, Maud recording that she had never been so glad to get away from any place. Their next stop, Pence Springs, had splendid views but the water tasted and smelled of rotten eggs. They had arrived in a region rich in medicinal sulphur springs, both hot and cold, but unfortunately Cecil was not one whose complaints – at that time, laryngitis, hay fever, asthma, rheumatics – seemed to benefit from sulphur. If anything, the water made them worse.

All around were creeks with little houses on their banks, looking to be ideal as a hunting ground, but Maud wore herself out knocking at doors without finding more than a couple of tunes. The scenery was incomparable, the woods inviting, but the people simply did not know what their callers were asking for. So they packed up and took the train to Clifton Ford, a journey made memorable by the lodging of a cinder in Cecil's eye. He had to sit in agony for two hours with both eyes closed. On arrival, Maud led him to a barber who was able to remove the offending object. They arrived at Blue Ridge on 1 June to find the temperature rising to 93°F. The heat was unprecedented: 'apparently we are breaking another record, about the sixth this year!'[24]

They found a hotel in a gorge, surrounded by trees. It had little daylight, no electric light, and no air to speak of. The dining room was full of 'idle over-dressed young girls – a gruesome sight', wrote Cecil. 'The young women of America do not attract me!'[25] He was in a thoroughly bad mood, having hardly collected a tune for a week. He would have liked to knock off for a rest, but 'after a blank week like the last one I cannot give up yet.'[26]

They were starved as well as in darkness, so while Cecil went out prospecting, Maud took the train to Roanoake and bought canned soups, marmalade, and raisins. It was at this point that their luck began to turn, for hereabouts they started to discover the most splendid singers of all, notably a Mrs Donald, who instantly produced ten tunes, six of them first-rate. She was a train journey away, but it was worth making it for days in succession and at the end of a week Cecil was writing, 'one of the best weeks I have ever had. I took down 62 tunes including some very fine ones indeed.'[27]

After a day off to make fair copies, they decided to go back once more and were introduced to a Mrs Bowyer, who sang a wonderful 'Silk Merchant's Daughter' and a nice version of 'Geordie', making up the week's

Laura Virginia Donald, Dewey, Bedford County, Virginia
EFDSS, Cecil Sharp Photograph Collection

total to eighty – a record. At a wonderful farewell party, which drew a crowd, a man came in and danced a spirited 'Hoe Down', after which Maud was inspired to dance 'Lumps of Plum Pudding' and 'None So Pretty' to Cecil's sung accompaniment. All their singers had been old people and they felt they had harvested the songs in the nick of time. On 11 June they packed up: 'a gruesome business as usual, rendered doubly difficult because of the stygian darkness of our rooms.'[28]

Elated by this success they decided to have their week's rest back at the hotel at Natural Bridge, where they had been comfortable before. This time their luck was out. 'Piano going incessantly & some common girls occupy rooms close to us & we heard their raucous voices up till 12.30', complained Maud.[29] They managed to move away, but to little good effect, for a couple of young sailors arrived and made day and night hideous by playing incessant ragtime piano. They had never heard so much noise made on a piano and were overcome with wonder at the forbearance – or insensitivity – of the forty or fifty other guests, who appeared to have no objection to the row.

Maud, however, managed to get on with indexing their recent finds and Cecil gloated over the 230 tunes they had taken down on this trip, concluding that it was the richest harvest of any he had made, either in England or in the USA. They made two copies of the best twenty-five, one to be sent to Aldrich, the other across the Atlantic to Mrs Vaughan Williams to await her husband's return from the war. They left for New York with mixed feelings, sorry to leave the beauty of the mountains, but thankful to be away from the sulphur water which made them both feel ill.

Chapter 11

On 19 June 1918, Maud and Cecil were hurrying back to New York for a three-week summer school at the Gilman studios. They were also planning a visit to Newfoundland. The tales they had heard about its songs had stuck in their minds, and the idea of going somewhere cooler for the midsummer months was attractive. They hurried to the British consulate to get visas, at the same time renewing their passports for another two years. They spent evenings with Ben Iden Payne, who was in New York between producing pageants in various US cities. They gossiped and sang him their new songs, enjoying the company of the only English person they had met for months. But a note of depression is obvious in both diaries, and Maud did not feel like writing hers up for ten days.

The principal reason for their gloom was that the school had opened with only six pupils. It was the project of their dear friend Susan Gilman and they were terrified of failure for her sake. By the second day the numbers had gone up to nine, but even so there were only two and a quarter students to each teacher. At the end of a day of morris and country dancing they discussed whether to cancel the whole thing, but decided to go on. Maud was dubious.

Their depression was briefly forgotten when Percy Grainger made a sudden appearance at their hotel, remarkably arrayed in khaki and trailing his ubiquitous mother. He stayed for three hours, discussing folk songs round the piano with Cecil, while it fell to Maud to keep Mrs Grainger amused – 'rather a trial', she confided to her diary.[1] They found Grainger 'very chastened and much older . . . far less boyish and buoyant'.[2] Both Graingers were clearly enamoured of the United States and Percy had become an American citizen and contrived to join the US Army as 'a military band-master, or something of the sort'.[3] He was understandably fascinated by the Appalachian finds. He sent them tickets for a concert at Columbia, letting them in for a dreadful first half, with 'Cheap music and a bad conductor'.[4]

Things improved, however, when Percy himself appeared to play a Liszt Hungarian Rhapsody: 'He played from a full score turning the pages himself – a masterly feat', wrote Maud.[5] The evening ended with a performance of his *Gum-Suckers' March*, which gave her intense pleasure and induced a fit of the giggles.

On Independence Day the four teachers gave their nine pupils an afternoon off, after a class in which all joined in to sing 'The Star-Spangled Banner' and 'God Save the King'. They went to see the procession, but what diverted Maud most was watching aerobatics from her hotel bedroom, with planes releasing a confetti of paper over the city.

It had been far from easy, but throughout the three weeks they had behaved as if the school were a flourishing, paying concern. They held examinations, though there is no record of how many of the nine passed. During the last week their generous friend Peggy Scovill arrived and, having enquired into the Gilman affairs, promptly paid the printer's bill and other overheads, averting a financial disaster. She contrived, in fact, to make it look as if the school had made a 150 dollar profit. This, Susan Gilman proposed to divide between herself, Cecil, and Maud, but they refused payment, with the result that they ended up considerably out of pocket and reluctantly had to make the decision that a Newfoundland trip was not possible. It would have to be back to the Appalachians after a week in Boston. There they held classes for Mrs Storrow's Girl Scouts, which gave Maud a good deal of pain. The girls were the clumsiest she had ever looked on, and undisciplined into the bargain, their ungraceful movements accentuated by the frightful costume they wore – blouses tucked into bloomers.

Lily Conant was in hospital in Boston, having problems in the early stages of pregnancy. Richard was in Europe with the army and she felt sad, insecure, and somewhat lost in her adopted country. By the end of their visit she had cheered up, elated, like the rest of them, by unusually sanguine reports in the newspapers about the Foch offensive. It looked as if the tide of war had turned. Maud and Cecil stocked up again for the mountains, buying new baggage, tea, biscuits, and raisins, asthma powder for Cecil, pipes to give as presents, and a load of film for the camera.

It was intensely hot when they started for Virginia, wearing 'the smallest amount of clothing consistent with decency'.[6] Bedford City seemed a clean little place and the hotel, at the foot of the Peak of Otter, comfortable. The log cabins looked promising, but first impressions were misleading. The song hunters had been forestalled by Presbyterian missionaries and anything but hymns was taboo. There was no lack of songs in the hotel each evening, but of the sentimental variety, to the piano – 'the very worst songs that the American mind had ever conceived'.[7] They had happened on a tourist resort. It reminded Cecil of Hampstead Heath on a bank holiday.

The air, however, was delicious at 2800 feet and they felt it incumbent on them to climb the extra thousand feet to the top themselves. They were rewarded with a stunning view. They moved hopefully from one small village to another, always meeting the same problem: no songs, but no lack of sermons and theological discussions. One old lady who would have loved to sing was in too much of a fluster, expecting the preacher to dinner. The far side of the range had yet to be 'converted', but the lack of roads, which had defeated the evangelists, proved too much for Maud and Cecil too. In the end, they gave up and departed to Roanoake in insupportable heat. To cheer themselves they went to the movies. Even here their luck was out. *Resurrection* was showing and it was 'very rotten'.[8]

Rescue came from the most unexpected of quarters: 'a very interesting Episcopal parson',[9] the Rev. Dr Bryan of Petersburg, introduced himself and not only advised them where to go but actually sang them a song. He directed them to Miss Davis at St Peter's mission, 'a new and substantial School Building, a new and unfinished Church and a comfortable dwelling house', where they were given a warm welcome and 'astonishingly nice adjoining rooms'.[10] A couple of good singers had, moreover, been invited to supper. To return this hospitality, Cecil offered singing classes to the children and was rewarded when one of them sang a delightful version of 'The Rebel Soldier'. Between classes, they tracked down some of the most prolific singers of their whole American adventure, returning elated to the mission.

They were unwise to rejoice publicly, for it turned out that the best of them were on Miss Davis's black list, who told 'bloodcurdling stories of the escapades of their fathers & near relations'.[11] 'Oh these missionaries', complained Cecil. 'Their whole life seems set upon nosing out what is objectionable in anybody – except themselves of course – and ignoring the good.'[12]

They stayed a week collecting, regardless of disapproval and enchanted with the results. Miss Davis resolutely refused payment for their board and lodging, 'and seeing that I should hurt her feelings by pressing the matter I accepted the situation as gracefully as I could'.[13]

The last days of August were spent in Virginia with all the familiar discomforts – bad food, missionary-corrupted singers, an all-pervading stench of tobacco from the factories in Winston Salem, and, to them, a frightening preponderance of black faces. On the 27 August, Maud recorded 'the worst ride we have ever had … on side of mountain with a drop of several hundred feet over the most terrible road'.[14] By now they were connoisseurs of this sort of travel and probably did not exaggerate. They went on their usual hunting expeditions, sometimes returning with empty notebooks only to be sung to after supper by their landlord: 'It so often happens that we get nothing when we work hard & a lot when we work not at all.'[15]

No matter the state of their health or their terror at bad drivers, they never ceased to be able to marvel at the mountain scenery. Their last few weeks were the most successful ever. They went back to their old catchment area of North Carolina, to Marion and Burnsville. The ride there was the most beautiful Maud could remember, the train climbing over 3000 feet to a pleasant town with good rooms and their own baths. 'If we get songs living in such luxury it would be wonderful.'[16]

They were indeed in clover, paying 2½ dollars a day each for lodgings and discovering a gold mine of singers along a narrow creek. The hotel people marvelled that they should spend long hours with such 'low trash', but they returned day after day, stuffing their notebooks with the repertoire of the Mitchell family and their friends, sometimes up to nineteen people in one room, plus dogs, the atmosphere suffocating. Cecil reckoned it the best place they had stayed in and decided to remain for the rest of their time, the longest stay they had ever made. They ended with a two-day farewell party all over the town, saying goodbye with genuine regret and the sad premonition that they were finally putting the Appalachians behind them. Cecil, who could not stop counting, reckoned 625 songs that year, making 1625 for the three years they had spent in the United States, gathered from more than three hundred singers.

A promised week's holiday was spent back at the Grove Park Inn and for once Cecil did not complain of the boredom of luxury. This must have been a relief to Maud, who was only too happy to bask in creature comforts so long as she was not, all the time, being prodded in the conscience by her companion. They arrived exhausted, but after an excellent lunch and a rare afternoon nap were able to sit on the terrace and admire the view and the autumn colours. An acquaintance came to tell them the Germans had

The Mitchell family with Maud (second from left at back), Burnsville, Yancey County, North Carolina. EFDSS, Cecil Sharp Photograph Collection

accepted President Wilson's proposals, so they dressed for dinner warmed by the hope that the fighting might soon be over.

The only blot on the horizon was that Maud was starting a cold, which put Cecil in a panic in case either of them caught the Spanish influenza that was decimating the inhabitants of Asheville, presumably a version of the epidemic flu that, in Europe, was to account for more deaths in 1918 than all the slain of the four years of war. But Maud's cold was not bad enough to prevent her shopping in the hotel store, where she tried on countless garments and celebrated their return to civilization by buying what Cecil described as 'a blue serge dress – very nice!'[17] So pleased was she with this purchase that she made him photograph her in various poses, 'chiefly I think to impress and crow over Helen'.[18] They finished up their stock of film with Maud taking pictures of Cecil. They had brought back about 120 mountain photos from this trip.

Each evening they attended an organ recital, the hotel's speciality and an entertainment growing in popularity at this time, accompanied by the sort of lighting and sound effects that were to become familiar in European cinemas in the next decade – 'all very childish but amusing'.[19] They showed the organist some of their harmonized songs and he began to introduce them into his repertoire, being most flattering about the accompaniments. Their appetites were tremendous for the first edible food they had tasted in months. Then they packed 'for the thousandth time',[20] regretting they must leave this pleasant place. For Maud, whether she realized it or not, it was to be the end of the happiest time of her life.

On 19 October, in a mood of melancholy, they watched their beloved mountains disappear. They had lived above 2200 feet for the last six weeks. In the train to Washington and thence to New York, Maud was all the time conscious that Cecil's mind was totally concentrated on the thought of England. For months they had almost forgotten home and their families, away from civilization at a time when the war would have made return impossible. With the imminent prospect of peace, the whole situation changed. Plans for a foray to Newfoundland were again abandoned and they decided not to accept offers of work in California. There were, however, immediate commitments which they felt obliged to carry out. With much heart-searching, they decided to go home in December.

This, when it came to the point, proved less straightforward than they had imagined. They hurried to the British consulate, only to be told that

Percy Grainger, 1918
Percy Grainger Estate

they must obtain permits from Military Control, who would need to be convinced that their journey was necessary. They filled in numerous forms. Two days later they waited nervously for two hours, only to be told that Cecil's permit would be issued; but, 'For some obscure reason there was a ban on women crossing the Atlantic unless for important war-work.'[21] Things had been easier at the height of the submarine danger before America had entered the war. Maud was plunged into dejection and Cecil cabled Constance: '*Army Control officer will grant me a passport but not Maud without permission by cable from War Office Can you procure this Cannot leave her here alone.*'[22] He was affronted to be charged nine dollars for this communication.

Meanwhile, they had been able to spend time with the Campbells, whom they had missed on their holiday in Asheville, but who had come to New York. They discussed and sang songs with Olive and John – 'They are nice people & no mistake'.[23]

On the last day of October they went for final classes in Boston and for a weekend at Lincoln. Mrs Storrow's beautiful house was full of nurses convalescing from Spanish flu, but room was found for them. They luxuriated in the comfortable beds, read and rested, went for walks to pick up hickory nuts among the fallen leaves, and called on Boston friends. Lily looked well, expecting her baby soon. Among the people who dropped in was Percy Dearmer. Cecil wrote: 'It was nice, though rather a shock, to hear a typical Oxford voice & pronunciation again.'[24] Mrs Storrow drove them back to Boston after the nicest weekend Maud had ever spent at Lincoln.

In Boston they had classes to take, but Cecil was laid low with a sore throat so that Maud had to deputize while he stayed in bed. 'About 1 o'clock', he wrote, 'the news that Germany had signed the Armistice reached Boston. The bells were rung, everyone crowded into the streets and there was the wildest and most unrestrained jubilation. While I was lying down and trying to realize that the 4½ years of terror had come to a glorious end Maud came back from Lincoln with the news that the whole thing was a hoax, perpetrated probably by some stock exchange people!'[25]

That day, 7 November, they had the pleasure of entertaining Emma Hensley to tea. They kissed her goodbye, wondering if they would ever see her again. The next day Cecil was well enough to set off for Cleveland, where they had their next teaching engagement. It was there, on 11 November, that they were 'Awakened at 4.30 a.m. by hooting & ringing of bells, & later firing of gun or rocket. Peace at last!'[26] This was from Maud's diary. She continued: 'Cleveland in an uproar all day long . . . My own feeling is one of immense relief but I cannot reach a pitch of high exultation. Now it is all over I think I realize the horrors of war all the more.'[27] And Cecil wrote: 'A wonderful day, but I do not feel like making a noise . . . I cannot forget poor Butterworth, Tiddy, Percy [Lucas] and the many others – Here they have made few sacrifices.'[28] He fought his way through the rejoicing crowds to buy a pair of bedroom slippers for Maud, whose birthday was the following day. She had left hers behind in Boston.

Maud celebrated her birthday, a fine sunny day after a severe frost and the third birthday she had spent away from home, by taking classes and exploring Cleveland. The world's doings, reported in frequent editions of the papers, provided 'all that the most voracious emotional appetite could demand',[29] so they felt no need to resort to the theatre or the movies. They taught their students 'Peascods', 'Black Nag', 'Rufty Tufty', 'Hey Boys', and 'The Parson's Farewell', and enjoyed amiable exchanges with about fifty young people, some of whom Cecil allowed to heckle him, amused at one young man's attempts to convince him that the quadrille was a dance of American origin. They had a demonstration and speeches of farewell and Maud wrote: 'So ends our week at Cleveland – one of the nicest we have had anywhere, & the relief not to have the thought of the terrible fighting always at the back of one's mind.'[30]

A week in Detroit was similarly successful and they returned to New York gloating over the fact that they had made about 425 dollars – more by fifty than Cecil had ever earned in a week. This satisfaction almost compensated for a sleepless night in the train where Cecil suspected that the sheets, as was usual in the USA, had not been properly aired. Their delight was enhanced on reading in the papers that restrictions on women's travel were about to be relaxed.

So they hurried to the White Star offices for news of sailings and to the British consulate and the American authorities, where they were asked to fill in innumerable forms in triplicate 'of the most offensively inquisitorial character I have ever seen'.[31] To get Maud's passport they had to stand in the open for two hours and talk through a window to 'an insolent official – a sort of bargee', as she described him.[32]

The information that they would still have to wait between fourteen and thirty days caused even the mild-mannered Cecil to swear. Eventually they were introduced to a major who promised to pull the necessary strings. They marked Thanksgiving Day by giving vent to growing frustration at the delays and irritation at American boastfulness about the war and 'the great part they propose taking in the Peace negotiations'.[33]

Maud's diary comes to an abrupt halt on 19 November, her last remarks being to the effect that all was looking well for their departure. Cecil kept up his records to the end of the year, but it is clear that, for Maud, a chapter of her life had suddenly ended. On 3 December she went shopping for a belated birthday present for Cecil, having failed to find anything that pleased them in Detroit. At Abercrombie & Fitch a nice Irish assistant persuaded her to buy a beautiful dark-green woollen sweater for him. But Maud was 'under the weather' for several days, including one made loud by the gongs and bells that sent President Wilson off to the peace conference at Versailles. She recovered and astonished Cecil by buying three hats: 'she said as presents but as she wore one of them at lunch and another at tea it looks as if she meant to keep them for her own little head!'[34] This date is notable in Cecil's diary because this entry is one of the few slightly personal references he ever makes about Maud.

A farewell week had been arranged for Boston, but the *Adriatic*, on which they were to sail, announced a postponement. This was more than Cecil could tolerate, so they sought another booking and decided on the *Lapland*. This was due to depart four days earlier than they had planned, which occasioned cables to England and the reluctant cancelling of their last visit to Lincoln.

It was now a scramble of packing, shopping, and farewells, the saddest of which were to the Gilmans and Charles Rabold. Mrs Storrow came to see them off, laden with presents. On the *Lapland* they found boxes of gifts from Mrs Callery and baskets of fruit from Peggy Scovill. They were overwhelmed with emotion as New York vanished over the horizon.

In contrast to the anxious dramas of their wartime crossings, this was an uneventful passage and most of it was spent discussing plans for the imminent vacation school at Stratford. At Liverpool on 19 December, one of Maud's suitcases was, somewhat predictably, missing, and there is no record of whether she found it again. Charles Sharp arrived at the Custom House while they were searching, looking splendidly recovered. They observed that nothing could beat England for raw, damp cold.

At Euston, Maud's father greeted them and she drove with him to Florence's flat, while Cecil went on to yet another new house, this time in

Maresfield Gardens. He recognized it before he got out of the taxi, from the furniture van at the door. Maud and her luggage arrived before dinner and they spent a merry evening in the 'roomy, light and very quiet' house,[35] with its small garden backing on to FitzJohn's Avenue, which was to be her home from now on.

London was crowded to overflowing, with queues at all the shops as Christmas approached. They had to get used to ration books again. On 24 December, Charles put Maud on a train to York so that she could celebrate Christmas with Helen and Douglas Kennedy.

Chapter 12

The house at 4 Maresfield Gardens delighted Maud. A room had been set aside for her so that she did not have to seek a nearby lodging for herself and her typewriter. Dorothea Sharp had left home to live with a friend and Charles was shortly to go abroad to take up a job as a botanist, so there was plenty of space. Maud's favourite of the daughters, Joan, remained at home, as did Susannah, who was to take, in due course, an active part in the folk dance revival. While Maud was in York with the Kennedys, Cecil had spent what he described as 'perhaps the happiest and most peaceful Christmas',[1] in the bosom of his family, something that had rarely occurred in the life of the Sharps. Despite the still severe rationing, Constance had contrived to procure a magnificent turkey which temporarily shattered his vegetarian principles.

Meanwhile in York, Maud made the acquaintance of her nephew, John, born while she was in the USA. She stayed three days, hearing about Helen's war, which had been dedicated to holding the EFDS together at a time when almost all the officials had been absent. Even in spite of her labours, they felt anxiety about the future of the movement, especially when they contemplated the gaps in the ranks of the morris team caused by tragedies on the battlefield. Maud, however, was to preface the post-war chapter of her biography of Cecil Sharp with a hopeful verse from a folk song: 'John Barleycorn sprang up again, / And that surprised them all.'

'The Morris is a man's dance': John Kennedy, c. 1920
EFDSS, Peter Kennedy Collection, Maud Karpeles Materials

Singing and Dancing Wherever She Goes *A Life of Maud Karpeles*

Chapter 12

Above: Summer Vacation School, Stratford-upon-Avon, 1919
EFDSS Photograph Collection

Left: Dancing for the troops, Le Havre, 1918
EFDSS Photograph Collection

Two days after Christmas, the sisters set out by train for Stratford-upon-Avon, where the vacation school was about to start. Cecil met them at the station, full of surprise and delight at the numbers who had entered. The sisters were at once whirled into activity among nearly seventy students, most of whom had learned the basics of folk dancing before the war. It was an emotional reunion, both for the greeting of old friends and for the discovering of yet more gaps in their ranks.

Having complained regularly through the winters abroad, Cecil now regretted the change of climate – 'the dull sunless cold winter after the exhilarating air of America',[2] though he greatly enjoyed the absence of his bugbear, American steam heating. To habitués of the school he appeared charged with dynamic energy, but he himself confessed to feeling 'more or less collapsed, as a man would feel who had lived on stimulants for some years and had suddenly given them up'.[3]

The returned travellers had much to contribute to the school, Cecil giving an evening talk on the Appalachian finds, which Maud illustrated by singing the choicest of the tunes. The great excitement was the passing on of the patterns of the 'Running Set' to their most expert dancers. However, for both of them, 'the most stirring occasion of all was one in which Cecil

Maud Karpeles, Cecil and Joan Sharp at Cirencester
EFDSS Photograph Collection

Sharp took no active part but listened, together with the rest of the "School", to four members of the staff describing how they had taught folk dancing to the troops in France'.[4]

The moving spirit behind this enterprise had been Miss D. C. Daking, who described the difficulty of persuading the men at a convalescent depot to try dancing. She had overcome their reluctance by the ruse of putting weapons in their hands. Once started on a sword dance, their enthusiasm carried them from strength to strength, and from that small beginning the 'sport' had spread like wildfire throughout France, to the armies on the Rhine and thence back to convalescent camps at home. The EFDS was hard put to find enough teachers for them.

On New Year's Eve the Stratford school went out carol-singing with Chinese lanterns to the hospital, to call on Marie Corelli, who lived in the High Street and had crowned herself queen of the town in competition with Shakespeare; and thence to the Shakespeare Hotel, ending up at the American YMCA.

The last of her visits to America had lasted nearly two years and Maud now found that England gave her a sensation of mental dizziness: 'Conditions had changed so much and it was hard to catch up on events and to adjust

Cecil Sharp and Maud Karpeles judging a children's dance competition, 1923
EFDSS Photograph Collection

oneself to the present situation, still so full of uncertainties.'[5] The moment the Stratford school was over, Cecil Sharp was plunged into a colossal programme of organization in which Maud worked harder than she had ever done to keep up with him. Indeed, the last five years of his life were to be the busiest he had known.

The first thing was to rent a London office for the EFDS and to engage a secretary, though it continued to be at Maresfield Gardens that the real work was done, mostly in lengthy conversations between the two of them. For two years after their homecoming, Maud held no official position in the EFDS beyond being a member of the Executive Committee, but in 1921 she took over from her sister as Honorary Secretary. She was afraid that Helen, especially after her valiant work during the war, might be reluctant to give up the office, but Helen felt that Maud, in constant touch with Cecil and without the distraction of a husband and family, would do the job more efficiently. Meanwhile Cecil wrote to Mrs Storrow: 'The way in which the E.F.D.S. is prancing along is quite miraculous . . . I feel very happy about it all. I knew from the beginning that things would turn out this way sooner or later but I never dared allow myself to hope that I should live to see it all.'[6]

Soon after their return, Cecil was called upon by the Board of Education to discuss the best way of teaching schoolchildren to grow up with 'a sense of rhythm and love of our old English national songs and dances'.[7] H. A. L. Fisher, brother of Adeline Vaughan Williams, was President of the Board and perhaps had been prompted in this direction by his brother-in-law. In April, Sharp was offered the post of Inspector of Training Colleges for Folk Song and Dancing, and in the next two years visited over sixty of these establishments, most of them three or four times. Again he wrote to Mrs Storrow: 'It is nice to find oneself no longer wasting energy and beating on the doors from the outside, but now entering in as a welcome visitor.'[8]

All over the country demands came in for people to organize local branches of the EFDS and Maud was occupied with training teachers as fast as she could. By 1924, three thousand would-be dancers were attending weekly classes in London and suitable halls became as hard to find as trained instructors. Maud was run off her feet, teaching, organizing, and examining. Five years after the war, 3800 Certificates of Merit had been awarded. It must have seemed to them as if the entire nation was dancing to celebrate the peace.

Each holiday period was the occasion for a vacation school, Easter being added to the Summer and Christmas ones. The summer of 1919 saw yet another at Stratford-upon-Avon, but it quickly became clear that another venue would have to be found. The enormous increase in students enrolling presented accommodation problems, Stratford, after all, had its own Shakespeare industry which was liable to fill all the available hotels and B&Bs, and the extra influx of folk dance students, while it added to the jollity of the birthday celebrations, was becoming an embarrassment. So 1919 proved to be the last vacation school that Cecil Sharp was to conduct there, and for the next three years an invitation was accepted from Cheltenham College to make use of their halls and playing fields for the lectures and demonstrations. Maud took an active part in all these schools and was the person chiefly responsible for the preliminary organization.

To the Cheltenham school came Sir Arthur Somervell, composer and educationist, who was, at the time, Inspector of Music for the Board of Education. In the past he had been an opponent of Cecil Sharp's ideas, conducting acrimonious correspondence with him via the newspapers on the differences between 'national' and 'folk' tunes. Now all was forgotten and he became an enthusiastic follower and even a pupil. Though just turned sixty-nine, he threw himself into the dance. To Maud he quickly became 'Cousin Arthur', and after the first Cheltenham summer school he wrote applying to join the Christmas one, to be held at the Chelsea Polytechnic. In his letter he revealed the way in which she had helped him: 'I'm more than grateful to you for your hint about going through the dances in bed, with a book to refer to. I can now dance about 22 with fair credit I believe. (I do them in my room night &

Arthur Somervell, Helen and Douglas Kennedy, 1926
EFDSS, Peter Kennedy Collection, Maud Karpeles Materials

morning). I have even learned 3 or 4 which I have never danced in class."[9]

These Polytechnic schools proved more popular than had been foreseen and were quickly overflowing, so that extra space had to be found, the situation becoming more and more desperate each year. By 1922, they had 578 students, twenty-one teachers and twenty-one accompanists, and had to employ a fleet of motor buses to ferry them to and fro between the central building and the outside classrooms.

THE TWO SISTERS.
BURLESQUE BALLET
IN 3 SCENES.

Music arranged by CAV. TOMMASINI GUINEABOXSKI.
Choreography by FOLKY.
Scenery by LEON BAKST AND NOEL FRONTST.
Costumes by KASTOFF.
Wigs by NATURE, LTD.!
The Short Curtain specially designed and painted by PABLO PIZZICATTO.
The whole production costing £000,000,000,000.
Synoptic Notes by ERNEST NOUVEAUHOMME, the celebrated and *only* authority on Nationality in Music,
Conductor ... ... MAESTRO ENRICO WOODI.

DANCERS:

The Two Sisters } .. .. { KARPSAVINA.
{ KARPALOVA.
The Scottish Knight ... ... MORIS BADENOFF.
Czar of the Efdeeski ... ... CSSSL SHARIAPINE.
Weebit Dekadent ... MARIE THE NIHILIST.
Corps de Ballett UPPA DUBBEL, TCHERNACZINGLE, SATAN ONERR, BAKTOBAK, SIDESKI, MORRIS OFFOVITCH, GALLEYITSKI, SHUFFELSHUFFEL, ROUNZZ.

Scene I. and III. *The Court at Chelsea.*
Scene II. *Appalachia.*

A. J. Stanley, Printer, Tudor House, High Street, Stratford-on-Avon.

Vacation School entertainment, c.1919
EFDSS, Peter Kennedy Collection, Maud Karpeles Materials

Chapter 12

A. H. Fox Strangways, Helen Kennedy, Peggy Kettlewell, and Cecil Sharp
EFDSS Photograph Collection

After the post-war Christmas school at Stratford, an Easter one had to be promptly added. With the Kennedys living in York, that city presented itself as the obvious choice for the first two years. The third year it moved to Manchester and thenceforward settled in Aldeburgh, where, on the invitation of its principal, Mrs Dudley Hervey, who had fallen under the folk dance spell, Belstead House School provided an ideal setting. It had spacious grounds and plenty of living accommodation and the whole set-up was to remind Maud and Cecil of the happy vacation schools they had run for Mrs Storrow in the USA. From 1922, a number of schools were held there and Belstead House became for Maud almost a second home.

It was there that the happiest gathering of all the summers took place in 1923, which, as it turned out, would be the last that Cecil Sharp was to conduct. The atmosphere was of a family party and among the many important musical friends who came were two who gave Maud and Cecil particular pleasure: Olive Dame Campbell, the instigator of all their Appalachian adventures; and Evelyn Wells, the teacher from Pine Mountain School where they had spent, perhaps, their happiest week of all in the USA. Both these ladies were persuaded to talk to the company and enchanted everybody with accounts of life in the wilds. 'Foxy', as Cecil's old friend A. H. Fox Strangways was known, was among the visitors and afterwards wrote a glowing account for *Music & Letters*. It was, he said, 'a week of pure pleasure ... in a house with twenty and a village with three hundred people as happy as the day was long. And the day was long. It began at seven with the bathing detachment, unless the riding squad had preceded them at six. By nine, thirteen pianos were going in schoolrooms, gymnasiums and refectories, and a normal day's work ... had begun.'[10]

Foxy was then taken a round of the classrooms and watched as Cecil sorted out the natural dancers from the clumsy, correcting their errors and combining them into compatible sets:

After a short adjournment for milk and biscuits, for dancing and singing are both exhausting things when they are done with vigour, work goes on till one; the afternoon is free, and there is another hour and a half before dinner. When the weather permits, as it mostly did, the dancing is out of doors, and very beautiful sights were a demonstration by the staff one day, a performance of *As You Like It* by the Hervey-Grey company on another, and, on a third an evening gathering of the whole 300 dancers till daylight died and all the colour went out of the frocks. These took place on a large lawn with rising sides fringed with elms and planes; the spectators luxuriated in shade and the dancers and actors revelled in the sun. For music there was fiddle and piano, or fiddle alone with pipe (with or without tabor).[11]

The incident that remained most vividly in Maud's memory was an open-air performance of the Abbot's Bromley Horn Dance as dusk was falling. 'The dancers, looking half human half animal with their antlers' horns, mysteriously emerged from the darkness of a clump of trees, went through the curious evolutions of the dance in the half-light and then slowly vanished, while the sound of the accompanying tune played on the violin by Elsie Avril continued to haunt our ears. It was as though we had had a visitation from the spirit world.'[12] But the most important feature of that school was the series of talks given by Sharp. Maud wrote: 'perhaps some premonition made him feel that he must unburden himself of his philosophy concerning the songs and dances.'[13] Later, in her autobiography, she made a summary of the contents of his 'sermons'.

Over the next two years there were two schools at Easter, at Aldeburgh and Harrogate, with Cecil Sharp dashing from one to the other to spend three days at each, and with Maud in charge at Aldeburgh in 1923 and at Harrogate the next year. With the help of Lady Mary Trefusis, they also opened Easter schools at Plymouth and Exeter. Sharp had appointed Lady Mary as President of the EFDS in 1912. She had been, as Lady Mary Lygon, Lady of the Bedchamber to Queen Mary, and she was a scholarly musician and a tireless accompanist for dancers. She became a good friend to Maud.

Apart from the vacation schools there were numerous other special functions for the EFDS to organize. Among the earliest of these, on 21 July 1919, was an enormous country dance gathering in Hyde Park for the

Buns and milk
EFDSS, Peter Kennedy Collection, Maud Karpeles Materials

Peace Day celebrations. This was the first of many open-air meetings to be held in London parks, as well as in the provinces. Maud described it in her autobiography: 'On four evenings preceding the day, classes were held in various halls in London at which simple Country Dances were taught. It fell to my lot to take the classes at the Chelsea Polytechnic to which an enthusiastic crowd of two hundred or more novices turned up. On the day itself about a thousand dancers participated and the music was provided by the band of the Fourth Royal Fusiliers. Around the enclosure there were many thousands of interested spectators, many of whom drifted into the enclosure and joined the dancing throng. During the course of the dancing we were honoured by a visit from Their Majesties the King and Queen.'[14]

Two years later, in the summer of 1921, the EFDS hired the King's Theatre, Hammersmith, for a week's folk festival to attempt to bring the songs as well as the dances to a wider public. Four different programmes were given, with performances every weekday evening and two matinees. A small theatre orchestra, led by Maud's discovery Elsie Avril, provided accompaniment to the dances, most of the music having been arranged by Sharp. 'No attempt was made to stylize the dances and they were presented in as straightforward and natural [a] manner as was consistent with a public show. During the dance performances the whole company was on the stage, except when the Morris dancers had to retire to the wings to put on their bell-pads. The dancers, when not performing, were seated on either side of the stage.'[15]

Between the dances came interludes of song, performed by the English Singers or the Oriana Madrigal Society, under Charles Kennedy Scott; and solo songs were given by Clive Carey, Mattie Kay, and Margaret Longman. 'Mattie Kay had illustrated Cecil Sharp's lectures for many years,' wrote Maud, 'but when she was not available he often called on Gwen Ffrangcon-Davies. She was a beautiful singer and I always felt sorry that her pre-occupations as an actress prevented her from making more public appearances as a singer, particularly of folk songs.'[16]

Gwen Ffrangcon-Davies, with her pure soprano voice, was about to win fame, in 1922, in the part of Etain in Rutland Boughton's *The Immortal Hour*, an opera that astonished everyone with the length of its London run. She remembers with pleasure, not long before that, being the first to bring some of the newly discovered Appalachian songs to the public. She recalled Cecil as looking frail and ill and coming to rehearsals muffled up in a shawl. It was about this time, too, that he described himself as 'a rotten Director doubled up with lumbago, coughing and spluttering with bronchitis, and otherwise displaying symptoms of galloping senility'.[17]

The King's Theatre was hired in three successive years and at the 1922 festival 'Her Majesty the Queen, accompanied by Lady Mary Trefusis, was present. During the interval I was presented to her and she expressed her great enjoyment of the performance. Unhappily, on that occasion I was prevented from taking part in the dancing owing to a sprained ankle.'[18]

It was in connection with these performances that Maud put her opinion of theatrical performances of this type on record: 'Some have questioned the suitability of giving stage performances of the dances and songs, but it has to be remembered that they are fundamental and universal forms of artistic expression and are by no means tied to their traditional setting. I am sure that at these performances they lost none of their essential qualities. Though the dances were so familiar to me, I was over and over again lost in wonder at their beauty as I sat watching them.'[19] 'At the request of the Board of Education', she continued, 'a special performance was given for representatives of the Overseas Department attending the Imperial Education Conference. Cecil Sharp gave an opening address and there is no question but that this event did much to increase interest in the revival.'[20]

All through these five busy years Maud's only settled home was a small bedroom in the Sharp household, to which she returned between her many sallies here and there to schools and other places where there was dancing. The lack of space that she could call her own taught her to develop the neat, economical methods of record-keeping that impressed her executors years later. She had, literally, no room to be untidy or to store superfluous papers. Sadly, this must have led to the destruction of letters that could have added colour to her biography.

During these busy years, with their arduous pattern of travel and work, Cecil's health, as Gwen Ffrangcon-Davies had observed, was deteriorating. In addition to asthma and his other chronic complaints, the mysterious fever continued to plague him, descending without warning and sending his temperature soaring. Each attack left him limp and weak. On one occasion, Maud had to watch while he was stricken in the midst of an illustrated lecture at the Old Vic. His determination carried him through to the finish, but in the taxi which she had summoned he became delirious. In 1923, the year in which he received the honorary degree of Master of Music from Cambridge University, she counted thirteen attacks.

His family managed to persuade him to take the occasional short holiday

EFDS group photo, Hyde Park, 1922
EFDSS, Peter Kennedy Collection, Maud Karpeles Materials

Chapter 12

and, since Constance's health also continued to be delicate and she had already cast Maud in the role of nurse and guardian, as well as secretary, to her husband, it was a foregone conclusion that the pair of them would go together. They managed to enjoy a few pleasant excursions, notably to Malvern and Sidmouth, hiring bicycles to explore the countryside. But nothing would induce Cecil to be completely idle, nor would he allow Maud much rest. Evenings were spent answering his large correspondence and, after this was disposed of, deciphering new patterns of steps from the pages of Playford's *Dancing Master*.

Indeed, they managed to do some collecting, as Maud related: 'near Oxford ... we noted Morris Dances from Abingdon, Berkshire and Brackley, Northamptonshire. We obtained the Brackley dances from two brothers, the only surviving members of the Brackley team. They were excellent dancers, despite their age, but it took a long time to note the dances, because every time for any reason they stopped in the course of the dance they had to go back to the beginning again before they could proceed. We also made a thorough search ... in many areas of the Midlands ... cycling from village to village. Over and over again we talked to people who had dim memories of the dances having once been practised, but nearly always they had been given up sixty or seventy years ago.'[21] While in Oxfordshire they made a visit to the Kettlewells, who now lived in Burford, and were fortunate enough to find some good folk singers there.

By the autumn of 1923 the attacks of fever had lowered Cecil's physical state to the point at which he agreed to take more drastic action. 'I do not want to live', he had written, '– especially in such a world as the present one – unless I can recover my strength. I hate having my wings clipped and dragging along as an invalid.'[22] It was Maud's idea that they should go to Switzerland, and they remained there for two months. Her eldest sister, Lucy Heilbut, had become a widow in 1921. With their small daughter, Katie, she and her husband had been living in Montreux, lodging in the apartment of a Dr Minnich, who afterwards became her second husband. When Cecil had an attack of the mysterious fever, Dr Minnich was consulted and promptly diagnosed malaria. He prescribed massive doses of quinine, a treatment that was immediately effective, and Cecil was to have no more of these attacks.

In Montreux, Maud and Cecil had what she described as a quiet and peaceful time, 'though again we were not completely idle'.[23] Since rest was anathema to Cecil, he had taken steps to see that he was kept constantly in touch with the business of the EFDS. In their luggage they had brought a book by Thoinot Arbeau, published in 1588, entitled *Orchésographie*, 'the first really elaborate treatise on dancing that was printed',[24] but never, so far, translated. This lack they now set out to remedy, though Cecil's French was rudimentary and Maud must have done most of the work. They little knew that when they returned it would be to discover that Cyril W. Beaumont had just completed a translation of the same book.

With this and other labours Maud's nose was kept well and truly to the grindstone. The small Katie Heilbut carefully observed the situation, noticing that her Aunt Maud was allowed to visit her sister on Sundays only and that her stay in Montreux was not what anybody normal would describe as a holiday. She remarked also that while Cecil was understandably ill-looking, Maud also seemed distinctly below par – pale, thin, and appearing a great deal older than either her own actual age or that of her elder sister. Katie's impression was that Cecil overworked her and that his insistence that both of them should keep to a vegetarian diet was doing Maud no good at all.

Not obviously rested, but with Cecil free at last of his debilitating fever, they rushed home to be at the Christmas school at Chelsea. It consisted, Maud wrote, of twenty-one simultaneous classes, with an attendance of about 550 students. After that, having been warned by Dr Minnich not to overdo things, Cecil seems to have made a brief effort to live sensibly in Maresfield Gardens. 'During the first winter weeks of 1924 he managed to keep fairly well by seldom leaving the house. In fact, he felt better than he had for the last few years; and he was full of plans for the future. He wanted above all a time of quiet and leisure in which he hoped, among other things, to write a comprehensive book on the English folk dance and to publish the remainder of his Appalachian collection.'[25]

But when spring brought the resumption of the EFDS activities it was too much to expect that this comparative quiet would continue. For April of that year Cecil's diary lists Easter schools at Harrogate and Exeter, and for May, apart from London meetings of the EFDS, lectures and adjudicating sessions at Torquay, Sheffield, Cardiff, Newport, Bath, Birmingham, Lincoln, Norwich, and Ilkley. 'I am flying all over the country', he wrote, 'and all my literary work is at a standstill.'[26]

Adjudicating the folk dance competition at Ilkley, from 26 to 28 May, turned out to be the last activity of Cecil's life. Maud was not with him but had arranged to meet him the next day at Retford, where they were to witness a hobby-horse ceremony. Together they were going on to preside at a three-day competition at Newcastle-upon-Tyne. Maud was the first to arrive. 'Some hours later,' she wrote, 'shortly after Mr Hercy Denman, with whom Cecil was to stay the night, had met him at the station, I heard their voices as they walked up to the house . . . Cecil was very hoarse and when I went out to meet them I was greeted with the remark from Hercy: "He has a very bad cold and is feeling very ill." Cecil went straight to bed and the next day I travelled to Newcastle alone.

'On June 3rd I re-joined him, meeting him at Darlington station and we travelled back to London together. Throughout the journey he was on the point of collapse and on arrival at Maresfield Gardens he immediately took to his bed. His illness was at first thought to be heart trouble but an X-ray showed it to be cancer of the throat.'[27] This was something, Katie believed, that Dr Minnich had foreseen, and she believes he had warned Maud that it might be expected.

For the three weeks of his illness, Maud was almost constantly at Cecil's bedside. The moment he realized he was incurably ill he started to make valiant efforts, with her help, to finish a projected history of the dance that he had been working on with a friend, A. P. Oppé. Maud recalled that he was strangely incurious about the nature of his malady, one that was scarcely mentionable at the time. Indeed, the word 'cancer' does not appear in the biography published in 1933 on which Maud collaborated with A. H. Fox Strangways, and it is still described only as 'a fatal illness' in the revised version that appeared under her own name in 1967. It is only in her own autobiography, written a decade later, that the forbidden word is used. For the last week he was semi-conscious, but, in lucid moments, was able to name Douglas Kennedy as his successor in the EFDS and to appoint Maud as his literary executrix. He died in the early hours of Midsummer Eve, 23 June 1924.

Chapter 13

The name Karpeles does not appear in the list of 'among those present' at the cremation in Golders Green, although Helen Kennedy is mentioned along with her husband. It would be typical of Maud at that period of her life to avoid giving her name at the chapel door. Constance and the four Sharp children are mentioned, as well as Cecil's sister Evelyn. Vaughan Williams was present, both as a friend and to represent the Royal College of Music; and the branches of the EFDS at Liverpool, Bristol, Bath, and Chelsea sent representatives. Many friends from the world of music and dance were there, together with most of the staff and many students from the Chelsea College of Physical Education. Henry Nevinson, journalist and war correspondent, who had recently become a great friend to Cecil and to Maud, was in the congregation. The service was conducted by the Rev. Percy Dearmer, musician and hymn-book editor, whose 'typical Oxford voice & pronunciation' had diverted Cecil at Lincoln, Massachusetts, when Maud and he had paid their farewell visit to Mrs Storrow.

Maud's name was equally absent from the flood of obituaries that appeared in the London press, and almost every local paper the length and breadth of the country, even though many of them went in detail into his researches in the Appalachians. This was perhaps not surprising in the European publications, but it is strange that her collaboration was not noted in the mass of obituaries and articles on his work published in the USA. Some of the writers, notably Richard Aldrich of the *New York Times*, had known her well. The wide coverage of his death, from all quarters of the globe, and the amount of space he was awarded, would have astonished Cecil Sharp, and must have gratified Maud. The cuttings, in all probability pasted in by her, fill many pages of the EFDS scrapbooks.

On 28 June, at St Martin-in-the-Fields, Martin Shaw played in the congregation with a selection of folk tunes at the start of a memorial service. On this occasion, Percy Dearmer gave the address, prefaced with a reading from Psalm 150 containing the verse 'Praise him with the cymbals and dances'. He spoke of Sharp as a prophet and pioneer and emphasized that he had left plentiful disciples to carry on his work.

Maud was left, as she described it, 'groping in a sunless world'.[1] For fifteen years, Cecil had filled her life, to the extent that she had abandoned her previous interests – politics, religion, social service – without really noticing that she had done so. During this time she had seen little of her own family, apart from Helen, who shared her enthusiasms. During the wartime years in the USA, Cecil and she had been together every day, and since then, while she lived in the Sharp household, they had only been separated during the very busy seasons when they had had to rush to opposite ends of Britain to cover simultaneous schools and festivals. Her autobiography gives little real idea of the sudden desolation that now fell upon her.

For the first few weeks, however, she was kept on an even keel by the enormous amount of work that went on without interruption and by the knowledge that nobody knew better than she how Cecil would have wanted it done. She turned first to Vaughan Williams, who gave her unfailing encouragement and, as she wrote, 'worked indefatigably for the welfare of the [EFDS] and it was largely due to his guidance and vision that it continued to prosper after Cecil Sharp's death'.[2] He was appointed Musical Adviser to the EFDS. Few summer plans were interrupted, the only engagements cancelled being the festival at Hammersmith and a country dance party planned for Hyde Park.

Shortly after Cecil's death a Board of Artistic Control – an 'objectionable term', complained Maud – was appointed, consisting of herself, Vaughan Williams, and Douglas Kennedy. Douglas, meanwhile, was arranging to retire from the post of botanist at the Royal College of Science in order to fulfil Cecil's dying wish that he should succeed him as Organizing Director of the EFDS. Though Kennedy had only started dancing at the same Stratford school as Maud and Helen, he had folk music in his blood. His grandfather had been a singer of Scots songs and his aunt was Marjory Kennedy-Fraser, the collector of songs from the Hebrides.

Within a month, Lady Mary Trefusis summoned a special general meeting of the EFDS to decide on a suitable memorial to its founder. It was agreed that the most appropriate form this could take would be a building where dancing could take place and where the large library Cecil had bequeathed the EFDS could be housed. Such a headquarters was something he had dreamt of. A Memorial Fund was set up, with H. A. L. Fisher as Chairman and Winifred Shuldham-Shaw, an enthusiastic worker in the cause, as

Honorary Secretary. Fisher wrote letters to *The Times* and many other papers, appealing for £25,000. A sum of £2000 was promptly contributed by friends.

The summer school for 1924 took place in Cambridge, which continued for some years to be preferred to Aldeburgh because, out of term, it was able to offer plenty of living space, fifteen or sixteen good classrooms, and a headquarters at the Perse School. Christ's Pieces provided a romantic setting for the white-clad morris men and the girls in their blue dresses and cherry-coloured ribbons, and Vaughan Williams's college, Trinity, opened its Fellows' Garden for three hundred dancers taking part in rounds and squares, 'as many as will', while the sun sank behind the trees until only a crimson afterglow remained. *Country Life* described the event, so soon after Cecil's death, as 'a species of funerary games'. Vaughan Williams gave up his summer holiday to act as director; Lady Mary Trefusis played indefatigably to accompany ballads at the Corn Exchange; Maud was mentioned in *The Times* as an 'able coadjutor', to Douglas Kennedy. The last, the paper said, 'has the knack of doing what is wanted in the right way; he is an excellent dancer, sings a good song and makes a good speech'. With 756 students signed up for the course, everyone made a strenuous effort to appear normal, cheerful, and festive, but though everything went smoothly the three weeks proved a strain to directors and students alike.

As always at a folk dance school, there was a sizeable detachment of Paulinas – as the pupils of St Paul's Girls' School, Hammersmith, were called – inspired to attend by their head music master, Gustav Holst. Among them, on this occasion, was his daughter, Imogen, then a schoolgirl of seventeen, and a classmate of hers, Jane Schofield, who kept a diary in which she recorded the joys of the dancing and the horrors of the exams, with an occasional glimpse of Maud and some slightly unexpected comments on other EFDS worthies. She had arrived at the school, by no means her first, in a state of depression, having recorded on 23 June her shock at Cecil Sharp's death: 'Returned to school feeling rotten. Just before the exam in the morning Imo met me with the dreadful news of Mr Sharp's sudden death. It was a dreadful shock to me, I had had no idea his illness was at all serious ...The Summer School will be dreadful without him.'[3]

Jane's brother, Kenworthy Schofield, was a prominent member of the EFDS and kept a stern eye on his young sister's progress. On 4 August she wrote: 'Classes began in real earnest. I am in Morris 2 with Sinner [Marjorie Sinclair] – Ken sent me down to be dealt with by that lady because my

Douglas, Helen, and John Kennedy, 1925
EFDSS Photograph Collection

Morris step is so bad. The Lady Mary Trefusis took the singing in the Corn Exchange – she made me want to scream. I know I ought to love everyone, but I would like to stick a pin into Lady Mary.'[4] The next day, 'Dr Vaughan Williams took the singing – he does make us work hard. He thinks we're awfully bad.'[5]

Examinations started on 8 August:

> I presented myself – my little mind a blank & my little knees a-knocking – only to find to my added dismay that Miss Karpeles & Miss Smallman were presiding . . . all went moderately well at first except that they would make me a woman when I like being a man, also I kept thrusting the wrong arm almost habitually at my unfortunate partners. Then came the Running Set, & they asked me to be a man! – I rejoiced hugely but somehow or other Mary Heffer, my partner, seemed to think she was a man too, & planted herself quite immovable on my left hand side & before I could do anything about it the wretched dance began – everyone began tearing about in different directions, and I got completely [lost] while the only thing that I could remember was that I was really meant to be a man only somehow I wasn't – the difficulty was that I couldn't make out which Mary thought she was – things got so desperate that at last I could bear it no longer so raising my voice above the hubbub I yelled to Miss Karpeles – 'I *am* a woman aren't I?' This had a most remarkable effect on the lady in question – she literally crumpled up – Miss Smallman was reduced to a similar state of hysterics & the whole examination room was in an uproar – the dance had to cease which was precisely what I wanted while Miss Karpeles said that she would not count it as she had been unable to attend properly – so we had to begin again, & this time being no longer uncertain as to my sex – all went well.
>
> Then came sword . . . then Miss Karpeles the brute conceived the cruel idea of making us do 'Sleights' – none of us knew it . . . I of course least of all. [Confusion followed until] 'Maud' at length came to the conclusion that she'd had enough of 'Sleights' – Exam ended – Concluded quite naturally that I'd failed – wondered what Ken would say. Still came to the conclusion that it was worth it – funniest afternoon I've had for ages. Then the miracle occurred – Miss Karpeles actually informed me without joking that I'd passed! – also said she thought I danced quite nicely! – But she then said that our standard was very high which made me have my grave doubts as to the truth of the preceding remark.[6]

It was at the finish of this Cambridge school that the reality of Cecil's absence suddenly hit Maud: 'After the School was over and everyone but me had departed, something seemed to snap. I felt very lonely and helpless and it was difficult to know what immediate step to take. Then for some unaccountable reason I thought of the Shap moors in Westmorland which I had often passed through on my train journeys to and from the north.'[7] She travelled alone to that wild, beautiful, and almost deserted country and spent ten days pulling her thoughts and feelings together. The mention of this brief retreat from society is all that her autobiography gives away of her feelings of bereavement.

When she returned to London, she was persuaded to join a party of dancers who, disappointed at the loss of the Hammersmith festival, had decided to go on a tour of the Netherlands, and spent a week performing in Amsterdam, Haarlem, Hilversum, Nijmegen, and Brussels. According to *Le Soir*, in the last of these places, where the British and Spanish ambassadors had been among the audience, 'On a beaucoup applaudit.'

The Christmas vacation school, held again in Chelsea, was almost embarrassingly successful, with forty classes and seventy instructors spread over all the rooms they could hire, outdoor carols in the churchyard of St Martin-in-the-Fields, and a large country dance party at the Imperial Institute. The *Daily Mail* thought this 'pure delight . . . the antidote to the deadly Jazz, the venomous fox-trot, to the pestilent one-step, to all the toxic dances which for some ten years now have turned the dancers of Britain into the semblance of a multitude of paralytic worms'. By New Year's Day, £4000 had been collected for the Memorial Fund.

Maud now began to rearrange her life, reconciling herself to the idea of having to stand on her own feet, as she put it, though it is clear that in the last few years she had been more of a support to Cecil than he had been to her, and her feet had been well and truly planted on the ground. She decided to take over two more rooms on the top floor of Maresfield Gardens, where she already had her bedroom, and turn it into a self-contained flat by installing a kitchen for herself. Here she was to remain until Constance Sharp died. After that, in 1928, Joan and Susannah took over the top flat, while Maud occupied the lower part of the house. During this time Maud was kept busy with the sorting of Cecil's library. She made herself responsible for the books he had bequeathed to the EFDS until such time as there should be a building to house them. His manuscript collections were left to his old college – Clare College, Cambridge – but before handing them over Maud

Chapter 13

Maud Karpeles and Douglas Kennedy
EFDSS Photograph Collection

took time to photostat the tunes and type out the song texts so that they might be ready to hand for study. The long hours spent on this monotonous work did her good.

In the spring of 1925 the Mansion House was the scene of a public meeting to boost the Memorial Fund. The prime minister, Stanley Baldwin, sent a speech to be read out and, not to be outdone, the previous prime minister, Ramsay MacDonald, contributed another. Messages were delivered from Sybil Thorndike and Dr Maud Royden, and from Vaughan Williams and Gustav Holst, neither of whom was able to be present. Two of Maud's old friends, Granville-Barker and Arthur Somervell, spoke in person. Sir Hugh Allen's eloquence was much admired by the press and Margaret Bondfield, a rare female MP, made a much-quoted speech deploring the dreary ritual dances of industrial workers whose factories she often visited, wishing that they, too, would take to folk dance. 'Everybody may not know', said a correspondent of the *Morning Post*, 'that the EFDS was specially exempted from the operation of the Entertainments Tax as a "national pastime". It must be a remarkable work that can soften the heart of the Inland Revenue.' Not everyone was so enthusiastic, however. A letter in *The Stage* read: 'Why not £25,000 towards English opera and let folk music look after itself, as folk music always will?'

Later that year, the BBC put on a concert to boost the appeal fund. Held on Cecil Sharp's birthday, 22 November, it included two verbal appeals: one from 2LO by Vaughan Williams, the other by Sir Hugh Allen from a studio in Oxford. All the singers gave their fees and the enterprise raised £650, making the fund up to £8080 by Christmas. By the following year it had swelled to £11,700, with the promise of a further £5000 from the Carnegie Trust. This, however, still fell short of the target.

It was to be another four years before the foundation stone of the building that was to become Cecil Sharp House was laid, and during that time Maud's energies were fully stretched in continuing the day-to-day work of the EFDS, helping to direct the Easter and summer schools, which spread further every year, and organizing special events to bring in money for the appeal. One of these events, broadcast by the BBC on 3 May 1926, was a somewhat unusual exercise. Supervised by Maud and Douglas, an orchestra led by Elsie Avril relayed folk dances all over the country and had groups in Preston, Cardiff, Malvern, and many other places, all dancing simultaneously to 'Nancy's Fancy', 'Hey Boys', 'Gathering Peascods', 'Newcastle', 'Haste to the Wedding', 'Sellenger's Round', and half a dozen other tunes.

Maud was to make her own first broadcast the next year. The BBC, still in the cramped studios of Savoy Hill, put out a series of illustrated talks on folk song and dance. While Douglas broadcast the first of these, Maud undertook the following three programmes, with a group of schoolchildren to provide background noises. Maud, who was later to give many talks and interviews, felt at ease with the microphone from the first. She was to receive an embarrassing shock, however, the first time she listened to a playback, suffering the experience known to most new broadcasters: 'I could not stand the sound of my own voice. It seemed to me like that of a "refined schoolmarm".'[8]

During this period vacation schools were being held annually in the USA, at Amherst and Long Pond, Massachusetts. Contributions came in from these American disciples, especially those who also came to take part in the schools in Britain. In 1927, Maud made her first visit to America without Cecil, travelling on the *Aquitania* with a company made up of the Kennedys, Peggy Kettlewell, Elsie Avril, Marjorie Barnett, and May Gadd. She wrote of the gathering at Amherst:

> The beauty of the College grounds with the distant mountain view cannot easily be surpassed, and to many of us the place held memories and associations which affected us even more than the beauty of the scene. For here ten years ago Cecil Sharp and I had directed the last Summer School of the American Branches. Many who had attended that Vacation School were present and it seemed at times as though the ten intervening years were but as one day. The enthusiasm of the students was boundless, and it expressed itself in such a way that by the third day hardly an able-bodied student was to be found. It says much for their native courage and perseverance that not a single caper was omitted on account of stiff and aching legs.[9]

Staying on after the others, Maud went exploring New England, especially the Green Mountains of Vermont, and was able to note some country dances. She made a sentimental journey to Pine Mountain School and revisited Cleveland, Ohio. She met old friends and was moved to find they continued to practise the dances Cecil had taught them. While in the USA, Maud was, of course, immediately in touch with 'Aunt Helen' Storrow. To her she poured out her enthusiasm and her worries about the progress of the Memorial Fund. Her confidences resulted in the Storrows becoming the biggest individual donors to the appeal. Whenever the flow of money dried up, they could be counted upon to come to the rescue with a substantial contribution.

All through the 1920s and 1930s the movement was gathering momentum. In 1925 a festival was held in the Great Hall of London University, in which fifteen hundred dancers participated to the accompaniment of the Band of the Coldstream Guards. The following year the festival was repeated in the London Scottish Drill Hall, with a public performance the next day in the Royal Albert Hall, the first of many such. 'The second session of the Festival finished at 10.30 p.m.,' wrote Maud, 'whereupon Douglas, Helen and I would retire to my flat and, after a hasty meal, proceed to draw up the programme for the following day. This was no light task and we did not finish it until the early hours of the next morning. Douglas then took the completed programme to the local printer and all was in order for the evening performance . . . The general dancing . . . was accompanied by a small orchestra led by Elsie Avril and conducted by Vaughan Williams. He always prefaced his remarks to the members of the orchestra with the following injunction: "Now gentlemen, if there appears to be any disagreement between Miss Avril and myself, take no notice of me but follow her." I would often stand beside him to indicate the tempo of the tune. On one occasion, I noticed that he had scribbled on his score: "Faster than I think."'[10] Maud always took some part in the dancing and particularly enjoyed performing in the Albert Hall, feeling, in that enormous place, in close touch with even the most distant members of the audience.

Next year, the New Scala Theatre was taken for the Cecil Sharp festival and the proceeds of the five days of performances went to the Memorial Fund. The English Singers, Plunkett Greene, Jean Sterling Mackinlay, Steuart Wilson, and other soloists gave their services to the cause. The London Chamber Orchestra consisted entirely of professional musicians, including Leon Goossens, with Vaughan Williams conducting. *The Times* gave a very warm welcome and was particularly impressed by '"The Running Set" from Kentucky, in which eight dancers kept up a *perpetuum mobile*, all with a single step woven into a hundred patterns.' The Scala festival was a success, repeated the following year with, this time, Gustav Holst as conductor and Maud as dancer, stage manager, and coach for the amateur dancers.

Meanwhile the vacation schools proliferated. At one in Malvern, Maud was delighted to meet her old acquaintance from Fabian Society days, Bernard Shaw, who revealed himself as an admirer of Cecil Sharp and spoke with enthusiasm of the dancing he had just witnessed. On these occasions

Maud was often conductor or lecturer, but seems to have been relieved when visiting musicians were able to free her for the dance arena. They included Vaughan Williams, Holst and his daughter Imogen, Reginald Jacques, Arthur Somervell, Steuart Wilson, and, on one occasion, Adrian Boult. Lecturers included Granville-Barker, H.W. Nevinson, Lord Raglan, and the Rev. Frank Etherington, vicar of Minehead, for whom Maud had given demonstrations in the days before the war. He was, like Nevinson, to become, in the 1930s, one of her most intimate friends and providers of moral support.

During these years Maud was gaining confidence and becoming a forceful personality. With Cecil alive she had been inclined to efface herself and keep respectfully in the background, and he had done little to bring her forward. Without him, but with the conviction that she knew better than anyone what he would have wanted for the movement, she grew more assertive and continued in this way throughout the rest of her days, to the extent that she was, in the end, capable of arousing hostility and making enemies. She had discovered with astonishment that speaking impromptu came to her with ease, so long as she stuck to the subjects of her enthusiasm. More and more she was being called on to give lectures. Many of these were more or less direct quotations from ones she had heard from her mentor, and it was only to be expected that she would adopt a similar style. Cecil Sharp had been well aware that his lectures were often described as sermons, so great was his proselytizing zeal. It is amusing to find the same accusation being made against Maud.

In 1925 an EFDS staff conference had been inaugurated, which was held, the first year, in Aldeburgh. Among the forty-five members was Helen, Douglas Kennedy's sister, an excellent dancer, singer, and teacher:

> During an interval [Maud wrote] her notebook was found lying on a chair. Someone out of curiosity opened it and found in it but two pencilled lines:
> Sermon by D.N.K.
> Ditto by M.K.

But despite this caustic remark it was a most enjoyable and successful event.[11]

Jane Schofield, Imogen Holst's friend from St Paul's Girls' School, gave a description of one of Maud's lectures at the Buxton summer school in 1927, having managed, after arriving at the last moment, to squeeze herself into an absolutely crammed hall:

Amherst summer school, including Douglas Kennedy (top left); Charles Rabold (centre of middle row); (front row) Helen Kennedy, Maud Karpeles, May Gadd (centre front). EFDSS *Photograph Collection (Lincoln W. Barnes, Amherst)*

Chapter 13

The lecture was very good indeed – Miss Karpeles just threw herself into it, and told the whole story very simply & very well. She sang some of the songs herself, and though her voice is very small it was so true, & the way she sang them so sincere. I enjoyed them far more than the songs which Mr Kennedy and Miss Avril sang later in the programme – though they are gifted with much better voices. She finished up with some slides showing pictures of the Appalachian scenery and the people from whom she & Mr Sharp collected the songs. I ought to explain that these people who live in the Appalachians & Alleghenies are really Elizabethan English who emigrated at that time, & became buried in these mountains.[12]

About a year after Cecil's death, Maud had started once more to do a little folk dance collecting. She felt both inadequate and melancholy attempting this on her own, but the activity gave her more of a feeling that she was carrying on his work than she obtained from sitting on committees or delivering her lecture-sermons. Her first attempt was on an expedition to Upton-upon-Severn, where she had been told there was morris dancing to be seen. An aged fisherman told her that they used to dance to make money whenever the weather put a stop to fishing. Thirty or forty men would then get together, but most of these were now dispersed or dead. However, he managed to collect a team, mostly consisting of his own family, who proceeded to demonstrate, in a rough and uncertain manner, how a stick dance and a handkerchief dance had been performed. Exercising phenomenal patience, Maud managed to reconstruct the movements to a sufficient extent for them to be taken into the EFDS repertoire. She felt she had had a small triumph and went on to find other groups in Worcestershire and in Shropshire.

A broadcast she made in 1927 brought her a letter from a Mr Charles Smith of Mitcheldean, Gloucestershire, who wrote: 'I hope you won't mind my addressing these few lines to you. It is to tell you how interested I was in your lecture on English Folk Songs last Friday afternoon. You was [*sic*] talking of the late Mr. Cecil Sharp and of how he went about the country gathering those old songs and tunes from old people. As I happen to be one of them, I thought you would be interested in what I am going to tell you.'[13] He went on to describe how two ladies had come to ask him about the mumming play in which he used to act and had invited him to visit them. With them, he 'met the dear old gentleman, Mr. Sharp, and I found it was him that wanted the Gloucestershire Mumming Acting. He was pleased to see me and he wrote down all about the mumming and I sang some songs as well.'[14]

His postscript read: 'Please excuse bad writing and spelling as I am self-taught. I was driving Oxen at Plough years before the School Board came out in the Cotswolds and never had but little schooling.'[15] Maud hurried to see him, taking one of her dance colleagues with her, and found him 'a delightful old man . . . much excited by our visit. He described several Country Dances and whistled the tunes. Poor man, he was much embarrassed as he had had a dental operation a few days before and he kept on interrupting his whistling to exclaim: "Oh dear, I be so lispy."'[16]

The find Maud considered the most important was the Royton Morris, tracked down in Lancashire in the summer of 1928. At the prompting of a friend, she wrote to a local newspaper for information and was put in touch with Mr Lees Kershaw, who had played the concertina for the dances for over forty years at its annual performances in Wakes Week. With Susannah, Cecil Sharp's plain, pleasant, youngest daughter, who was her frequent companion, she set out to visit Royton. As usual with folk musicians, she immediately established friendly contact with Kershaw and he gave her a number of tunes. The dance performances had lapsed since the war, but he managed, after a few months' effort, to collect a complete team and Maud was able to travel back and check her notation of the figures. She was particularly delighted with her work on this dance because a bogus version had grown up and was widely practised at local fairs. The figures she collected at Royton preserved its traditional character and had not, as one of the performers put it, 'been infringed'. She brought Lees Kershaw and his leading dancer to London to instruct the EFDS demonstration team and later the whole Royton team danced at an Albert Hall festival.

Another Lancashire morris dance she was able to rescue from utter oblivion was the mysterious Circle Dance from Abram, near Wigan. She never managed to see it, since it had not been performed since 1901, but a piece of ground in Abram was dedicated to the dance on condition that it took place there once in every twenty years, so to preserve its claim it ought to have been danced again before 1922.[17] Maud visited the ground, which was now surrounded by the workings of the Maypole Colliery and marked out by a concrete post at each corner. 'It was a bare and desolate spot', she wrote. 'As I stood there gazing at it a queer sensation came over me. I seemed to be carried back into the past, or perhaps it would be more true to say that time seemed to have disappeared and the past was merged into the present.'[18] She managed to acquire the steps of the dance from a local enthusiast named

Richard Porter. He was old and ill, and he died a few months later, but during what remained of his life the two of them kept up a constant correspondence which inspired him with the ambition to recover so that he could dance at the Albert Hall. Maud greatly regretted that this was not to be.

Maud also collected in Northumberland. The results of her work there over five years came out in due course as *Twelve Traditional Country Dances* (1931). The piano arrangements were by Vaughan Williams, with a note on the title page: 'in collaboration with Maud Karpeles'. This, she wrote, was 'an honour I do not merit, for my collaboration was purely negative. I was not satisfied with Vaughan Williams's first draft because I felt that he had not sufficiently stressed the dance rhythm. Whereupon with the greatest tolerance he amended the arrangements until they met with my approval. He insisted on my name appearing ... and I believe that his reason for so doing was not that I might have the credit but that he was not altogether satisfied with the final result.'[19]

At the end of 1928 Maud took a step that was to free her for even more independent collecting. After long heart-searching she resigned the post of Honorary Secretary of the EFDS that she had taken over from Helen in 1921. Over the intervening years it had become difficult to distinguish between the work she did in this capacity and her functions as one of the three directors of the Board of Artistic Control. She accepted nomination to the Executive Committee and continued to teach, adjudicate, take part in performances, and give occasional lectures for the EFDS, but she was able to feel now that her life was, at least in part, her own.

It was also in 1928 that the Memorial Fund reached and passed its £25,000 target. Inevitably, by this time, what with inflation and more ambitious ideas of what the building was to fulfil, the figure needed had leapt to £31,000. Extra efforts were made to attract subscriptions and well-disposed bodies were persuaded to improve their offers. Thus the Carnegie Trust, which had agreed to contribute £5000, when decision day came increased this sum to £6500. An anonymous donor offered to add five shillings to every pound subscribed from then on. The Storrows, inevitably, came forward, this time with a cheque for £5000.

Gloom had been cast over these activities by the death in 1927 of the President, Lady Mary Trefusis, who had been the moving spirit in getting the Memorial Fund launched. Her loss galvanized the rest into even greater efforts, particularly the Honorary Secretary, the indefatigable Winifred Shuldham-Shaw. Known as Holly, from her maiden name of Holloway, she was a singer, dancer, and pianist, whose impersonations of the other EFDS members had been the high spot of many social gatherings. She, and her small son, Patrick, later to become famous as a dancing master and singer of folk songs, were always present at EFDS functions, and it was at the Buxton summer school in 1927 that Jane Schofield wrote a description of one of Holly's 'turns' which, incidentally, makes reference to the ethereal quality of Maud's dancing:

> Then Mrs Shuldham-Shaw appeared – and she really surpassed herself. She started off with some of her old skits – Jean Stirling Mackinlay singing 'William Taylor' – Mr Plunkett Greene singing the 'Crocodile' – Mrs Kennedy Frazer talking about experiences in the Hebrides – etc. etc. – received with much enthusiasm. Then she did 'Miss Karpeles teaching singing games' – she'd evidently been present on Wednesday last & taken note of the said lady teaching 'Roman Soldiers' – she reproduced it absolutely perfectly – squeaky voice & everything – it brought the house down of course – awful shame! Finally she proceeded to enact a little episode – She was a French governess – and she had 5 children in her charge – Hélène, Maudie, Douglas, Ralph, & Walter.[20]

The first three were, of course, the Kennedys and Maud; Ralph is unknown but probably not Vaughan Williams; and the last is Sir Walter Rea. There followed a dissertation by the governess instructing the children how to dance, ending: 'Maudie you must dance *on* ze ground not off it!' Holly's little biography, *Cecil Sharp & the E.F.D.S.*, was written to attract shillings to swell the Memorial Fund, which it did with great success.

So, at the end of their years of collecting money, the Kennedys, Maud, and their helpers switched their activities to the search for a place to put their building. The architect was to be Henry Markham Fletcher, FRIBA, who came with a strong recommendation from Vaughan Williams – pushed, moreover, in their direction by his daughter, who was an ardent folk dancer. It was he, and his colleague Mr Pinkerton, who, late in 1927, had summoned Douglas Kennedy to join them on a derelict site in NW1, at the point where Gloucester Avenue meets Regent's Park Road.

> When I arrived [Douglas wrote] they were obviously excited by their find. I thought the site singularly unattractive as it had been used for some time as a dump for all measure of rejections and smelt to high heaven.

Maud Karpeles and William Kimber laying the foundation stone of Cecil Sharp House, 1929. EFDSS *Photograph Collection (Special Press)*

Chapter 13

While they were dilating on its attractions, an island site with no near neighbours to complain of our stick clashing and incessant ring of Morris bells, I could only just withstand the smell. When I remarked on it they brushed my complaint aside and said it was just a dead goat which had been tethered to graze on the lush vegetation. When I asked of what it had died they supposed it was the quiet and loneliness. Anyhow the sanitary inspector had arranged for its removal so I could stop worrying. The upshot was that we bought the site at a knock down price.[21]

The price was in fact £5588, which left the Memorial Fund better off than had been expected. Work was promptly started on the foundations and the building emerged above ground level by June 1929, making it possible to lay the foundation stone on Midsummer Day, five years and one day after Cecil Sharp's death. To perform the ceremony, the unanimous choice fell on Maud, who, as Douglas wrote, 'had been Cecil's right hand "man" for the last ten years of his life, assisted by William Kimber who had been his right hand man for the first ten years of his Morris dance collecting and teaching'.[22]

Maud's face was half-obscured by a smart new cloche hat typical of the period. After she had laid the stone, Kimber cemented it into position with particular expertise, bricklaying having been his trade. The proceedings had been set in motion by H. A. L. Fisher, who asked Maud, before she laid the stone, to say a few words about Sharp's ambitions and achievements, adding, 'Nobody is more fitted to speak of them than she is.'[23]

Her speech was brief and reticent; she was clearly overcome with emotion. The passage she chose to remember in her autobiography ran as follows:

> To the many who knew Cecil Sharp this ceremony inevitably arouses conflicting emotions. We rejoice that we have been able to realize his great wish but there is sadness in the thought that he – our friend whom we loved so dearly – is not here to share in our rejoicings. It is f[iv]e years since Cecil Sharp died and our sense of personal loss is still acute, but our sorrow though it colours our thoughts does not obscure our vision. Cecil Sharp, the man, is no longer here, but we believe that his personality is still making itself felt – perhaps more strongly than when he was alive – and that it will continue to do so long after we have left this earthly scene. And so this building which we are erecting in gratitude for the past is likewise an expression of our faith in the future.[24]

On the foundation stone was carved: 'This building is erected in memory of Cecil Sharp, who restored to the English people the songs and dances of their country. Midsummer Day 1929.' Under it, the customary new-minted coins were buried and along with them the badge of the EFDS, representing locked swords – both symbols of sacrifice, as Maud remarked in her speech.

After the cementing of the stone, Lady Ampthill, who had succeeded Lady Mary Trefusis as President, made a presentation of silver and ivory trowels to Maud and to William Kimber. It was left to this folk dancer, who had really been the original source of all this activity, to wind up the proceedings. He spoke of the Boxing Day meeting in 1899, when he had been twenty-seven years old and Sharp had been on a Christmas visit to his mother-in-law a mile east of Oxford, at Headington. Looking out of the window upon a snow-covered drive, Sharp had seen a strange procession: 'eight men dressed in white, decorated with ribbons, with pads of small latten-bells strapped to their shins, carrying coloured sticks and white handkerchiefs; accompanying them was a concertina-player and a man dressed as a "Fool"'.[25] Kimber had been the man with the concertina. Cecil Sharp had rushed out of the house and that had been the start of the movement that now brought the present company to Regent's Park Road.

Chapter 14

The collecting trip to Newfoundland that Cecil and Maud had planned in 1918 had been abandoned for lack of money. Their next target date, 1925, had been forestalled by his death. Ever since, Maud had cherished in the back of her mind an ambition to go there on her own, 'to compensate in some small measure for Cecil's unfulfilled intention'.[1]

She was deterred, at first, by the fear that she might not be competent to note the tunes. Working with Sharp, she had always left it to him to put the notes down, while she recorded the words in shorthand. 'I had little musicianship,' she wrote, 'in the sense of being able to see what I heard and hear what I saw.'[2] But, one day in 1929, she found herself telephoning a shipping office to enquire about sailings: '"Well," I said to myself, "I suppose that means that I have decided to make the venture."'[3]

She had, however, other commitments directly after laying the foundation stone. She had been booked to direct that year's summer school at Amherst, and had already decided to make that the opportunity to do some collecting in the United States and also in Canada. Newfoundland would have to wait until the autumn. Vaughan Williams was among the friends who put her on a train at Euston in mid-July on her way to board a boat for Canada. She felt she had great need of the luck he wished her.

'Arriving in Montreal,' she wrote, 'I had a few hours to spare, so I extravagantly took a taxi and did some sightseeing. My driver was charming. He apologized that he could not have me to sit with him on the front seat, but the law, he said, did not allow ladies to sit with the driver unless there was a chaperone in the back seat. He was most fatherly and I am sure the law need have had no fear in this case. He pointed out all the sights, which were certainly very impressive, and he insisted on my getting out of the taxi to see anything of special interest. He always took my arm to escort me across the street.

'My first objective was Lakefield, Ontario, where, as I had been informed, "old time" dances were practised. These took place at the Pavilion . . . a big wooden hut with open sides, and it was crowded with young men and women from the neighbourhood. You paid nothing to watch but if you wanted to dance the charge was ten cents which entitled you and your partner to participate in a group of three dances. After each group of dances the floor is cleared and then you buy a fresh ticket for the next group, and so on. It is a wonderful way of making money . . . !'[4]

She wrote at once to Helen, describing the arrangement: 'I suggest to Holly that she runs Country Dances for the Fund on that system.'[5] She was disappointed that the dances, 'square' or 'round', were all accompanied by a band playing well-known, published tunes. 'There was a caller,' the letter to Helen went on, 'who shouted through a megaphone. I couldn't understand a word he called, but most of the people followed the instructions pretty well and evidently knew the dances. They were for the most part just quadrille figures and nothing like as interesting as the dances I saw two years ago . . . I am going to a "house-dance", i.e. a private dance, tonight, which is being got up for my benefit, but I don't expect I shall see anything very different.'[6]

She was correct in this supposition, but found it, all the same, an interesting experience. She was collected in a car by the son of her hosts and shown first to a bedroom where she had to sit for an hour conversing with the other ladies, mostly about the dozen or so babies present, while the men stood about in another room, smoking. The dance started at 10.30 p.m., and she was able to watch and make notes for two hours except when the fattest and hottest man in the room insisted upon dancing with her. At half past midnight she excused herself, to the mortification of her hosts who had been hoping she would stay to 'lunch'.

Lakefield, by the side of a lake, proved a most beautiful place, but her hope of finding songs was dashed by the evident prosperity of the inhabitants. As in the Appalachians, she found it much more difficult to call on well-housed strangers than on people who lived in huts or cabins. But one day in the neighbouring town of Peterborough, she 'had the good luck to hear some children singing "The Frog and the Mouse". I immediately knocked at the door and found four children alone in the house. They said they had learned the songs from their mother who knew many old songs, so I arranged to call next day and I got several good folk songs from her.'[7]

In her letter to Helen she described the most memorable of the friends she made in Canada:

the most lovely Irishman, Michael Sullivan by name . . . He is a fiddler and plays beautifully, but his tunes are unfortunately all the well-known Scotch and Irish ones. I took down three tunes of no great value . . . [but] I wish I could have taken down every word that he said in shorthand. He is a real artist and philosopher and has a wonderful way of expressing himself. He has a real vision of what all this folk-stuff means and it was quite wonderful to hear so many of Mr Sharp's ideas coming from him . . . he was quite thrilled with what I told him about the Society etc. He said he always felt that somewhere there must be something of this sort, and now he felt so proud to think that he was allowed to play a small part in it. He was much impressed by my laborious attempts to take down his tunes and he implored me to stay in Canada and not to go to the States, saying, 'You should keep your talents for your own country.' When I had taken down one tune he said, 'Yes, you've got the notes all right, but remember it's what lies between the notes that makes the music' . . . When I finally said goodbye to him, he said, 'I feel highly complimented by your visits. It has been a wonderful thing. It is not only that you and I have met, but that it has been music which has brought us together. But let us not be over-proud. Let us remember that we are a very small part of a very big thing.'[8]

She confessed to Helen that she had been extravagant in the matter of hiring cars and that her conscience later compelled her to walk when she could. Often she managed to get a lift. This good fortune sometimes landed her in trouble: 'I had a walk of 6 miles to go, but a kind gentleman who knew the country well – so he said – gave me a lift for 5 miles or so and then dropped me just about 11 miles from my destination. However fortunately I managed to get another lift for 4 miles in the right direction.'[9]

After leaving Lakefield, Maud crossed the border into the United States, where she went first to Vermont, staying with the Dimmocks, who had become friends during her first visit after Cecil's death. She attended a couple of dances, but did no better here than in Canada. In the modern 'round' dances the practice of 'cutting in' was prevalent. 'That means', she wrote, 'that as you are toddling round with your partner another man will tap him on the shoulder and then take possession of you. In one dance I changed hands five times, so I felt I was quite a social success.'[10]

She went on to Boston where Helen Storrow enabled her to 'prospect' in other New England states by lending her a car and chauffeur. None of the dances she attended came up to her expectations. She found their style degenerate and objected to the waltz-fashion of swinging partners, wishing, on the very hot nights, that she could be transported back to the good old days. She was able to report on the progress of Cecil Sharp House and air her continuing worries about getting the place completed. The Storrows' reply was a further cheque for £5000 to be dedicated to furnishings, and the decision was made to put Helen in charge of this part of the work.

After the Amherst vacation school, Maud at last set out for Newfoundland, leaving Boston on 5 September on the night train to Halifax, Nova Scotia. She started in a highly nervous state, having been taken to a 'thriller' – 'a most blood-curdling affair and not at all a good preface to my lonely journey'[11] – after a farewell dinner with Lily and Richard Conant. She spent the 6th in Halifax and boarded a boat next day for St John's, delighted to find the sea like a millpond and the boat comfortable. She got little sleep, however, as her cabin turned out to be above the fog siren, which moaned continuously.

It took two days to reach St John's – 'quite the shabbiest town I have ever seen', she described it to Helen. 'It is really rather pathetic, especially as they are all so proud of it. The people seem very nice and very English . . . The people in the shops, etc. talk either in a nice ordinary English or more frequently with a strong Irish accent.'[12] She had a good room overlooking the harbour, but her pleasure at a private bathroom was somewhat diluted by the fact that the hot water came out of the tap bright red. The hotel was expensive but the food fifth-rate. She suspected, nevertheless, that in time she might find herself looking back on it as the utmost luxury.

Maud had arrived with a couple of introductions: to Dr Paton, head of the Memorial College; and to Fred Emerson. No sooner had she unpacked than the latter rang up and she spent her first evening dining with him and his wife, Isabel. Both were to be numbered, eventually, among her closest friends. The Emersons introduced her around and helped plan her itinerary, after which she was soon feeling at home, but it was a blow to discover that she had been preceded, a couple of months earlier, by two collectors sponsored by Vassar College. The weather, however, was 'splendid. The air yesterday was wonderful – very warm and bright and sunny with a sparkle in it, rather like Switzerland. But it gets very cold at night.'[13]

On the 11th, the day she wrote to Helen, she took down her first tune, 'a little jingle which is sung for the Cushion Dance. I got it from an elderly gentleman' – in fact, the St John's harbour master – 'who called on me at the hotel. He created great amusement amongst the page boys as he danced round whilst singing the tune, and finally knelt in front of me offering me the cushion (actually my newspaper).'[14] She was quite cheered by this scoop as she had arrived prepared to find Newfoundland barren soil and wondered whether she had come on a fool's errand.

Maud described in her autobiography the difficulties of planning her campaign:

> There were few towns of any size and the majority of the people, who were fishermen, lived in small settlements or 'outports' as they were called[,] which are dotted along the shores of the mainland or on the off-shore islands. The interior, which was almost uninhabited, consists of lakes, rivers, virgin forests and moorland ('barrens' as it is called). The coast line is very irregular and the great island-studded bays and narrow inlets penetrate the land to a great depth cutting it up into a series of peninsulas. Thus it was a difficult country to get about in, particularly as at that time there were no through-roads whereby one could get from one peninsula to another.
>
> The main railroad service, which was called the 'express' though it stopped at every station on the line, ran only three days a week. There were branch lines . . . but connections were bad and usually long waits (which always seemed to occur in the middle of the night) were involved. The majority of outports could only be reached by sea. Mail steamers plied the coast, calling . . . at the more important ports. They were very irregular and no attempt was made to run on schedule. A steamer announced to arrive in the afternoon might not turn up until the next morning, so that one dared not go to bed but loitered about waiting for the hoot which announced the steamer's arrival. It always seemed my fate to board the steamer in the middle of the night . . . to get to many places I had to charter an open motor-boat. I am a wretched sailor so, as can be imagined, I did not enjoy these sea voyages. Altogether much time was wasted in travel and it was difficult to decide whether to take advantage of a passing steamer before I had fully explored a settlement or to risk being stranded empty-handed for a week or more.[15]

Her secret dream, that Newfoundland might prove as fruitful as the Appalachians, was doomed to disappointment. Over and over, she was told that she had come too late and that songs that had existed had been forgotten.

Chapter 14

Her first ten days' exploring brought forth practically nothing and she was deeply depressed. But luck changed when she ventured further afield, to Bonavista Bay, where she fell in with a community of people of Irish descent who were ready to sing. As she had feared, she found it difficult to capture the tunes on paper, especially as the singers were inclined to introduce variants into every verse and sometimes took a long time before they produced any determinate tune at all:

> They were very puzzled to know why I wanted the songs. Was I on the stage or the agent of a record company? And even when I had disposed of these ideas they were convinced that I was going to make a lot of money out of the songs. 'If I could do that I should never have to do another day's fishing,' one man said to me, after I had noted his song and sung it back to him. Yet they never grudged me my supposed reward or expected to share in it.

At Stock Cove I was accepted almost as one of the family. They thought I was the nicest person that had ever been amongst them. 'Wherever she goes there is singing and dancing,' they said. They were

EFDSS, Peter Kennedy Collection, Maud Karpeles Materials

very sad when I said good-bye for they were expecting me to marry and settle down among them. 'Are you a young girl or a married woman?' was usually the first question I was asked. Everyone expressed surprise that a stranger should be so much like themselves. As one singer said: 'She's like someone you have known very well who has gone away for a time and then come back.' This recognition lay, of course, in our common interest in the songs.[16]

She found the scenery as beautiful as any she had seen in the Appalachians, with island-locked bays like large lakes and carpets of blueberries now in their vivid autumn foliage. She went north to Fortune Harbour. This lovely inlet, framed in steep wooded cliffs, failed to live up to its name as far as collecting was concerned, for here Maud came up against the same sort of opposition that had dogged her and Cecil in the USA – namely missionaries. Some Holy Fathers arrived at the same moment as she did and the population were called on to spend most of the daylight hours in church and had little time for folk songs. She contrived, all the same, to gather a few tunes that had not been noted by the couple from Vassar a few weeks before.

EFDS on tour in Canada, 1929
EFDSS Photograph Collection (Canadian Pacific Railway Co.)

She remained but a short time, going on to Harbour Grace, Conception Bay. There she found herself back in civilization, with things she had recently been missing – electric light, two mails a day, taxis, and, above all, the first bath she had had since leaving St John's. As often happened, 'creature comforts were not combined with songs',[17] though she did get a few. Still in Conception Bay, she crossed over to North River, the most beautiful of the inlets, and was 'lucky enough to run into a bevy of good singers, mostly related',[18] from whom she took down some really first-rate tunes.

Back at St John's, she was enthusiastically welcomed by the Emersons. She went through her manuscripts with them and was delighted to find that the quality of tunes was better than she had thought at the time of noting them. Fred Emerson made hasty piano accompaniments for the best ones and, at the invitation of Dr Paton, Maud gave an illustrated talk at the Memorial College.

It was the end of October when she started back to Boston, on what she described as a wearisome journey: 'I forget how long the train took, but the line circled pretty well two-thirds of the island to reach Port aux Basques in the extreme south-east, where one transferred to a ferry steamer to North Sydney on Cape Breton Island. But my adventures were not ended, for on arrival at Port aux Basques we found that the steamer that should have taken us to the mainland of Canada had stuck on a sandbank on the day we were due to sail, and we had to wait three days for the arrival of the supply ship.'[19]

This delay must have caused Maud acute anxiety, as she had only just allowed herself time to be on the spot to join Douglas Kennedy and a picked band of the best dancers from England for a four-week tour of North America. This was another scheme to raise money for the building now growing in London. The National Education Committee of Canada sponsored the tour and the Canadian Pacific Railway laid on a coach in which everybody could live. Before setting out across Canada, performances were given in the USA at Carnegie Hall, New York, the Boston Symphony Hall, the Eastman School of Music in Rochester, and in Cleveland. Then, in the beauty of the Canadian autumn, they set out to give performances in Yorkton, Regina, Vancouver, Calgary, Winnipeg, and Montreal, sleeping and mostly eating in their coach. 'We were a merry party', Maud wrote. They were accompanied by Clive Carey and Henry Nevinson, 'who greatly enlivened the proceedings by playing the Hobby Horse when the Morris

EFDS on tour in Canada, 1929
EFDSS Photograph Collection (Canadian Pacific Railway Co.)

Chapter 14

Dances were being performed.'[20]

Somewhat less than a year after Maud had laid the foundation stone, on the afternoon of Whit Sunday, 7 June 1930, she attended the opening of Cecil Sharp House. This was a grander ceremony than the first one, given that the building was now complete, furnished throughout under Helen's eye, and with a minstrels' gallery in the great hall ready to receive the first

George Bernard Shaw and Maud Karpeles at the opening of Cecil Sharp House, 1930. EFDSS *Photograph Collection*

performers. From here, the English Singers delivered a motet by Byrd and arrangements of folk songs. H. A. L. Fisher declared the house open and dedicated it for all time to English folk music and dance. Messages were read from the Prince of Wales and Princess Mary, both of whom had had music lessons from Cecil Sharp at Marlborough House in the days before he and Maud had met. Rooms were dedicated with the names of benefactors – Trefusis, Storrow, Carnegie. The speakers were Vaughan Williams and Harley Granville-Barker. Granville-Barker declared: 'In so far as a building can be like a human being this building is like Cecil Sharp himself. It is as his taste was – classical without being severe and pervaded by an extraordinary gaiety'.[21] 'For Miss Karpeles', the EFDS journal noted, 'and the faithful Chelsea pioneers the place must have been thronged with ghosts; kindly approving ghosts; one with a white hat and a note book, another with a green willow; many more, light-footed and tuneful, galleying and waving handkerchiefs in the Elysian Morris.'[22]

But for many of the people present – Maud not the least – a shadow was cast by the absence from the celebrations of Holly – Winifred Shuldham-Shaw – who was too ill to be present. For the previous six years she had worked as hard as anyone for that day's achievement. During that time, her home had been the scene of innumerable parties, large and small, for discussion, relaxation, and impromptu music-making. She died two months later and Maud was to feel her loss acutely.

Chapter 15

On 12 November 1930, Maud turned forty-five. Her hair was black, her dark eyes were sharp and bright, she was still slim and dressed 'pleasantly', wearing clothes of good, expensive quality. She spent money on hats, which were a distinctive feature of her wardrobe, and on pleated skirts, which she told the astonished assistants in Peter Robinson's she required for striding over the moors. She was by now clearly set for spinsterhood. The loss of Cecil Sharp was to make itself felt for the rest of her life, but the pangs were somewhat lessened by the six years that had passed and soothed by the knowledge that she had spent them working to further his ambitions. This work had culminated in the opening of Cecil Sharp House, the centre he had dreamt of for the movement. When the ceremony was over, Maud must have felt a certain flatness, almost a fresh bereavement.

All her life, ever since she had fallen in love with Frank, the bathing-machine attendant at Lowestoft, she had found it necessary to have a focus for her adoration. This could be anybody, alive or dead, distant or available, fact or fiction. A friend declared that, after Cecil Sharp, the real love of her life was Mr Rochester. She had a deep devotion to Vaughan Williams, but there she was one of an army, for he fatally attracted nearly every female who came in contact with him. In the early 1930s the object of her passion was Henry Nevinson, the excellent Hobby Horse on that merry railway excursion across Canada in the autumn of 1929.

Nevinson had known Cecil Sharp slightly, through Cecil's sister Evelyn, a notable suffragette, whose activities he had supported before the 1914–18 war. He had only become an intimate friend of Cecil, and consequently of Maud, after they had come back from the Appalachians. The account of their adventures across the Atlantic had drawn him closer into the Sharp circle. Watching good morris teams and the newly imported 'Running Set', he had become fascinated by dancing. 'To me,' he wrote, 'there is something intensely moving in a performance executed to absolute perfection, whether by orchestra, dancers, or a battalion of the Coldstream Guards on parade. I had always longed to move in time to music, but as the Evangelicals of my boyhood regarded dancing as one of the numerous avenues to hell-fire, I had been given no opportunity ... Now I perceived a chance, though it was not till close upon seventy that I was able fully to enjoy it, and the time left me was then inevitably brief.'[1]

Maud described him thus in her autobiography:

A great writer, poet, essayist, journalist and war correspondent, besides being a classical scholar, an eloquent orator and passionate social reformer; above all he was a good friend and comrade, not only to a few choice spirits but to all sorts and conditions of men. The catholicity of his sympathies made him sensitive to any injustice and quick to act in the cause of the wronged and the oppressed. No tale of distress or suffering left him unmoved; but besides his compassion for the sorrows of his fellows he had the almost rarer gift of being able to participate in their joy and happiness; and it was with this side of his character that we folk dancers became the more familiar ... he started at the age of seventy to learn to dance and he was a familiar figure at parties, classes and vacation schools. 'I have one foot in the grave, but so long as I am alive I shall dance with the other' was a favourite remark.[2]

Evelyn Sharp, Henry Nevinson, Douglas Kennedy, and Maud Karpeles
EFDSS Photograph Collection (G. F. Green, 48 Marchmont St, London WC1)

Henry Nevinson was full of contradictions. He had been brought up in a strict Evangelical atmosphere but ended up enjoying all the frivolities of life, dancing and flirtation in particular. He started with a passion for anything to do with soldiering, but his experiences on a number of fronts as a war correspondent had bred in him a hatred of war. This, however, made no difference to his passion for military history and for the panoply of bands and uniforms. His anti-slavery work in Angola had impaired his health but seems in no way to have abated his energy in good causes or in the enjoyment of parties. He was an agnostic, an anti-Marxist, a member of the Labour Party, and a campaigner for women's rights.

With all this, he had an extremely attractive personality and was a handsome man, even into his eighties, described by a friend of Maud's as 'absolutely delectable – and such fun!' He was deeply attached to Maud, as she was to him, and his second marriage, in 1933, to Evelyn Sharp, must have caused her more than a passing pang. But though Maud longed for marriage in theory, she would have been unlikely to have enjoyed it long in practice. She avoided domesticity and was by now becoming adept at distributing tiresome household duties among a number of accommodating friends and relatives.

During the latter part of the 1920s, while the work of collecting money and building Sharp's memorial was going on, Maud had already embarked

EFDS dancers at the Anglo-Basque festival, Bayonne, 1927
EFDSS Photograph Collection

EFDS dancers at Bayonne, 1927
EFDSS Photograph Collection (Keystone View)

on something that was to become more and more important to her future career. She had started to take an interest in the dancing of other nations. This was a part of folk culture that might have appealed less to Cecil Sharp than it did to her. His pursuit of songs in the USA had been exclusively of those that had originated in the British Isles. It is clear that he, like Vaughan Williams (who was inclined to dismiss foreign carols as 'nasty'), had little interest to spare for the music of other countries. Both were too busy rescuing their own.

After the first Albert Hall festival, it had become the custom for the EFDS to invite a group of dancers from abroad. The EFDS dancing team also began to enjoy an occasional foray to give demonstrations in foreign countries. Maud made a visit to the Anglo-Basque festival at Bayonne in the spring of 1927 with the demonstration team, accompanied by about fifty camp followers. The spectacular quality of the Basque dancing made a great impression on them, but she was sorry when English morris dancers tried to emulate them by introducing the showmanship of the Basques into their own, more reserved style.

'It was at Bayonne', she wrote, 'that I first met Dr František Pospíšil, the eminent Czech expert on the Sword Dance, who had the greatest admiration for Cecil Sharp's work. When he met our English dancers processing through

Admiring a Basque hobby horse, Bayonne, 1927. Dr František Pospišil is on the extreme right of the photograph.
EFDSS, Peter Kennedy Collection, Maud Karpeles Materials

Chapter 15

the streets he became greatly excited and started to film them, with shouts of "Vive l'Angleterre!"'[3]

The following year the EFDS was invited to take part in an International Congress of Popular Arts in Prague. With Douglas Kennedy absent in America, it fell to Maud to make most of the preliminary arrangements – quite a task, since the British delegation, the largest national group, consisted of over fifty people. They took a repertoire of Welsh songs and songs from the Hebrides collected by Marjory Kennedy-Fraser, as well as a group of morris dancers and sword dancers. Douglas arrived in time to read a paper about the dances and Maud delivered one about the country dance. She was thrilled to meet Béla Bartók, but grievously distressed that Leoš Janáček, who had been expected, died just before the Congress took place.

There were some heated discussions, she wrote:

> On one occasion, a German delegate by way of illustrating his paper gave recorded examples of typical folk songs of various countries, and on coming to England the sound of 'Tipperary' fell on our ears. The fifty-strong British delegation rose as one man and protested loudly, much to the astonishment and chagrin of the lecturer. At the final session, the setting up of an International Commission caused some difficulty and embarrassment owing to the insistent demand of two female delegates (one from America and a Rumanian) that a proportion of the Commission should consist of women. The male members of the Congress, who were in the majority, were evidently too chivalrous to voice their disapproval of the motion, and a wordy argument as to how it could be implemented broke out. On the spur of the moment, I got up and proclaimed in no uncertain terms that our business was to select those who were best qualified to further the study and practice of folk arts irrespective of sex or any other consideration.[4]

She sat down, trembling at her own temerity, to loud applause. When a British National Committee on Folk Arts was founded, Maud was appointed Honorary Secretary. She never thought much of its achievements, but it helped pave the way for international developments on the folk music scene.

Maud had been so pleasantly surprised at the quality of the songs she had brought from Newfoundland, on which she had been working with Vaughan Williams, that she decided a second visit was justified. She just had time, between the opening of Cecil Sharp House and her return to Amherst for

Chapter 15

another vacation school, to fit in seven weeks there. She sailed direct to St John's with the Furness Withy line. She wrote only a brief account of this second visit in her autobiography:

> I spent my time visiting outports along the south coast travelling mostly by boat of one kind or another. I found the people even more ready to

EFDSS, Peter Kennedy Collection, Maud Karpeles Materials

sing to me than those on the east coast. Indeed, it was often an embarrassment, for many of the songs I listened to were not folk songs and it caused great disappointment when I did not write them down ... On one occasion when a kind man had come to the end of his long

EFDSS, Peter Kennedy Collection, Maud Karpeles Materials

repertory of modern songs which I had not noted, he rather wearily ended up by saying: 'Well, all I can think is that some other young lady must have been here before you and got all the songs printed off.'

It would be impossible to calculate the number of miles I tramped to visit people who had reputations as singers. A great number of these visits had to be made after dark when the day's work was over. On one occasion I was warned by my host not to walk along a certain lonely road for fear of meeting ghosts and fairies who might spirit me away. The prospect did not alarm me and my only fear was the ubiquitous presence of the dogs that constantly prowled around.

More often than not these long tramps ended in disappointments. Nevertheless, I eventually managed to get quite a number of good folk songs . . . During the time I was there I noted about 90 songs (150 tunes including variants).[5]

Maud does not say on which of her two visits she collected the song with which her name will always be especially associated, the beautiful 'She's Like the Swallow'. On her return from Amherst, she again handed over her gleanings to Vaughan Williams, who made another fifteen pianoforte accompaniments.

Freed of much time-consuming work now that Cecil Sharp House was open and functioning, Maud settled down for a couple of years of editing the songs brought back from the Appalachians in 1917 and 1918. The 1916 tunes, together with thirty-nine previously collected by Olive Campbell, had already been published in New York by Putnam's and were to be republished in England in 1932 by Oxford University Press. For the new book, she wrote: 'I obtained help and advice from several friends, including Vaughan Williams and Anne Gilchrist, in what was to me an arduous task. Above all, I owe much to Fox Strangways for the assistance he gave me in the modal classification of the tunes.'[6]

While working on this with 'Foxy', Maud discussed what had become her next objective in the work to keep Cecil Sharp's name in the public eye. The time had come for his biography to be written. She doubted her own literary ability and did not feel, anyway, that she should be the one to write it. Chatting one evening with Foxy and reminiscing about Cecil, she suddenly asked him if he would consider being the author. 'Without hesitation he replied: "There is nothing in the world I would rather do." That settled the matter.'[7] It was a settlement that Maud came to regret.

Fox Strangways had been a schoolmaster at Wellington School, but had devoted most of his life to his work as a musicologist and music critic on *The Times* and the *Observer*. He was the founder and editor of the journal *Music & Letters*. He had met Sharp when the latter had just returned from Australia, hence he had known him longer than had Maud. Over the years, the two men had spent long hours discussing music and, as has been seen, Foxy was a frequent attendee at vacation schools, writing accounts for the press. 'Argument', wrote Maud, 'was the breath of life to Foxy and he indulged in this not from contentiousness, but because he wanted to get to the truth of a subject and to examine it in all its aspects. I was privileged to be present at the long drawn-out arguments he had with Cecil. Their controversies covered every subject under the sun and it would be hard to say whether they ended in agreement or disagreement.'[8]

It is evident that a good deal of disagreement was now to go on between Maud and Foxy, and from the very first she was unhappy about the progress of the book. *Cecil Sharp* came out three years later, published by Oxford University Press and ascribed to A. H. Fox Strangways 'in collaboration with Maud Karpeles'. Concerning what led up to this attribution, she wrote, with moderate tact:

> I had intended to restrict my collaboration to the assembling and sorting of documentary material and to the contribution of my own memories of Cecil. However, as time passed it became evident that the book was not progressing, presumably because of Foxy's many other commitments. I therefore suggested and Foxy gladly agreed that I should produce a rough written account of Cecil's life which might serve as a basis for the final biography. I had intended that my contribution, except for two chapters on collecting in the Appalachian Mountains, would serve merely as raw material from which Foxy would extract what he required, but instead of telling his own story he was for the most part content to patch and modify my crude statements. The result was naturally not entirely satisfactory.[9]

In this paragraph Maud clearly smoothes over what must have been a period of extreme exasperation. When she wanted something done, she wanted it done at once, and three years seemed altogether too long to keep the public waiting for Cecil's life. The book that came out ought, more properly, to have been ascribed to Maud Karpeles, 'with additions by A. H.

Fox Strangways'. She was never happy with it, but had to wait for twenty-five years, till Foxy's death, to revise it for a second edition. Eventually, in 1967, she rewrote it again, adding new material. In this final incarnation a lot of spontaneity has disappeared from the book and the 1967 version, if more stuffed with accurate facts, is distinctly less alive and readable than the first one, put out in stress and conflict.

In 1931 the EFDS made a proposal of marriage to the Folk-Song Society (founded in 1898), suggesting that it was obvious the two societies should become one, with the family home at Cecil Sharp House. Vaughan Williams chaired a meeting of the Folk-Song Society and found that the general opinion among the members was that this would be a desirable move. A few dissenters feared that the scientific study of song might be lost sight of, swamped by the larger and more boisterous dance faction. Maud rose to her feet and insisted that a proper understanding of folk music depended on a mixture of practice and scholarship. The motion was carried and the two societies celebrated their nuptials on 1 March 1932 as the English Folk Dance and Song Society (EFDSS). The marriage proved a success and the benefit was an increased interest in the songs.

Even before this, Cecil Sharp House had seen folk song concerts, recitals by Plunkett Greene, Steuart Wilson, Clive Carey, Gwen Ffrangcon-Davies, and Campbell McInnes. The last-named had been an early collaborator with Cecil Sharp but had been living in Canada during the time Maud had been involved with the movement. She heard him for the first time on his visit to England in 1931, and wrote:

> His singing of folk songs stirred me perhaps more than that of any other professional sing[er] I have heard. I shall never forget his singing of the last lines of 'Dives and Lazarus', in which the serpent addresses Dives with the words:
>
>> Rise up, rise up, brother Diverus,
>> And come along with me;
>> There is a place prepared in hell
>> For to sit upon a serpent's knee.[10]

Another greatly admired singer was the Danish-Icelandic soprano Engel Lund, whose recital of Folk Songs from Many Lands, given with the pianist Ferdinand Rauter, her musical partner for many years, gave Maud great joy. They were to become firm friends.

With the amalgamation of the two societies Maud was able to organize a series of evenings in the new mecca of folk music, where members would meet each other, talk and sing songs, mostly unaccompanied, but with a pianist always at hand in case of need. These were social evenings, wrote Maud, with light refreshments, and with a little persuasion even 'the most bashful were induced to sing and we got to know many hitherto unfamiliar songs. These meetings might be regarded as the precursor of the present-day "Folk Clubs", but the material with which we entertained ourselves was for the most part very different, for it would not have occurred to us to sing anything but authentic traditional folk songs.'[11]

EFDSS tour of the Netherlands, 1932
EFDSS Photograph Collection

Chapter 15

The following year, 'an ambitious week-end course was held at Cecil Sharp House which seemed to cover every aspect of folk music . . . My contribution was "Rhythm in the Dance", in which I endeavoured to show by precept and example the interdependence of music and dance and the way in which rhythm gives unity and purpose to what in its absence would be a series of unco-ordinated sounds and movements.'[12]

In 1933, Maud's duty for the Easter vacation was to direct at Minehead. When she heard she was to take charge of that particular school she remembered the days, between her meeting with Sharp and the beginning of the 1914–18 war, when she and Helen had gone to that parish at the invitation of its vicar to teach dancing in the village hall. The Rev. Francis Etherington had been a collecting companion of Sharp's in the very early days. He was no longer incumbent at Minehead, but had moved to the parish of Withypool, not far away. Sharp had had a high opinion of his knowledge and his attitude to folk music, so Maud at once booked him to come over and give a talk to her students. 'I had known Frank Etherington only slightly during Cecil's life time,' she wrote, 'but after the Vacation School was over I spent a few days at Withypool and shortly afterwards he visited me in London. From these meetings there sprang up a close friendship between us which brought me much happiness. Frank was a most lovable man, with broad human sympathies and our admiration and affection for Cecil Sharp was a strong bond between us.'[13]

Etherington told Maud that he was contemplating writing a life of Father Charles Marson, whom Cecil had first known in Australia, who had married him to Constance, and with whom, when Marson became Perpetual Curate of Hambridge, he had been on his first expeditions to collect songs. Maud had not met Marson, but had heard many stories about him during her days with Cecil. She suggested she might possibly be of some assistance to Etherington. 'My help was', she wrote, '. . . more or less restricted to acting as typist, assembling the data and making suggestions as to the general construction of the book, assembling data and typing. This collaboration, such as it was, gave me many opportunities over the ensuing years of enjoying Frank's company. He often came up to London and I visited Withypool.'[14] She got to know his son, Gordon, who also became a priest, and his daughter, one of whose missions in life was to improve the lot of the ponies on Dartmoor.

This must have been the time when Maud finally returned to her pre-Cecil Sharp interest in religion. Church-going and sermon-tasting had been one of the chief diversions of her late schooldays and her twenties, but over the folk collecting years this had been allowed to lapse, pushed out, along with politics, by a more consuming passion. Now, however, her life began once more to be tied to church-visiting and gradually she began to bring discussions of her possible baptism into the Christian faith into her long talks with Etherington. It was another six years before she actually took the final step to the font. The collaboration with Etherington gave Maud far more pleasure than she had ever found in her literary activities with Fox Strangways, but the biography of Father Marson was destined never to be published.

From the moment that it became one society, the EFDSS began to plan a great international festival to be held in London. Several years' work, a large proportion of it by Maud, went into the preparations. An Executive Committee was set up under Lady Ampthill, with Maud as Honorary Secretary, and the date was set for the summer of 1935. The Queen agreed to stand as Patron, Lord Halifax as President, with Ramsay MacDonald and Lord Rennel of Rodd as Vice Presidents. The participants were restricted to groups from Europe, but even with this limitation the festival was set to be the most ambitious ever attempted. Maud visited a smaller one of the kind in Vienna the year before, hoping to do some advance publicity, as well as to pick up useful tips. 'At one of the performances', she related, 'I had the great pleasure of sitting next to Princess Ileana of Rumania who was then married to the Archduke of Austria . . . I hoped that she might be able to attend our Festival the next year . . . I committed a *faux pas* when in the course of conversation I commented on her excellent English. "Well, after all, I am the great-granddaughter of Queen Victoria!" was her amused response.'[15]

More than five hundred dancers eventually arrived, representing seventeen countries, and three hundred British dancers from the EFDSS, the Scottish Country Dance Society, and a number of regional groups also took part. On the first day, Lord Rennel greeted the heads of delegations at Cecil Sharp House, speaking in a number of languages. The next afternoon saw the groups of dancers, in national costume, each preceded by their country's flag, walking in procession into Hyde Park, in mercifully fine weather, to dance in the Cockpit by the Serpentine. Maud watched the 'magnificent and impressive sight',[16] finding it difficult to believe that she had been largely responsible for summoning these multitudes. She realized, with something like panic, that though she might have started it, it was very certain that she could not stop it, even if she had wanted to!

The Archbishop of Canterbury, Cosmo Gordon Lang, with a Swedish dancer
EFDSS Photograph Collection (Marion Crowdy)

All five public performances had been sold out weeks in advance, three in the Albert Hall, one in the Open Air Theatre in Regent's Park, and one in the gardens of Lambeth Palace. The last of these was the occasion that chiefly stuck in Maud's memory. The Archbishop of Canterbury had given permission for the use of his four lawns, where dances went on simultaneously, and Maud was confident that he did not grudge the flowers that the dancers picked in order to present posies to each other. She was much affected at the sight of German and French groups embracing and exchanging these bouquets, all memory of the last conflict forgotten and apparently unconscious of any shadow of coming events. This was the occasion when Maud nearly found herself excluded, having omitted to provide herself with a ticket. 'I explained to the gate-keeper that I was the Honorary Secretary and was responsible for the organization of the Festival. "Oh we've heard that one before," was his response and he steadfastly barred my way. I was in some perplexity as to what my next step should be and I had wild thoughts of ringing up the Archbishop, when fortunately a member of the audience turned up with a spare ticket.'[17]

It was a busy week for Maud and, indeed, for all the dancers. 'They were taken by steamer from Westminster Pier to Greenwich, where they gave an informal display in Greenwich Park; and on another occasion an excursion

United by tea: dancers at the International Folk Dance Festival, 1935
EFDSS, Peter Kennedy Collection, Maud Karpeles Materials

was made to Hampton Court. Also when not otherwise engaged they were taken by their guides on sight-seeing tours of London.'[18] The whole of the capital was full of colourful parties in national dress: 'covies of Croats and bevies of Bulgars in unexpected quarters'.[19]

Maud lamented, later, that no film was made and there was as yet no public television. She regretted this particularly on account of what she thought the most memorable performance, that of the Romanian *Călușari*, 'who showed us a dance connected with an ancient Whitsuntide ritual ceremony in which the healing of sick persons played an important part. The vast audiences were thrilled and transported by the sense of mystery and magic which the dance evoked.'[20] But Maud was, nevertheless, proud of the British contribution and felt that her country had held its own among the glories presented by the dancers from other lands.

She was able to congratulate herself that no catastrophes due to bad management had marred the occasion, though there had been some narrow shaves:

> The first was when it was discovered that the luggage of the Russians with their dance paraphernalia was missing. Monsieur Maisky, the Russian Ambassador, was distraught and was only to some extent pacified when

Boat trip to Greenwich, International Folk Dance Festival, 1935
EFDSS Photograph Collection (London News Agency)

The Romanian Călușari, International Folk Dance Festival, 1935 (note the garlic on the pole). EFDSS Photograph Collection (The Times)

Chapter 15

he heard that the Germans had also arrived without their luggage. However, the luggage of both the Russians and the Germans eventually turned up, so all was well. Subsequently M. Maisky proved to be one of the most enthusiastic members of the audience. The Russians stayed over a few days after the Festival and M. Maisky gave a garden party for them in the Embassy grounds to which the Festival organizers were invited. It was not long before dancing broke out, and I had the honour of acting as partner to His Excellency and piloting him through the mazes of 'Gathering Peascods'.[21]

The second alarm came towards the end of the first rehearsal, 'when the leader of the *Căluşari* exclaimed: "But where is the garlic? We cannot dance without it." They needed a garlic with its medicinal properties to tie on top of the pole which accompanied them. A messenger was sent post-haste to Soho and he returned with the garlic before the rehearsal had finished.'[22] There were other problems. Lithuania was not on terms with Germany or Poland and would not be seen to walk beside them. This question was simply settled by Maud with a decision to put all the countries into alphabetical order.

The more scholarly side of the festival took place in Cecil Sharp House, where speakers from many lands paid tribute to Sharp, to Maud's gratification. At the final session a small body called the International Folk Dance Council was inaugurated, and once again it was Maud who was appointed Honorary Secretary.

The festival broke up after a tremendous party at the Royal Horticultural Hall. Nobody had known in advance how dreadful the acoustics were, with the result that the dancers could hardly hear Imogen Holst's band. Nevertheless, almost every female member of the English folk dance teams ended the week having been proposed to at least three times. Arthur Batchelor wrote in the *EFDSS News* that everybody had to thank 'the extraordinary combination of business ability, untiring zeal and organizing genius which is Maud Karpeles. To her we owe the fact that the continent can now discard its hitherto rooted idea that Britain has one dance, the Scotch Reel, performed by flappers in kilts over swords.'[23]

Chapter 16

When the clearing up after this immensely successful festival had been completed, Maud felt, for once, that she owed herself a holiday. Typically, she chose to take the 'busman's' kind. For some years she had corresponded with the Yankovitch sisters, scholars and dancers from Yugoslavia, and had been particularly disappointed that that nation had not been able to raise the money to send a team to England. The sisters now implored her to come out and see something of their folk culture for herself. She decided to make the journey in the spring of 1936. Since Newfoundland, Maud had begun to dislike travelling on her own and she chose as companion her nephew John Kennedy, the elder of Douglas's and Helen's two sons, who was now twenty. She retained vivid memories of this trip and described it at length in her memoirs, beginning:

> That year the dates of the Orthodox and Catholic Festivals of Easter coincided. We arrived at Belgrade in the evening of Good Friday. On alighting from the train we were nearly swept off our feet, both literally and figuratively, for the platform was one seething mass of happy and excited men, women and children, many in peasant costume, and all talking, laughing, shouting and running hither and thither. We said to each other: 'We have evidently arrived in the East,' and it was only later that we realized this was not a normal scene, but was due to the approaching Easter holidays.[1]

The Professors Yankovitch met Maud and John at their hotel and gave advice about mapping out an itinerary.

> We could only spare Good Friday in Belgrade, but ... made good use of our time, and were delighted with what we saw, particularly with the glorious view from the old fortress in the National Park overlooking the waters of the Danube and the Sava.

> With great reluctance we left the next day and started on an eight-hour journey southwards to Skoplje [Skopje] in Macedonia, which until recently had been under Turkish rule . . .
>
> That evening we went to the Midnight Mass. It was an impressive service, particularly when as it approached midnight the priest followed by his acolytes bearing lighted candles paraded round the church with the Eucharist. Then at the stroke of midnight a great cry went up: 'Christ is risen.' Whereupon members of the great crowd that had assembled in the church yard endeavoured to light the candles they were carrying from those of the Church dignitaries and to throw them while still alight into the nearby river. We snatched some sleep and were awakened early by the mingled sounds of music which seemed to issue from every house and street – bands, gipsy orchestras, singing, strange-sounding reed-pipes, and drums. This music prepared us for the lively scenes which confronted us as we ate our breakfast outdoors in front of our hotel, and afterwards as we wandered round the town. Skoplje is surely the centre of Europe, where East and West meet, and where civilizations, old and new, form a rich and colourful mosaic. In the streets, men and women in gaily coloured peasant dresses, veiled Mohammedan women, and gipsy women in Turkish trousers mingle with the wearers of smart up-to-date costumes and complexions.
>
> [From] Skoplje we made two expeditions to the mountain villages … to see and join in the dancing. We were accompanied by a kind professor and his wife, who spoke French and interpreted for us; and the Governor's car was placed at our disposal.[2]

She went on to describe in detail the dances that they watched, in particular one in many versions called the *Kola*, a social dance corresponding to English country dancing:

> It would be impossible to exaggerate the beauty of the setting: the kaleidoscope of colour – for all wore festival dress – the grandeur of the mountain country, and often a mediaeval village with its Byzantine church in the background; nor is it possible to convey the cumulative, almost hypnotic, effect produced by the rhythmic chain of dancers as it progresses on its interminably winding course to the accompaniment of pipes and drums . . . We visited some half a dozen villages and everywhere it seemed like entering a happy family party.[3]

From Skopje they took the train to Mirovča (Miravci) to see a performance of a dance called the *Russalija*, usually enacted at Christmas, but put on especially for their benefit. The local school inspector met them with a couple of well-behaved ponies 'with really sensible saddles which had a hump at each end to catch hold of',[4] on which they rode to the village.

> The dance was in progress when we arrived, and we could hear the throb of the drum and the piercing notes of the reed-pipe from afar. The dancers, about twenty in number – all men – form a big ring and dance round, one behind the other, in a counter-clockwise direction. Each dancer carries a wooden sword and with it he performs strange passes, cuts and thrusts in the air, whilst he moves forward with a slow elaborate motion accompanied by extraordinary gestures of body and limbs, interspersed with wild leaps and crouching movements. The effect is that of stalking, and warding off, some unseen object. Like the Rumanian *Căluşari*, the dance is said to have healing effects.[5]

The village had been rebuilt after an earthquake five years before. Here they had half a night's sleep but had to get up at 3.30 a.m. to catch a train to the Greek border, an experience Maud found rewarding for the beauty of the starlit sky, though she was by nature far from being an early riser.

For some days in Greece she and John behaved like ordinary tourists. At the end of April they set sail from Piraeus in a comfortable Yugoslav boat, the *Princess Olga*. She had been built in Britain, but the only sign they saw of her origins was a laconic notice reading '11 times round the deck is one mile'. After a beautiful cruise along the Greek and Albanian coasts, they landed at Dubrovnik. Maud fell in love with this 'Pearl of the Adriatic' as the guidebook called it and, though they saw no dancing, they found it delightful to live for a few days as if in the Middle Ages.

Their next port of call was what she described as 'the enchanted island of Korčula', where they were met by a welcome so warm that they felt as if they had lived there for years. The town, with its steep, stepped streets, was as beautiful as any they had seen on the mainland. There they saw a performance of the *Moresco*, reputed ancestor of the morris dance, though they found it bore but little resemblance to the English version. This dance had been specially laid on for them, but it had been spoilt through becoming a tourist attraction and proved a disappointment. They were to have a much more satisfying experience a few days later. The mayor drove them across the rocky, fir-clad island to Blato to see a dance being performed on its proper occasion to a vast crowd in the square outside the church. Maud was enraptured and described it at great length. This was an elaborate sword dance, with interesting resemblances to British and other European ones, and was preceded by a lengthy ceremonial. Permission was first asked of the mayor, with much flag-waving, and a deputation was sent into the church to ask for a blessing before the dancing started. It was the high spot of Maud's tour.

The next day they left Korčula and started reluctantly homeward by way of Split and Venice. The experiment of travelling with her nephew had been a success and Maud looked forward to having him as a companion on many further adventures. One of these did come to pass. The next year, they made a shorter but hardly less memorable trip to the Aran Islands, west of Galway, where they stayed in the house that belonged to Robert Flaherty, director of the famous *Man of Aran* film. The 'man' himself had been Pat Mullen, whom Maud found a delightful person and a marvellous storyteller. She was to entertain him at a later date in London. The islands charmed John and he started to draw plans for a cottage he would build on Inishmore, where Maud believed she would like to end her days. This was a short holiday as Maud had an engagement to lecture in Paris at the *Archive internationale de la danse* exhibition of national costumes. Here she met, for the first time, Claudie Marcel-Dubois and Maguy Andral, who were to become important friends.

But these excursions in the company of John were among the few happy things in the later part of the 1930s. In spite of the friendliness of the dancers at Lambeth, everybody was becoming increasingly aware of international tensions and the growing plight of the Jews in Germany – especially Maud, whose Jewish ancestry caused her much tribulation. Before she began actively to concern herself with this, however, she had to deal firmly with a matter of more personal anxiety. For some time now, she had been in dispute with the EFDSS over the vexed question of copyright in Cecil Sharp's collection of folk dances. His will had appointed her literary executrix and agent for his estate, and consequently it was she who controlled the dances and tunes he had transcribed. His publishers, Novello & Co., paid royalties to the estate. Maud wrote:

> The [EFDSS] took the view that the Society's work was hampered by not having control over the dances, although there had not been a single occasion on which they had been refused permission by me or by Novello to do what they wished with them. They also felt it was unjust

that the Society should have no share in the financial proceeds. This without regard to the fact that Cecil Sharp had done his collecting work without financial assistance from the Society or from any other body . . . In the circumstances it seemed only right that he should be entitled to make provision for his family after his death.[6]

Maud herself had never received any payment for her considerable part in Sharp's work, whereas Novello's made a good profit on the sale of sheet music.

The EFDSS was most indignant when Novello's joined the Performing Right Society 'without consulting them',[7] a stand Maud found ironical when, later, the EFDSS itself became a member. The Executive Committee now decided to take counsel's opinion. This, to their mortification, came down in favour of Maud's position. Maud explained this in her memoirs:

> there is much confusion of thought . . . as regards copyright in folk music. It is rightly argued that folk music is part of our common national heritage and belongs to the whole English people, but it is often not understood that the 'right' is not in the original material as obtained from the traditional performer, but in the 'copy', i.e. the collector's transcription, and that it is only just that he, the collector, should receive some return for the time, skill and money he has spent on his work. Anyone is free to collect material that is still practised by traditional performers . . . but the same material may not be transcribed for public use from an existing notation falling within the legal copyright period without the consent of the copyright owner.[8]

At the end of this dispute, Maud felt so embittered at the behaviour of the EFDSS and so far estranged from their ideas that she resigned her seat on the Executive Committee. She remained a member and retained some interest in EFDSS activities, continuing to sit on the Editorial Board of the society's journal. And she always retained a lively interest in the library, remaining on its committee, of which, in later years, she became Chairman.

She was, as usual, very far from idle. She had an ambition to write a history of the country dance and was busy with research into this project, which she never found time to complete, and she was still engaged in helping Frank Etherington with his biography of Charles Marson, another book that never saw the light of day. 'Father' Etherington, as she called him – Maud preferred her clergy to be High and encouraged this form of address – was a fattish, red-faced, jolly type of man, somewhat unlike the majority of the objects of Maud's devotion. He made frequent visits to confer with her in London and gave her an excuse for many excursions to Withypool to stay with his family, occasions she greatly enjoyed.

For years she had been hovering on the brink of joining the Anglican Church. In 1938 she took the final plunge. The occasion that precipitated this was the onset of trouble that culminated in an operation to remove her gall bladder. She told Etherington that she no longer wished to delay taking the final step of baptism in order, as she put it, 'to get my papers in order in case of non-recovery'.[9] His comment was: 'Not an unworthy motive'. Her actual decision was made, she thought, almost subconsciously, as she listened to a performance of the *St Matthew Passion* by the Bach Choir, conducted by Vaughan Williams. The words 'O what is this to us?' seemed to call for action. Etherington arranged for the baptism to be conducted by his son Gordon at the parish church of St Mary the Virgin and All Saints at South Mimms, where he was vicar. Maud was out of action for several months as a result of the operation, which seems also to have put an end to her career as a dancer. She was now fifty-five.

While she recovered from her operation the thoughts that chiefly troubled Maud were about the growing persecution of the Jews in Germany and, now that she was free of committee work for the EFDSS, she determined to use that extra time in doing something of practical help. A refugee organization had been opened at Bloomsbury House in Holborn and she started work there in the children's department. Her somewhat poignant duty was to go to Liverpool Street Station to meet parties of refugee children and help to settle them in suitable homes.

It was during her work in Bloomsbury that Maud made one of the greatest friendships of her life, with Ursula Wood, later to become Ursula Vaughan Williams. Ursula came from an army family but was deeply bored with all things military and had escaped from life on Salisbury Plain to be, for a short time, a student at the Old Vic Drama School. This was just before her marriage to Michael Wood, a serving officer. At a performance at the Old Vic she had been instantly bowled over by the ballet *Job* and had written to Vaughan Williams suggesting that they should collaborate on a musical work. The composer had replied by putting her on to Douglas Kennedy, with the suggestion that they should devise a masque or a folk opera together. But Ursula was not to be put off and, while becoming friends with Douglas and Helen, insisted on being taken out to lunch by the composer of her choice. They became instant friends. At that time she was wondering what useful job she could find to do in the climate of growing unease and Vaughan Williams sent a message to Maud asking her to consider 'my Ursula' as a helper with the refugees. According to Ursula, Maud received her 'with deep distrust', but agreed they had better have lunch together. At half past twelve they set out for the nearest Lyons Corner House, where an excellent three-course meal could be had for 1/6d. At about four in the afternoon they were still at the table, and Maud declared it was not worth going back to the office and that they could consider themselves friends. They had dealt with God and sex and need not bother with anything else.

For some months, while her husband was in Jamaica, Ursula went daily to Bloomsbury House to help vet the people who offered homes to the children. In particular, she remembered rejecting, with Maud's approval, a West Country farmer who said he would take one, 'God willing and the child obedient'. They found the work distressing but felt they were doing something of practical use.

In August 1939, Maud suggested to Ursula a visit to the Three Choirs Festival but then wrote her a letter putting the project off, showing her state of mind on the eve of war:

> There doesn't seem much hope of Hereford, but if the miracle happens I'll make arrangements and write again. It just all seems a bad dream. Most people I meet still cling to the quite unreasonable belief that war will be averted – but none can say how. Well, if it comes we must try and keep our memories of what is good and lovely and try to keep our sense of decency.
>
> I was in Shropshire two days, looked in at S.-on-Avon and got back Friday evening. I went to the refugee office Sat. morning and found it partly evacuated. I shall go on working there as long as I am wanted until something else turns up. I have put my name down at the LCC for evacuation of mothers and 'under 5s'. I evacuated my niece and her small boy yesterday and on my advice they went to Church Stretton.
>
> Don't give up the flat just yet, because if better times come you may be able to find some job that will bring you to London now and again. And now good-night. I want to do nothing but sleep and fortunately manage to do so fairly well. If the miracle happens I shall give myself at least a fortnight's holiday.[10]

Maud found that the actual declaration of war came almost as a relief, and the fateful 3 September saw her escorting a group of pregnant women and infants to country homes that had been offered. She also helped to house refugees from Belgium. 'In addition to my other work at Bloomsbury House', she wrote, 'I formed . . . a Refugee Musicians' Committee, on which many illustrious English musicians served, including Hugh Allen, Harriet Cohen, George Dyson, Myra Hess and Vaughan Williams. The object was to cater for the welfare of refugee musicians, and wherever possible to provide them with employment. This was not easy, for the Home Office was most reluctant to issue work permits to foreign musicians and I had many altercations with the official in charge and also with the Incorporated Society of Musicians, who were very obstructive.'[11] Her great support in this work came from Sir Hugh Allen.

Maud's work for refugees, both children and musicians, was immensely useful, but it failed to satisfy her passion for service. She longed to get her teeth into a job that would actively forward the war effort. Over and over again she made applications to government departments in the hope of landing something she considered constructive, only to be turned down once more on the grounds that her father had been born in Germany. Eventually she secured a place on a factory bench where she sat by the hour fiddling with solder and wire to make portable radio sets for the navy. The venture was a disaster. With no rest for her back, she began to suffer from aches in her spine and shoulders. Almost as bad as the pain was the nervous strain induced by the loud and monotonous accompaniment of *Music While You Work*, which never abated and soon drove her to distraction. She was delighted when an offer came to act as General Secretary for the Christian Council for Refugees and she abandoned her high-minded self-torture and settled, until 1944, into a job infinitely more suited to her talents and background. She had much pleasure in being welcomed to this post by a letter from Bishop Matthew, which said, 'From the first announcement of the vacancy I always felt there should be but one candidate.'[12]

Under the Council's auspices she arranged regular tea-time concerts at the Queen Mary Hall of the YWCA. In those days of blackouts, entertainments had to be confined to daylight hours. The artists, most of whom were refugee musicians, offered their services and included such eminent performers as the Czech Trio with Walter Susskind as pianist, Max Rostal, Jelly d'Arányi, Nina Milkina, Engel Lund and her accompanist Ferdinand Rauter, and the Rosé Quartet. This last group consisted, wrote

Maud, 'of only two members of the original quartet (Arnold Rosé himself and Friedrich Buxbaum) while Walter Price was the 2nd violin and Ernest Tomlinson the viola player. Arnold Rosé's sense of hearing was by then somewhat defective and consequently his intonation was not always perfect, but he made up for it by his unsurpassed sense of rhythm. I hope it will not sound derogatory if I say that his playing was the nearest approach to that of a folk fiddler that I have heard in any professional musician. When he first arrived in England he was in great straits, and among my pleasantest memories is the fact that I was able to do a little to help him and that my friendship meant something to him.'[13]

It was observed that he meant a good deal also to Maud, who wrote to Ursula: 'I have lost my heart to Rosé. He has the old-world courtesy and grand simplicity of a noble gentleman.'[14] She was being pursued, in a somewhat unwelcome manner, by another member of the quartet, the cellist Buxbaum, and was forced to implore her friends to stand by in order that she should not be alone with him.

Arnold Walter, the musicologist who was later to make an important mark on the musical life of Canada, was another refugee. In an autobiographical article he expressed what many foreign musicians were feeling at this moment: 'I have never met nicer people, never acquired dearer friends than in England. Maud Karpeles, Imogen Holst, Douglas Kennedy, and Vaughan Williams helped us, protected us, sustained us.'[15]

Maud was now no longer living in Cecil Sharp's old house. Shortly before the war she had moved to a top flat, 80 Holmefield Court, Belsize Grove, also in Hampstead, which had a glorious view south across London to the Surrey hills, with, as its centrepiece, the dome of St Paul's. During the many air raids, when the all-clear had sounded and the inhabitants of the flats returned upstairs from the ground-floor corridor to which they had retreated, the first thing she would do was to reassure herself that this landmark was still standing. In this flat, early in the war, when food and drink were not yet too scarce, and her devoted maid Florrie had not yet been called up, Maud gave many parties, such as one she described to Ursula Wood in a letter to the Isle of Wight in April 1940: 'The lovely flowers arrived just at the right moment – in time for my party. I beat my record and had 16 people – 14 to supper and the Nevinsons coming in after. It really went with a swing.'[16]

She listed her guests, mostly musicians. At fifty-five, Maud had lost none of her enjoyment of flirtation and she appears to have had four gentlemen engaged in the delightful game, three of them welcome, the pursuing cellist less so. 'Emmy Heirn arrived late and breathless, would not wait to eat anything, but said she *must sing*, which she did most gloriously. Loewe [Ferdinand Rauter] kept whispering confidentially in my ear that he loved me. Buxbaum embraced me rapturously which made dear H.W.N. [Nevinson] look so green that I had to tear myself from B's arms and throw myself upon H.W.N., much to Evelyn's disgust. However I told her she ought to take a lesson from Mrs B, who didn't turn a hair. Then followed a fight between the two men . . . I do wish you had been there altho' it would have meant that you would have robbed me of my three. Still I would have been quite content to have been left with dear Rosé!'

After Florrie's departure, Maud was thrown back on her own very basic cooking, help from obliging friends, or the 1940s version of the take-away. This consisted mostly of a cold roast chicken from the local delicatessen, which she would eat her way through until visitors pointed out that it had gone beyond human consumption and was no longer good even for the stockpot. When eggs were to be had she would essay an omelette, retorting to friends' criticisms, 'But I *like* leather omelettes!' She took many meals at the MF Club, run by May Mukle, the cellist, in a cellar by Oxford Circus. The membership of this cost five shillings a year. It offered an excellent meal for 2/6d. in a dining-room almost always full of congenial musical friends.

As the air raids increased, Ursula was a frequent companion. On visits to London she would stay the night in the Belsize Grove flat. At bedtime they would brush their teeth, put on their dressing-gowns, and collect a basket of comforts, including a book to read and a pillow, and retire to the ground floor as soon as the air-raid siren sounded. Maud plaited her black hair into pigtails and, while waiting for the sirens, would sit on the bed and sing ballads to Ursula in a pretty little voice, with exact intonation. It was during these times that they devised an anthology of the words to folk songs under the title, supplied by Ursula, of *The Crystal Spring*. They were never able to get a publisher to take it, but, years later, Maud used the name for a book of folk songs. If a raid took them downstairs, they would return to the flat at 3 or 4 a.m., check on the safety of St Paul's, and drink china tea in the summer dawn.

One night, when Ursula was staying, Maud decided she ought to go to Helen – the Kennedys lived a few minutes' walk from Belsize Grove and Douglas was out doing his shift as an air-raid warden. The bombing on that occasion was 'absolutely awful' and they decided to take an umbrella because they felt safer, under its flimsy protection, from objects descending from above. They sat listening with Helen to the continuous dropping of bombs, Maud amusedly observing Ursula. Afterwards, she told her that every time a big one exploded she would put on a fresh coat of lipstick.

Maud was not feeling well. Her letters complain of back pain such as had troubled her on the factory bench and, in June 1940, continued internal twinges demanded another operation. Her pencilled letters were headed, Hospital of St John and St Elizabeth, NW8. She described her stay there as 'just a picnic compared with 2 years ago. I had a certain amount of pain and discomfort for the first day or 2, but I've known worse in Nature's ordered sequence. If only one had an easy mind I should enjoy the rest.'[17]

The convalescent period gave her an excuse to visit Frank Etherington on Exmoor. Her previous gall bladder trouble had precipitated her official acceptance into the Christian church and her baptism as a High Anglican. Now, the second operation was to lead to her confirmation. For some time she had been wondering if she should take what seemed the ultimate step and become a Roman Catholic. Always for Maud, the higher the ritual the greater the appeal, so she took instruction from the Jesuit Fathers at Farm Street. The whole idea was abandoned, however, over the question of divorce. Maud, in her fifties, was far from contemplating matrimony for herself; the idea of marriage had always been romantic, but she knew she would never endure the practicalities. She put it to the Fathers that, in theory, she would wish to be able to put away a husband and, possibly, marry another. The church's refusal even to contemplate the idea sent her scurrying back to the Anglican fold.

She was prepared for confirmation at St Paul's, Knightsbridge, giving, in the opinion of her friends, almost as many headaches to the clergy there as she had to the Jesuit Fathers. She took Ursula Wood along to the service and Ursula, though not herself a churchgoer, played her part in the correct manner, including taking Maud to tea at Fuller's tea rooms after the ceremony. After confirmation, and now a regular communicant, she offered her services to the church as a fire-watcher and was enthusiastically welcomed. Two nights a week, she would sally forth to Knightsbridge in her siren suit, coming away, after the all-clear had sounded, in the dawn. One morning, in early summer, she stopped in the street and looked back at the building she had been protecting. The realization struck her that it was absolutely hideous and that nothing would be better for the landscape than its removal by a bomb. After this she gave up her fire-watching, though she still attended services there on a moderately regular basis.

Following the death (from a heart attack) of her first husband, Ursula Wood lived in London at 7½ Thayer Street, the flat she had taken in the first year of the war and had kept on, partly at Maud's suggestion, while living with her husband on the Isle of Wight. Jean Stewart, the viola player, who performed often with the Menges Quartet, lived in the flat below and it was there that they began to hold social gatherings on Wednesday evenings.

During these years, in spite of bombs, anxiety, and sorrow, people in London contrived to find society and entertainment. The pleasure of parties, when enough food and drink could be scraped together, and concerts, which might at any moment be interrupted by the sirens, was, if anything, enhanced. There were the splendid National Gallery concerts every midday, where Myra Hess gathered all the best musicians available. Many of these same musicians would gather at Ursula's Wednesdays: Jean Stewart of course, Engel Lund and Ferdinand Rauter, and composers including Gerald Finzi, Arnold van Wyck, and Howard Ferguson. Ferguson remembers coming in to one party and thinking, 'My God, there's Richard Wagner!' It was, in fact, Winifred Wagner, whose resemblance to the great man was striking. She had been brought by Maud.

In spite of this multitude of friends, it has to be said that Maud was not universally popular. Single-minded determination to do what she thought right, or, more often, what she believed Cecil Sharp would have thought right, in spite of opposition, had turned her by now into a ruthless fighter. She had no time to suffer fools and did not scruple to show what she thought of them. She would dismiss those she despised with 'Oh, *poor* So and So!' She was often tactless and showed no consideration for those whose opinions she did not share. She demanded high standards, pulled no punches, and had a sharp, fierce manner of putting down opponents at public meetings.

After the war, when shopping again became a regular pastime, she would drag her friends on clothes-buying trips and embarrass them by being rude and crushing to assistants who tried to find her garments in a colour she approved. Having firmly decided what activities were a waste of time, she appointed people to look after certain tiresome chores. Thus it was Ursula's duty to organize her fairly frequent house-movings; her niece Katie's privilege to shop for her; and Jane (later van Boschan), an excellent dressmaker who sewed for many of Maud's circle, was entrusted with her mending, often having to rescue undergarments long beyond reasonable repair, for Maud had a distinctly frugal streak.

Eventually Maud's block of flats received a direct hit and several of her fellow residents were killed or injured. She was fortunate enough to be away that night, on a visit to Withypool. She described her return and the vicissitudes that followed, writing to Ursula on 22 October 1940 from the Savoy Hotel:

> I hope you are duly impressed by the heading of [this] paper. Am homeless and so am sleeping here for a few nights until I can make plans. Holmefield was bombed whilst I was away. I was lucky not only to have missed it, but also because very little damage was done to my flat. It was a direct hit on the back near the swimming pool, and the flat which was used as a First Aid room was completely blown in. Mine was one of the few flats that was uninjured. One man was killed and about a dozen injured but not very seriously, I believe. I can't face sleeping in that scene of devastation, and I am hoping I can get out of my lease, but I doubt it. I had meant to stay with the Nevinsons on my return, but found them in a shaken condition, and herding together in their bedroom. They had suffered badly from blast – most of their windows broken and a bomb case landed on their roof wh[ich] made a hole in it . . . Apart from danger there is horrible inconvenience in getting about and a shortage of gas and water and breakdown of telephones. It really is like living in a besieged city.[18]

She wrote later of her own flat: 'all doors and windows and most of the ceiling and walls were down and everything was covered with dust, but miraculously the only thing damaged was a china bowl'.[19]

She moved from the Savoy to the more modest Berners Hotel, which was conveniently situated for her work at Bloomsbury House. 'I remained there for a short time', she wrote, 'and then moved to a service room in Campden Hill. I lived there comfortably until one evening a bomb fell within a few yards. It was an anxious moment for the house swayed, literally, and it seemed like an eternity before it righted itself, though probably it was less than a minute. After that I lost my nerve and went to live with my sister and her husband . . . sharing their table-shelter bed whenever the bombs were approaching.'[20]

Maud's first encounter with bombs had been when Cecil Sharp House suffered a direct hit. During the period known as the Phoney War it had managed to keep going, to the pleasure of countless refugees who gravitated there as a home from home. With a blackout designed by the custodian, an

John Kennedy in naval uniform
EFDSS Photograph Collection

unflappable ex-Royal Navy submariner called Bushell, it had managed to keep open with a condensed programme of meetings and dances known as 'Beating the Blackout'. On 27 September 1940, however, the blow fell. Bushell was outside at his air-raid warden's post at the time and flung himself down in a gutter as he heard the screech of the bomb. Shaken but undamaged, he was able to climb inside and turn off gas, water, and electricity at the mains. He found the stairs down, a huge hole in the roof, and most of the inner wall that carried the musicians' gallery in ruins. Douglas Kennedy came in the morning but could hardly bring himself to look. Maud's chief feeling was one of relief. Her principal concern was for the contents of the library, and most of these had prudently been removed for safe keeping before the bombing began. To her mind the total destruction of the Queen's Hall, with its incomparable acoustics, had been a worse catastrophe.

The greatest tragedy of the war for Maud was the loss of her beloved nephew and recent travelling companion, John Kennedy. Before the war he had joined the RNVR in the so-called Yachtsman's Reserve, and in April 1940 was reported missing in action on board HMS *Glowworm*. For many successive nights, Douglas and Helen went to Maud's flat and listened to broadcasts from Germany, hoping that Lord Haw-Haw might read his name out in the list of prisoners of war that came at the end of his propaganda talks. 'It is just refined torture', Maud wrote to Ursula, 'to have to sit round that mechanical instrument waiting for the pronouncement of that satanic voice. Still even at the worst it is a relief to know that survivors were picked up.'[21] It fell to Ursula to bring the news of his (mercifully instantaneous) death. She received a flimsy little note from Frederick Corfield, a friend of her brother, John Lock, written from his prison camp in Germany. He was a survivor of the sinking of the *Glowworm* and had actually seen John Kennedy killed.

Maud resigned from the Christian Council for Refugees in the summer of 1944 to become secretary to a refugee department of the Red Cross, a post she continued to hold for some time after the end of hostilities. She had had a busy war, the only holidays she had allowed herself being the occasional visits to Withypool. She went with a guilty conscience, pricked every time she saw a placard on a station demanding 'Is your journey really necessary?'. She could not persuade herself that hers really were.

She described one such visit just before D-Day: 'the morning after my arrival at the village inn I was sitting peacefully having breakfast when a party of Americans came into the dining-room. I took little notice, but presently the waitress came up to me all of a fluster and whispered in my ear: "That's General Eisenhower." And General Eisenhower it was – the last person I would have expected to see in that remote Exmoor village. Apparently he had been inspecting some American forces who were stationed nearby and he was taking the day off in order to go riding – the only free day he had during the War, I was told. He had tea with the village post-mistress and gave her an autographed photograph of himself.'[22]

Chapter 17

At the end of 1945, Maud was able to return to her pursuit of folk song and dance, and her first piece of work was for a chapter on the subject for the *New Oxford History of Music*. The invitation to write it had come from Dom Anselm Hughes. Surprised and flattered, Maud was nonetheless intimidated and replied that, much as she would enjoy the commission, she had grave doubts as to her competence. Dom Anselm replied with an invitation to lunch in Oxford and the comment, '"grave doubts as to competency" are, to my mind, the requisite for good work, and this is reinforced by theology as well as what I have seen of the quality of other people's work and still more of what I have myself thrown off in the last 33 years'.[1]

The meeting proved delightful, especially given Maud's relish of the society of learned clerics, but she was hardly reassured. She went to express her doubts to Professor Dent, who advised her to keep to the present folk revival and to leave history to the editors. All the same she spent a good many hours at a desk in the British Museum library researching the subject. It was there that she made a friend who was to be important to her in the future, especially as an interpreter, Tola Korian Terlicka. Maud wrote: 'I noticed that my next-door neighbour was reading music and when she left for luncheon I inquisitively peeped at the books that lay on her table and found that they were collections of folk songs. So when she returned I introduced myself to her and from that time we became firm friends.'[2] In spite of encouragement from Vaughan Williams and Steuart Wilson, Maud was never happy about her article and was not sorry that, in the end, it was not printed; but she felt she had enlarged her own knowledge.

Maud's first excursion abroad after the war was to Geneva in response to an invitation to attend a conference of the *Commission internationale des arts populaires* (CIAP). Coming from food-rationed England she was overwhelmed by the abundance in Swiss shops – bunches of bananas especially – and by the marvellous meals that were set before her. She had left a London gripped by a shortage of gas and had been mildly cheered, on the morning of her departure, to hear her lodger scraping his toast which, for a wonder, had got burnt under the grill.

Maud was then living in a non-self-contained flat above some offices in Earl's Court, which was the best accommodation she had been able to find at the end of the war. She had let a room to Alec Jenkins (son of the prominent civil servant Sir Gilmour Jenkins): 'the caretaker always referred to Alec as my nephew,' she wrote, 'because she "thought it sounded better".'[3] She remained in these unsatisfactory rooms for several years, but eventually moved back to Hampstead to share a house, 14 Clorane Gardens, with Marjorie Heffer and Mary Maurice. She was to remain there until 1958.

It was in the course of one of her many moves towards the end of the war that Maud had rung up Ursula in a state of excitement. She was going to get things out of store. 'I am about to be reunited with 4lbs of Lapsang', she announced. 'You shall have some!' It had been carefully packed, wrapped in a blanket among elaborate anti-moth precautions. It turned out to be Mothball Tea!

Ever since the triumphant festival of 1935, Maud had nourished the vision of an international organization for folk music, her memories of that splendid week reinforced by recollections of the wonderful dancing she and John Kennedy had seen on their trip to Eastern Europe the same year. After the festival, the intention had been to hold such gatherings every four years, but the plans projected for 1939 had been thwarted by the impending war. In 1946, Maud felt it was time to get going again, and she therefore set out hopefully to attend the first general conference of UNESCO. Its deliberations left her unsatisfied. The talk did not seem to lead to any practical conclusions and she was disappointed that folk music was not adopted as a regular activity. Later, UNESCO was to develop a more sympathetic attitude, but these first proceedings aroused nothing in Maud but acute impatience. On her return she sought an interview with Sir John Maud, Permanent Secretary to the Ministry of Education, with the object of reconstituting the former International Folk Dance Council and broadening its scope to include folk song. From that moment onwards, she wrote, the rest of her life was devoted to the international aspect of folk music and, indeed, from that date her autobiography almost ceases to include any domestic detail and becomes a history of the International Folk Music Council (IFMC). Maud was now sixty-one.

In the name of this council she set about arranging a meeting at the

Chapter 17

Belgian Institute to take place in the autumn of the next year. Invitations were sent to everyone who had attended the 1935 festival and to every folk music expert that Maud had ever been in touch with. The Foreign Office was persuaded to assist and invited governments to appoint and send delegates. Eventually, twenty-eight countries were represented and UNESCO sent an observer. Vaughan Williams was Maud's obvious choice for chairman and, always anxious to oblige her, he agreed, though his life in music was extraordinarily full and he never shared her enthusiasm for international dance. When he was unable to attend meetings the chair was taken by Steuart Wilson, another of the handsome objects of Maud's devotion. With two such genial personalities to preside over the members, it was clear from the start that the conference was going to be a success. It took place in late September 1947 and was the occasion for happy reunions between friends who had been separated by the years of war, as well as for the making of new friendships. There were many good parties.

An initial fear, that the proposed council might be seen as a rival to the CIAP, was brushed aside and the IFMC was created without delay, its objects being the 'preservation, study, dissemination and practice of the folk music of all countries'. Vaughan Williams was elected President, with Dr Marinus of Belgium and Mr Lorenzen of Denmark as Vice Presidents. Maud, inevitably, was appointed Honorary Secretary. She wrote: 'Once constitutional matters were out of the way . . . Dr. Vaughan Williams asked from the Chair: "Now has anyone got anything more they want to say? I hope they haven't."'[4] This was greeted with applause and the conference passed eagerly to discuss a multitude of plans for the future.

The creation of the IFMC was an act of faith. There was no money. The conference had been paid for out of a fund held in trust by the EFDSS from the profits of the 1935 festival. The EFDSS added another £100, and a delegate to the conference, who insisted on remaining anonymous, added a further £100. This was later revealed to have been Patrick Shuldham-Shaw, folk singer and collector, son of the late-lamented Winifred. The whole future of the IFMC was precarious in the extreme. Its office was a room in Maud's own small flat, a temporary expedient which was destined to continue for a very long time.

The first official event for the IFMC was a full-scale conference in Basle, with fifty delegates from seventeen countries. In spite of lack of funds, the IFMC contrived to mount such meetings yearly in widely separated places. Thus Maud, between the ages of sixty and eighty, found herself packing every summer to go off to Italy, the USA, Yugoslavia, Spain, Brazil, Germany, Denmark, Romania, Austria, Canada, Czechoslovakia, Israel, Hungary, Jamaica, and Ghana. During this time there were also conferences in Edinburgh and at Cecil Sharp House. As Honorary Secretary, a large part of her year was spent in organizing the whole complicated business.

The Basle conference was the occasion for many convivial gatherings. The British delegates were entertained in a manner to which, with wartime austerity lingering at home, they were far from being accustomed. The programme assumed the form that future meetings were to take, described by one delegate from England as being 'a gentle admixture of the gay with the serious'.[5]

The vexed question of authenticity was raised and a first attempt was made to define folk music, a problem that was to bedevil the IFMC's debates for many years to come. Maud was pleased that UNESCO again sent a representative and that this led, later in the year, to the formation of the International Music Council, of which the IFMC was one of four constituent bodies. This led to even more travel as, for the next few years, Maud attended its yearly meetings in Paris. On each visit she was the guest of Claudie Marcel-Dubois and Maguy Andral, friends she had made at pre-war folk dance festivals.

The Basle conference opened with a message from its President, which Maud felt to be the keynote of the assembly. Vaughan Williams wrote: 'I feel that our researches into the origins of our art have more than a scientific value because they will help us to understand each other's point of view in so many other things and will thus contribute to the much desired unity of nations.'[6] The two most important decisions were to hold a conference each year and to publish a yearly journal, with a twice-yearly bulletin of information and announcements. Maud cheerfully undertook to edit these and contributed a lengthy editorial to the first of them, which appeared within the year. She went on from the Basle meeting to Germany, visited Freiburg, and was horrified to see the destruction wrought by Allied bombers on the medieval city.

The next conference was held in Venice and showed, as Maud wrote, 'that there were some fundamental differences of opinion with regard to the Council's approach to folk music and dance. There were some who held the view that while it might be necessary to take account of the educational and propagandist as well as the scientific objects of the Council it was necessary to separate these aspects. Others expressed the view that the only "authentic" folk music is that which is performed by peasants. Indeed, in the early days I had a heated correspondence with a few learned members who wished us, as it were, to place a *cordon sanitaire* around the "folk" and to taboo the performance of the songs and dances by anyone other than a peasant.'[7] This last view must have been anathema to Maud, who had spent so much of her life dancing and teaching others to dance in the authentic manner. The conference also explored the possibility of branching out to embrace the music of black Africa, but it was to be sixteen years before the annual meeting was held on African soil.

In 1949, in Venice, the IFMC held the first of two festivals of music and dance. Later, they gave up organizing festivals at the same time as their meetings, partly because the business of setting them up proved overwhelming, but even more because the entertainment laid on by each successive host country, though an interesting background to the lectures and debates, was not an international programme. Maud's friend Tola Korian described the scene in St Mark's Square in Venice, where a gigantic stage had been erected:

> what remains in my memory and steps out of that colourful, swinging, whirling and enchanting multitude is the gay and excellent performance of the English delegation, the charming costumes of the Scandinavian people, the touching simplicity of the Irish, Austrian and Sardinian groups, then the raisins of the pie: the French with their Basque and Vendée dancers, the Spanish stick-dancers, the women-dancers from Saragossa, the sword dancers from Piemont [*sic*] and the sound of the Alpenhorn from Switzerland, which filled the Piazza and, as it seemed, the whole sky with its deep, melodious tone.[8]

Not everybody was delighted by this display, however. Douglas Kennedy wrote that some of the examples of dances had been 'affected by sophistication and artificiality', and that there was a need to guard against such large festivals turning into mere spectacles.[9]

Soon after her return from Venice, Maud was delighted to receive a cable inviting the IFMC to hold its next conference at Indiana University in Bloomington. She had been longing to get back to America. So, the following July she set sail in the *Queen Mary*. The sight of the New York skyline brought memories flooding back. On this occasion she stayed with Esther and Meredith Langstaff at their home in Brooklyn. There she was joined by Evelyn Wells, her friend from Pine Mountain School, and the two of them set off for Indiana, sharing a sleeping compartment on the train, though they had but little sleep as they talked all night.

The IFMC meeting had been arranged to precede the Midcentury International Folklore Conference, for which many of the delegates stayed on. Most of the members were from the USA and Maud again made friends with whom she was to keep in touch for the rest of her life, notably Charles Seeger. She learned more about American music: 'the range was from the cowboy square to American religious songs, Gospel hymns of a Negro church in Chicago, songs of the Great Lakes sailors, and the Dragon Myths and Ritual Songs of the Iroquois'.[10] Maud wrote of this conference: 'I chiefly remember the moonlight evenings in the roof of one of the buildings, when we not only engaged in conversation but sung and played to each other and listened to records . . . As for the conference itself, it was one of the most alive meetings I have ever attended.'[11]

Maud read a paper on her pet subject, 'Authenticity in Folk Music', in which she quoted Cecil Sharp's definition, 'folk music is music that has been submitted, through the course of many generations, to the process of oral transmission'.[12] In the past, she declared, folk music had come about by a process of natural selection. Modern conditions now made this process impossible, therefore the collector was left with a heavy responsibility – a solemn trust was laid upon him. 'An old Morris dancer from Lancashire', she told the meeting, 'once wrote to me: "I have given you dances that I have given to no one else, not even my own son, for I know that you will treasure them as much as I do." It goes without saying that we must not falsify the material we receive from traditional sources. But I think we have a further duty . . . to exercise discrimination in the selection of the material that we present to the public. For by selecting the best and most authentic folk music we may in some measure counteract the damaging effects produced by modern conditions.'[13] Maud's paper led to lengthy discussion. At the folklore conference that followed she was asked to speak on the work of Cecil Sharp.

At the end of this happy week, Maud was able to do something she had been dreaming of for over thirty years. She returned to the Southern Appalachians on a trip that was partly for song collection, sponsored by the Library of Congress in Washington, DC, but was even more a sentimental revisiting of places she had been to with Cecil Sharp between 1916 and 1918. Her companion was Mrs Sidney Robertson Cowell and, to make the work easier, this time she carried a machine for recording the singers. It was early autumn, the country as beautiful as she remembered, but she found enormous changes, as she described in her revision of the life of Sharp: 'Roads and electricity have brought "civilization" to the mountains ... The log-cabins have nearly all disappeared. People no longer ride mule-back, but they go spinning along the roads in motor-cars; and journeys that used to take several days can now be done in a matter of hours. It is all very much more comfortable, but not entirely a change for the better.'[14] Nor was the region any longer a paradise for song collectors, for which Maud blamed the radio, with its easy dissemination of 'hill-billy and other "pop" songs'.[15]

Most of the singers whom she remembered (the best had been old in 1918) had died, but all the same she managed to rediscover between forty and fifty friends – singers or their children. The great joy was to be reunited with Emma Hensley, now Mrs Donald Shelton, living in one of the few remaining cabins on a mountain top. Emma could remember all the songs, and she and Maud spent happy hours singing them together and talking about the past. In the case of most of the others, the songs had been pushed to the back of their memories, but often a talk with Maud would bring them flooding back and she was moved to find how many of them had lively recollections of Cecil.

At the end of this emotion-stirring expedition Maud had a month's contract to work at the Library of Congress, acting as a consultant to the Folklore Division. This involved listening to and reporting on about three hundred records of Anglo-American songs and passing on her findings to the BBC with a view to making an exchange of material. While she was in Washington, both on this occasion and in later years, she made her home with Charles Seeger, a 'musician, musicologist and educationist' for whom she developed a great admiration.

The return visit to the United States had been an enormous pleasure, but perfect enjoyment was marred by the absence of Maud's oldest American friend, 'Aunt' Helen Storrow. She had died in 1944, aged eighty-one, at the beautiful house in Lincoln, near Boston, where Cecil and Maud had enjoyed so many luxurious weekends. Her obituary in *English Dance and Song* reported: 'It is said of her that she was the gayest of the gay at her eightieth birthday party, dancing for hours on end.'[16] Without Mrs Storrow and her husband it is unlikely that Cecil Sharp House would ever have been built.

The year 1951 was an important year for Maud and for the IFMC, whose conference was held in Yugoslavia. It was on this occasion that the IFMC decided to set up a special Broadcasting Commission, something that was to

Emma Shelton, Flag Pond, Tennessee, 1950
EFDSS, Peter Kennedy Collection, Maud Karpeles Materials

be implemented in London the next year and was to increase Maud's activities even further. The conference itself was accompanied by a festival, during which 'For 5 successive nights we were held spell-bound while dancers, singers and instrumentalists from the 6 Yugoslav Republics (75 villages) performed for us ... At the end of the first evening, when 15 Serbian villages had taken part, I was asked to give a radio comment on the performances, but I was so overwhelmed with excitement that all I could do was to stammer and stutter a few quite inadequate words of appreciation.'[17]

Back in London, Maud at last attempted to do something about the standards of folk dancing to be found among members of the EFDSS. For some years she had been feeling that these had degenerated and that the ideals set by Cecil Sharp were fast being forgotten. The craze for square dancing which had invaded England from the USA was largely to blame. She felt that English country dancing was gradually being destroyed. Since her disagreement with the EFDSS over Sharp's royalties, she had had little official contact with the society and she felt that her influence was slight. In recent years she had made a good deal of use of the premises of Cecil Sharp House, particularly the library for study and the canteen for meeting old friends and conferring with Helen and Douglas Kennedy. Just now, however, when she most needed Douglas to advise her, he was absent in America, and had, moreover, been taken seriously ill there. She therefore decided to approach Frank Howes, now Chairman of the Executive Committee. She wrote to him, 'suggesting that it might help to improve the situation if I were to impart my knowledge and understanding of the dances to others by training a group of dancers who would be willing to learn from me what I had to give them'.[18]

No reply arrived for several months and when it did it came as a distinct snub, to the effect that the EFDSS Executive Committee was 'convinced that the time had gone by when any such scheme of teaching as you offer us could be made to work smoothly'.[19] There is little doubt that by this time there were a good many people in the EFDSS who looked on Maud as interfering and bossy. Her manner of presenting herself as the sole repository of the truth put many a folk dancer's back up.

The 1952 conference was held at Cecil Sharp House where, for the days of talk and entertainment, Maud must have come into contact with her growing number of enemies. But it was reckoned one of the IFMC's great successes. Vaughan Williams was for once able to give his presidential address in person, Steuart Wilson was Chairman, the Kennedys were tireless in arranging hospitality, Sir John Maud read a speech, and a paper compiled by Maud from reports from sixteen member countries was read and discussed. There were interminable discussions in the hope of arriving at an agreed definition of folk music, ending with the usual decision that no single proposal would satisfy all members. In his opening address, Dr Vaughan Williams firmly showed where he stood on this matter. Indeed, he revealed himself as entirely out of sympathy with the subject of these debates. 'It was,' he said, 'I think, Lord Haldane who said that he could not define an elephant but he knew one when he saw one. I feel the same with folk song, and for the moment we will leave it at that. In the course of the many formidable essays to which we are to have the pleasure of listening during this conference there will probably be acrimonious discussion on this point and may I *not* be there to hear. I want to enjoy folk songs and not to quarrel about them.'[20]

Vaughan Williams had taken on the presidency of the IFMC out of affection for Maud, as he had supported all her projects since the death of Sharp. But the truth is that he had no real interest in international folk dance, was totally out of patience with the internal quarrels that had always rent the EFDSS, and was profoundly relieved that, with nine out of ten IFMC conferences held in foreign countries, where he had not the time to go, his role was more or less that of a figurehead. 'Despite their President's admonitions,' wrote Marie Slocombe, 'when the Conference got down to a consideration of the Report . . . they did begin, inevitably, with the vexed question of definition.'[21]

The most important business of this meeting was the implementation of the previous year's decision to set up a Radio Committee (later the Radio, Television and Sound/Film Archives Committee). This was to lead to another important friendship for Maud, with Marie Slocombe of the BBC, who, for the next fifteen years, was secretary to the new committee. She seems to have hit it off with Maud from the start. Later in the year the two of them went song collecting in Somerset for the BBC. The success of this trip – from the personal point of view, for they did not discover many songs – led to their becoming regular travelling companions on conferences abroad. The BBC had recently started a systematic search for folk songs and was also employing Peter Kennedy, the younger son of Douglas and Helen, as one of its full-time collectors. Later that year Maud made a second expedition, this time to Devon, in her nephew's company.

It would not seem that folk music could have left Maud with much time for other interests. Nevertheless, she kept a lively ear open for the music of her friends and contemporaries, particularly that of Vaughan Williams, going regularly to hear him conduct Bach Passions at the Dorking Festival and attending the first performances of his own compositions. He preserved a letter she wrote him in January of the next year after her first encounter with his 6th Symphony, a work that left many of his admirers puzzled and stunned. 'My dear Ralph,' she wrote, 'what can I say! The only word that seems to have any sense in connection with it is "apocalyptic". It was tremendously exciting and breath-taking – at times the suspense was almost unbearable, and then just as one thought one was lost a familiar passage would come to reassure one. We left at the interval. We felt we could not listen to anything else immediately after.'[22] Maud's degrees of pleasure, Jane van Boschan recalls,

Chapter 17

Peter Kennedy in the 1950s
Topic Records / British Library

could be measured by the contortions of her face. The more screwed up it became, the greater was her ecstasy. In contrast, distaste and disapproval left her countenance blank and expressionless.

Later that same winter, Vaughan Williams and Ursula Wood were married, and Maud wrote to them: 'Dearest Ursula and Ralph, Indeed you have my blessing and all the good wishes I can gather. May you have many years of blessed happiness together. I think it is lovely for both of you and very satisfactory for me to have two such dear friends united.'

In 1953 the conference, with attendant festival, started in Biarritz, from whence 'the whole membership, i.e. some 400 dancers, singers and instrumentalists migrated for 2 days from Biarritz to Pamplona'.[23] Maud went on to describe their arrival:

> Our arrival at Pamplona at mid-day was almost unbelievable. The whole town had turned out to welcome us and both sides of the beflagged streets and the windows looking down on them were filled with cheering spectators as we – the 600 of us – processed from our buses to the Mayor's Palace. That afternoon we were taken to witness a bull-fight. As a guest of honour I was seated in a prominent position, but nevertheless I have to admit to the discourtesy of sitting with closed eyes for most of the time.
>
> That same evening the bull-ring was the scene of a very different kind

Ursula and Ralph Vaughan Williams on their wedding day, 1953
Reproduced with the permission of the British Library

of spectacle – that of the Festival performance. And I can say with truth that the audience was no less enormous and no less enthusiastic than that of the afternoon.[24]

Marie Slocombe wrote: 'Some of the effects were . . . marvellously spectacular under the night sky of Spain – I recall especially the moment when the Swiss alphorn players came on and at the first plaintive notes a thousand pigeons rose in the sky. Nevertheless it was felt by many in the conference that this Festival raised acutely problems of large scale presentation for large audiences . . . "the subtleties are lost in space" and "not everything lends itself to demonstration in an arena in the presence of 15,000 spectators".'[25]

The more serious work and deliberations of the delegates came near to being swamped, but Maud must have cherished a speech made by a delegate from Ceylon, though she did not quote it when writing her memoirs: 'All through the proceedings there was one person always modest, never obtrusive, but none the less the heart-throb of the whole organization. She commanded our attention and our respect because it is her unflagging enthusiasm that has kept the Council going.'[26]

It was in connection with this occasion that Maud wrote with some satisfaction: 'I may say that throughout the course of its history the IFMC has managed to steer clear of politics. Before the Biarritz Festival of 1953, a foreign office representative of a certain communist country wrote me that it had been noticed that Spanish dancers were taking part and that of course dancers from his country could not appear on the same platform, so what was I going to do about it. I answered that we did not mind from which country the dancers came so long as they showed authentic traditional dances. Almost by return of post my letter was courteously acknowledged. I was informed that my letter was "quite satisfactory" and the dancers appeared in due course.'[27]

Maud's health was now not as robust as it had been, and she was anxious to have more time to devote to song collecting and to free herself of the more irksome duties that being Honorary Secretary of the IFMC involved. Except for occasional help from a shorthand typist, she had carried on the job single-handed since its inception and the strain was beginning to tell. No suitable replacement was to be found, however, and she found herself compelled to go on, which she did for another ten years.

The main object of her expeditions of the previous year had been to discover whether in the West Country any songs were remembered by the descendants of the singers from whom Cecil Sharp had collected between 1903 and 1913. She had managed to trace eighteen children of people whose repertoires had been particularly large and valuable. But the harvest had been only ten songs from four singers and a recording of the music that accompanied the Minehead Hobby Horse. Over and over again, these people lamented that they had not taken more interest when they were young and regretted the loss of tunes which, they realized, were better than any they heard now.

Maud made an exploration of the Forest of Dean and parts of Herefordshire with Patrick Shuldham-Shaw, but they met with little success. She went on to stay with a school friend, Violet Rumney, at Sissinghurst, where they explored some of the villages of Kent. There she became friendly with a delightful family of gypsies and was later able to bring Peter Kennedy to visit them. In this connection she wrote: 'Whenever I have visited gypsies – be it in tents, caravans or houses – I have always enjoyed their company. They are sociable, friendly people and very often have a store of good folk tunes, though they are apt to mix up the words of the songs.'[28]

Like Cecil Sharp, Maud was evidently adept at extracting songs from complete strangers, and she had no doubt learned some of the technique from him. She wrote on this subject:

Throughout my collecting experiences I have never been confronted with a downright refusal to sing on the part of the singer, except on one occasion and that was short-lived. I had heard of a singer in Camarthenshire who was said to know many 'old songs'. When I called at her house she was out, so I left a message with her daughter saying I would come back, rather unwisely telling her of my mission. When I returned later in the day I was met at the door by a rather austere looking lady. 'Are you Mrs. Brown?' I asked. 'Yes, I am,' she replied. 'But I'm not going to sing to you.' However, I was not daunted. I said I was sorry, but perhaps I might come in and have a chat with her. Her innate courtesy persuaded her to invite me in, and within twenty minutes she was cheerfully singing to me. I got only one authentic folk song from her, which she called 'The Mermaid'. After she had sung it, she remarked: 'Queer thing, those mermaids. Seems like they can sing well and that they are very good-looking.' Then she added: 'My husband once met one. It was in America.' Wise man to keep her so far off, I thought.[29]

Chapter 17

The IFMC's seventh conference was held in São Paulo in 1954, and Maud's journey to Brazil was the longest she had so far undertaken. Her speech, at the opening ceremony, was as long as any she had given and was full of wonder at the beauties with which she found herself surrounded. In the event, however, the trip was to prove a frustrating one. Again they debated the 'Definition of Folk Music', with Maud reading her own paper of that title, and again they ended up with a formula that left many unsatisfied. Then Maud was frustrated at being totally unable to see the local dances, which were performed for the delegates on a high platform in the open air. She wrote of this fiasco: 'though seats had been reserved for us our line of sight (or at any rate, mine) was soon obliterated by members of the enormous crowd who pushed in front of us. Dr. Almeida searched for Douglas Kennedy and me among the crowd and invited us to come up and crouch on the platform, but the boos from the audience soon forced us to descend.'[30]

When the conference was over, Maud had hoped to be able to wander around on her own and see some dancing on its home ground, but here again fate stepped in to prevent her. The president of Brazil chose this moment to commit suicide and the visitors were warned not to venture far from their hotels for fear of political unrest. Maud had to content herself with becoming an ordinary tourist and spent a few days sightseeing in Rio de Janeiro before flying home from Recife.

The next year took the conference to Oslo. It turned out to be a more sober and useful affair than the goings-on in Brazil had allowed. Maud commented, in her editorial for the IFMC's journal that this was 'in part due to a stricter adherence by the speakers to the subjects that had been laid down for discussion'.[31]

After this meeting Maud decided to take three months leave from her endless paperwork in order to pay a prolonged visit to the USA and Canada. This was far from being a rest cure because she ended up giving nearly twenty lectures on a tour of mostly US universities, but it was a great pleasure because of the number of old friends she was able to visit. The primary object that took her across the Atlantic was a summer school at Harvard organized by Professor Bertrand 'Bud' Bronson, whom she had met at the Indiana conference five years before. She was well acquainted with his monumental work on 4000 versions of the Child ballads in England and America. After Harvard, Maud went to stay with Evelyn Wells and the two of them set off for the Appalachians on another expedition with the recording machine.

On her return to England, Maud was quite pleased to accept 'a small honorarium' from the Executive Board of the IFMC for her services as Honorary Secretary. She was still unable to find anyone she thought worthy to replace her and, indeed, the task of discovering anybody willing to put in so much time, for hardly any financial return, seemed hopeless. Maud's earnings, throughout her life, from lectures, articles, and published collections of folk songs, were negligible. She lived on an income from her Raphael forebears, which kept her in modest comfort, without extravagance, though she tended to become parsimonious with clothes in later life. She was never short of the money to take her anywhere she wanted to go, though travel was, of course, a good deal less expensive at that time, relative to other living costs, than it was to become later. She was often able to stay with friends abroad, or was the guest of the universities to which she went to lecture.

The next conference was held at Trossingen and Stuttgart. In an article in *The Times* on the eve of her departure, Frank Howes described her as she appeared in 1956: 'Secretary and organizing spirit of the meeting is a slender, soft-spoken Englishwoman in her seventies, whose dark hair hardly shows a trace of grey though she has pursued the strenuous calling of a folksong collector for more than 40 years.'[32]

Maud was able to revisit Freiburg on her way to the meeting, where she was happy to see that, with the help of the Americans, the city had been restored nearly to its former glory. In September of that year a Commonwealth Arts Festival was held in various British cities, during which Maud attended a five-day conference on Folk Music and Education held in Liverpool under the presidency of Yehudi Menuhin. This was made particularly enjoyable by the presence of many friends, notably Hugh Tracey, with whom Maud had much conversation on the subject of music in Africa. It was here that she made the acquaintance of Martin Kingsbury, who had recently joined the staff of Faber & Faber. He was to become the publisher of some of her collections of songs and one of her great friends.

Life at this time seems to have been one festival after another. No sooner had that of the Commonwealth ended than Maud was packing to go to Budapest at the invitation of Zoltán Kodály for a festival in honour of Bartók. This was a tremendous excitement, for the susceptible Maud had lost her heart to Kodály a year or two before when he had been on a visit to London. She wrote of this episode: 'I called on him (uninvited!) at Claridge's Hotel where he was staying. During my conversation with him I had the temerity to say that I felt there was an affinity between his music and that of Vaughan Williams. His reply was: "But, of course, we both speak to the people. We speak so as to be understood." A few days later I arranged a luncheon party for him at the English-Speaking Union to which I invited Vaughan Williams and others. After lunch we all went together to Cecil Sharp House to attend a performance of folk songs and dances with which Kodály was greatly impressed.'[33]

In Budapest she heard an inspired performance of Kodály's *Psalmus Hungaricus* and joined in the seemingly never-ending applause for her new hero. 'I do not know', she wrote, 'how many people were aware of the impending revolution, but the atmosphere was electrifying and it was obvious that the country was working up for some soul stirring event.'[34] In spite of these uneasy feelings, preliminary arrangements were made for the next IFMC conference to be held in Budapest. Plans got so far that notices were printed and invitations sent out, but, less than a month after the Bartók festival, Hungary was in revolt and the whole plan had to be cancelled.

Zoltán Kodály and Maud Karpeles at a meeting of the International Folk Music Council. EFDSS Photograph Collection

Danish members of the IFMC came to the rescue and the 1957 conference was transferred to Copenhagen.

The venue for the following year was Liège, where the Brussels International Exhibition was in progress, with some excellent performances by dancers from Africa. Hugh Tracey was able to add to the interest by showing the delegates some of his films from that continent. But 1958 was a sad year for Maud, as for many of her friends and for the IFMC. The Liège conference was destined to be the last at which a message from the President, Dr Vaughan Williams, was read out. Suddenly, on 26 August, at the age of eighty-six, soon after the first performance of his 9th Symphony and in the middle of much new work, he died. Maud had known him since the beginning of her folk dancing days and it had been on him, in particular, that she had leaned when Cecil Sharp died. In every crisis of her life, for the thirty-four years since then, it had been to Vaughan Williams that Maud had immediately rushed for comfort and advice, as she herself described:

> I used to pour out to him all my hopes and fears concerning folk music and other matters. He was always a patient and sympathetic listener and I derived great comfort from him. I was present at the Golders Green crematorium a few days later and at the Westminster Abbey service on 19th September when his ashes were laid in the North Choir Aisle near to those of Purcell and Stanford. The service with its music, mostly Ralph's own, was so moving that it was hard to contain oneself. I was privileged to be one of the small company that followed the casket to its resting place.
>
> His loss to folk music was truly irreparable.[35]

Chapter 18

It was several months before the IFMC had the heart to appoint a new President, and when they did their choice fell on a man who was to die little more than a year after he took office, Jaap Kunst, musicologist and authority on Indonesian music. So the choice had to be made again after a very short time.

The 1959 conference, however, was one that Maud would never forget, nor, indeed, would her travelling companion and friend, Marie Slocombe. The host country was Romania and they were splendidly housed in the former royal palace at Sinaia, where Maud and Marie occupied a marvellous suite with a marble-tiled bathroom, once the living quarters of Madame Lupescu. The scenery in the foothills of the Carpathians was as breathtaking as the Appalachians, and they were entertained in the evenings to traditional dance and song staged in a beautiful open-air setting.

Maud was in her element. The twenty-six nations represented offered a programme of records and films and joined in the usual indecisive arguments about what could really be defined as folk music. As Maud wrote: 'the view was frequently expressed that in a class society folk music necessarily reflected the struggle against the ruling classes. I endeavoured to refute this argument, saying that in the finest folk song (at least those of England which might until fairly recently be termed a class society), the traditional singer entered into a world of romance which had little to do with any political system or social condition and which would outlive these temporal phenomena.'[1] One important feature of the conference in Romania was the provision, for the first time, of simultaneous translation into five languages. This greatly speeded the discussion and enabled papers to be read in Romanian and Russian.

In that year came another emotional milestone for Maud. On St Cecilia's Day, 22 November, occurred the centenary of Cecil Sharp's birth, and she was able to oversee a large programme of concerts and dances staged by the EFDSS, as well as to give a number of broadcast talks. At this moment she must have felt the recent loss of Vaughan Williams particularly acutely.

That December, to Maud's relief, a small advisory committee was set up to assist the IFMC. She found it helpful to have, at last, some authority with whom to share her problems and enable her to clear her mind. The Chairman was Sir Gilmour Jenkins, a man who was extremely active in a number of musical fields. He was an old friend whom Maud had met originally at the parties given by Ursula Wood in the 1940s and he had been associated with the inauguration of the IFMC. He was partly able to fill the place left empty by Vaughan Williams, and Maud appealed to him in moments of doubt.

Vienna was the scene of the 1960 conference and on that occasion the principal discussion was the subject of folk music on radio. Among the papers was one that Marie Slocombe had prepared from replies received to a BBC questionnaire which had been sent out to organizations that dealt with the broadcast of recordings and methods of presentation of such material. Early the next year, with great satisfaction, Maud was able to announce to the members that Zoltán Kodály had accepted the presidency of the IFMC. 'This', she wrote, 'was only after much correspondence and persuasive effort on my part. His first sign of acceding to our request was a letter in which he quoted a Hungarian proverb: "If a horse cannot be found a donkey must do." I was perplexed. Did he mean he was the "horse" or the "donkey"? An early reply to my (I hope, tactful) enquiry set my mind at rest.'[2]

The year Kodály took up the presidency was to be an eventful one in other ways, bringing Maud both joy and sorrow. On 10 June, the Queen's official birthday, she was engaged to unveil a plaque to Cecil Sharp at the vicarage in Hambridge, commemorating the fact that he had heard his first folk song there. It was on this morning that the papers announced the award of the OBE to Maud Karpeles for services to music, an honour that gave her much pleasure. The day was chilly for midsummer, but several hundred people converged upon Somerset from all parts of the country to listen to Maud's speech and be entertained by Roger and Hazel Wallis, the present vicar and his wife. Maud spoke at considerable length, paying tribute not only to Cecil but to the earlier incumbent, Charles Marson, Perpetual Curate of Hambridge in 1903, and to his gardener, John England, from whose lips Cecil had heard the song 'The Seeds of Love', which had precipitated the start of the folk song movement. The day ended with a concert in the vicarage garden. 'One of the singers', Maud wrote, 'was Fred Crossman, a son of one of Cecil Sharp's former singers. He was an oldish man and his voice was almost gone, so that one could hear practically no sounds above the gusts of wind, but somehow he managed to hold his audience by means of his intense concentration.'[3] Maud found the experience almost unbearably moving.

Any excuse was welcome that would get Maud across the Atlantic, though in 1961 she went with some hesitation because her beloved Frank Etherington was failing in health. For some years the IFMC had been preparing to take itself to Canada. The invitation had been issued by its Vice President, Marius Barbeau, who had been planning for some time for a very special conference. The venue was Laval University in Quebec, and the highlight was to be a special convocation at which the honorary degree of Doctor of Letters was to be conferred on five of the delegates. One of those was Maud. No honour or tribute in her life gave her more pleasure than this.

The conference fitted in conveniently with a meeting of the International Music Council in New York, which promised Maud the opportunity to call on many friends. She settled in with Willard and Lillie Rhodes, who had been her hosts on several recent occasions, but her attendance at the meetings was cut abruptly short by a heart attack. Maud was now seventy-six and had been overworking systematically for most of her life. The Rhodes were kindness itself, but Lillie's nursing was so strict that it led Maud to complain that she was not allowed so much as to write a letter. She contrived surreptitiously to scribble a few under cover of the bedclothes and have them smuggled out of the house.

When she was pronounced fit to travel she felt she must hasten back to England, anxiety for Father Etherington making her skip some of the visits she had hoped to make. She had been shocked by his appearance when she had made her last visit to Minehead in April of that year and feared she might not be seeing him for much longer. This turned out to be only too true, for he died in November, at the age of ninety. Maud was to miss him acutely for the rest of her life. She wrote: 'He was a rare and understanding person and we had had so many happy times together in Somerset – at Withypool and Minehead – and on the occasions when he visited London. Since Cecil Sharp's death he was the person to whom I most readily turned for understanding and help in sorting out the tangled thoughts that were passing through my mind.'[4] But, she added: 'My absorption with the affairs of the I.F.M.C. left me but little time for personal sorrows. Before one conference was out of the way I had to start preparing for another.'[5]

Maud Karpeles unveiling a plaque in Hambridge, 1961
EFDSS Photograph Collection (L. G. Channett)

Chapter 18

The one she was now getting ready for was to be held in Czechoslovakia, at Gottwaldov, in the summer of 1962. The presence of Kodály along with his second wife, Sarolta, attracted many extra visitors and over two hundred members from twenty-four countries were housed in the vast Hotel Moskva. The conference coincided with the annual folklore festival at Shagnice where the delegates were able to watch spectacular sword dances. Afterwards a number of IFMC members accompanied Maud to Bucharest for yet another festival and she saw again the *Kumpanija* dance from Korčula that had so impressed her twenty-six years earlier when she had witnessed it with John Kennedy on its native heath.

It was the year of Kodály's eightieth birthday and Maud was busy composing a tribute to be translated into Hungarian for the *Magyar Zene*, a musicological journal. She was enchanted to be asked to break her journey home to spend a few days in the Tatra Mountains at the home of the Kodálys. There she had a chance to relax and enjoy long leisurely talks about music with the composer, with whom, as with his young wife, she felt deeply at home.

Towards the end of this year some relief for Maud's heavy burden of paperwork arrived in the shape of Robin Band, who was appointed part-time secretary to the IFMC. She began to see some hope, at last, of resigning the post she had held for nearly eighteen years. Her actual resignation was timed for the 1963 conference, which took place in Jerusalem. At the opening ceremony the delegates were welcomed by Abba Eban, then deputy prime minister; Mordecai Shalom, the prime minister; and Golda Meir, at that time foreign minister.

During the course of the meeting expressions of esteem were heaped upon Maud from all the nations represented and she was offered the position of Honorary President, with a permanent seat on the Executive Board. At a meeting of the General Assembly, Kodály presented her with a cheque and a handsomely bound volume containing a tribute written by himself and signed by over three hundred members. Maud was nearly struck dumb with emotion, but managed to stammer out a speech of thanks. It seemed wrong, she insisted, to be given so splendid a reward for doing a job that had given her so much pleasure. The Jerusalem meeting was her only visit to Israel and she was delighted to have had some introduction to the music and dance of the country of her ancestors.

Many people have been described as being wedded to their work. Of nobody was it more literally true than of Maud. For the past eighteen years, the IFMC office had consisted of a room in her flat, 'wherever it happened to be'.[6] Even before the IFMC had existed, most of her paperwork had been done in her own home or Cecil Sharp's house, often in very cramped conditions, sometimes actually in her bedroom, especially during the bombing in the war. This had the unfortunate effect that her work, as in a real marriage, stretched itself out to fill all the hours that God gave and had bred in her a habit of overwork. The good effect was that it had made her, by now, even more meticulous in her record-keeping than she had been during Sharp's lifetime, so that she left immaculate papers for her successors to take up.

It was not to be expected, however, that she would relapse into a life of leisure now that the burden of organizing was lifted. She continued, as she put it herself, to 'meddle' from her seat on the Executive Board and missed no meetings up to her ninetieth birthday. She continued to attend all the conferences, enjoying them more than ever when she was no longer responsible for setting them up. Since Quebec in 1961 she had greatly enjoyed being addressed as 'Dr Karpeles', and it must have been about now that, at a meeting during which the perennial question of double meanings in the words of folk songs had come up again, Sir Steuart Wilson, the Chairman, got up and said: 'There are seven different kinds of indecency and Dr Karpeles knows them all.' This was the kind of remark that Maud enjoyed.

The first conference that she was to attend in the new, relaxed style was held in Budapest, compensating for the disappointment of seven years previously when the Hungarian revolution had put a stop to plans to meet there. The entertainments included a visit to Kodály's birthplace, a water trip up the Danube, and concerts of choral and orchestral music by her idol Kodály and by Bartók. This was the seventeenth conference since the founding of the IFMC.

Following her heart attack in the USA – and fast coming up to her eightieth birthday – it had begun to be clear to her many friends that it would be better for Maud to move out of the flat she had lived in for seven years to a place where she could be looked after. In June 1965 she mustered her following of regular helpers – Ursula Vaughan Williams being the one who was in command whenever she moved house – and vacated her Bayswater flat to settle in a residential home for the elderly on the borders of Knightsbridge and Chelsea, near Sloane Street. She left her neatly ordered papers behind, allowing the IFMC to occupy her flat for a few months until a new temporary home was found for it in Cecil Sharp House.

There was no general conference in 1965. Not to travel abroad on folk music business would have been a great deprivation to Maud, had it not been that, in September, there was what she described as a 'magnificent' meeting of the IFMC Radio Committee in Stockholm. The Swedish Broadcasting Corporation was host to twenty other such bodies and Maud was invited to give the opening address. She told her audience that, in her opinion, the future of folk music was in the hands of those who worked in radio and television.

Maud's eightieth birthday, on 12 November, found her feeling astonished at her age, for she felt, heart attack notwithstanding, no older than she had been at seventy, 'and certainly no wiser'.[7] The event was celebrated by the BBC with a talk by Frank Howes; an interview with her was reported in *The Times*; and at the Annual General Meeting of the EFDSS, she was awarded the Freedom of the Society.

At the same time, Maud was busy 'meddling' with the plans her successors were making for the 1966 conference, one that was to provide almost the greatest excitement of any. It was the first to be held on the African continent, in Ghana, only a few months after the deposition of President Nkrumah. The venue was the campus of Legon University, a few miles outside of Accra, and, as Maud described, 'it would be impossible to find a more idyllic setting.

Maud Karpeles, c. 1960
EFDSS Photograph Collection

The noble, spacious and dignified terraced buildings, a heritage of British rule, were in perfect harmony with the natural beauty of the scene with its profusion of fragrant flowering trees and bushes, animated by the song and flight of birds of innumerable variety and the bright, busy little lizards darting hither and thither.'[8]

The conference itself 'was enlivened by the numerous groups of dancers, singers and instrumentalists who performed for us on the university campus and whom we visited in their native towns and villages, thus being able to see for ourselves that traditional music forms part of the everyday life of the Ghanaian. At Kumasi, the capital of Ashanti, I fell into conversation with a professional "letter writer" who was sitting in the market place. I asked him if he were a dancer, and his reply was: "But, of course. A man who does not dance is not a member of the community."'[9]

She found that this attitude to the arts of dance and music seemed to be common to all the people of Ghana, and was impressed by the place they were given in education and in religious ceremonies. She was also pleased by some of the composed music, and attended a number of concerts, writing: 'The beauty of the music and the picturesqueness of the singers were enhanced by the sight of a number of women singers who carried their small babies on their backs throughout the performance. It occurred to me that were this custom adopted by, say, the members of the Bach Choir, it might save some of the problems of baby-sitting.'[10] She left Africa with happy memories of a friendly, cheerful, and hospitable people, whose strong sense of humour particularly appealed to her. It had been one of her happiest conferences.

Early in 1967, however, came the shattering news of the death of Zoltán Kodály, which plunged Maud into acute grief. During the six years he had been President of the IFMC he had come to be a great friend, supplying, in some ways, though they met only infrequently, the places left empty by Vaughan Williams and Frank Etherington. Willard Rhodes, frequently her host on her visits to New York, who had been on the Executive Board for ten years, now stepped into the role of President.

This was the moment when the IFMC was forced to admit that it could no longer afford to operate from London. After much heart-searching, it was decided that a move would have to be made if another country came forward with a suitable invitation. A generous offer of hospitality was made by the Danish Folklore Archives, and all hands turned to sorting out papers and preparing for the transfer of office and secretariat to Copenhagen, in

September 1967. Maud, who though officially retired was still deeply involved, found the whole process 'fearsome' and spent several weeks knee-deep in dusty files in the temporary offices in Sicilian Avenue, Bloomsbury, discarding all that could possibly be dispensed with.

While this was going on, the last conference to be organized from London took place at Ostend. Maud read a paper on 'The Distinction between Folk and Popular Song', restating her oft-repeated belief that 'a song that is composed by an individual and passes into the common repertory does not *ipso facto* become a folk song', stressing that it is not the popularity of a song that determines whether or not it qualifies as a folk song, but the inherent qualities it has acquired through the process of oral transmission. This meeting decided that conferences should, in future, be held only every other year, so that no gathering was planned for 1968. Maud's passion for travel and meetings, however, was again satisfied by the Radio Committee, which held an important congress in Copenhagen that summer.

Travel was not so far afield as usual in 1969, but Edinburgh appealed to Maud as an ideal setting for a conference and she was glad to make closer acquaintance with Scottish dancing. Besides, she was already planning another trip across the Atlantic. The Danish Folklore Society, in its turn, found it impossible to continue to play host to the IFMC after two successful years, so another home had to be sought. The new Honorary Secretary was to be Professor Graham George, Head of Music at Queen's University, Kingston, Ontario, and he offered office accommodation for the IFMC. In the autumn after the Edinburgh conference, arrangements were made to take the headquarters to Canada.

Maud went across in May of 1970, but not, this time, on IFMC business. She had been invited to go, all expenses paid, to receive the honorary degree of Doctor of Letters from the Memorial University of St John's, Newfoundland. This she was delighted, proud, and gratified to accept, the more so as she had a longing to revisit the scene of her two solo collecting trips and to seek out old friends and folk singers. The convocation was an impressive ceremony and the Public Orator, Dr G. M. Story, presented her to the President and Vice Chancellor, winding up his discourse with the words: 'To list the activities of Miss Karpeles is to summarize the accomplishments in her field during this century . . . But I present her not solely as a scholar and editor, but as the rare woman who came to our shores as no stranger had come before, and of whom a Newfoundland singer said: "There is singing and dancing wherever she goes."'[11]

Chapter 18

Maud spent a blissful week in St John's, royally entertained by the university and by old friends. She wrote that many changes had come about since her 1930 visit, not the least of them being the founding of the university. Roads had been built and bus services had replaced passenger trains. She was taken for drives to revisit the beautiful country, and even went on a collecting expedition during which she managed to get several songs from a woman who had been twelve years old when they had first met. For a restful few days she went to stay with the Emersons, who had helped her so much on her previous visits. They had moved to Nova Scotia, where their house was on the shores of a beautiful lake. She then went on to the USA,

Maud Karpeles receiving an honorary degree from the Memorial University of St John's, Newfoundland, 1970
EFDSS Photograph Collection

where she was again the guest of Willard and Lillie Rhodes, first in New York and then at their country home. After four weeks of real holiday, she returned to London just in time to organize the meeting of the IFMC's Executive Board which, this year, was held in the Bedford College hall of residence in Regent's Park.

Chapter 19

Maud's resignation as Honorary Secretary of the IFMC left her with a little more time for her work of writing and editing. Her determination to put all of her own and Cecil Sharp's folk songs in order resulted in her being as busy in her late eighties as she had ever been. About 1959, she had started sorting Sharp's collection, which consisted of nearly five thousand tunes, excluding dances. She now got down to completing this formidable task. Only about 360 had been printed during his lifetime, so there was a rich harvest of unknown treasures to be given to the world. She could not hope to deal with the entire collection, so she decided to restrict herself to songs and ballads, omitting the singing games and shanties. 'Even so,' she wrote, 'these numbered 2470, so a further reduction had to be made. Finally I made a selection of 1165 tunes, or rather tune-versions (413 separate song titles) and though this is somewhat less than half the number of tunes that were noted, I believe nevertheless that it may be said to represent the corpus of the collection.'[1]

Anything of doubtful provenance was thrown out; variants so slight that they threw little fresh light on a song were scrapped; and a number of the commonplace tunes of the 'come-all-ye' type were rejected. The results were published by Oxford University Press in 1974 as *Cecil Sharp's Collection of English Folk Songs*. From this, she chose seventy-two of the best and, with guitar chords supplied by Patrick Shuldham-Shaw, had them published separately as *The Crystal Spring*, the title being that of the anthology of folk song words that she and Ursula had compiled during the war but which had never found a publisher.

Before completing this, she published in 1971 her own *Folk Songs from Newfoundland*, a collection of 150 tunes and variants, eighty-nine different songs, and three dances. The next year *Eighty English Folk Songs* came out, comprising the best of the tunes she and Sharp had found in the Southern Appalachians. Also, she had often been asked to supply an authoritative account of English folk song, as none had appeared since Sharp's *English*

Folk-Song: Some Conclusions, of 1907. So she wrote *An Introduction to English Folk Song*, which was published in 1973.

It was as she approached ninety that she began, in response to suggestions from friends, to start work on her autobiography, which, as has already been remarked, turned out to be less about her own life and more about that of Cecil Sharp, the foundation of the EFDS, and the history of her own particular creation, the IFMC. At the same time, even though weakened by heart attacks, she managed to deliver a number of lectures and a quantity of BBC talks and interviews. In connection with the broadcasts she wrote: 'I have always found the greatest difficulty in expressing myself and extempore speaking is a particular nightmare to me. I have on several occasions been interviewed for radio programmes, but wherever possible I have prepared my remarks prior to the recording. So much so that on one occasion when Michael Oliver was interviewing me for *Kaleidoscope* he decided that the only thing to do was to let me go ahead during the recording and later fit his "questions" to my "answers".'[2] She also complimented the producers with whom she worked at this time, including 'Alec Robertson, Roger Fiske, Anna Instone and Julian Herbage (of *Music Magazine* fame) and Stanley Williamson'.[3]

For Williamson, she also appeared on television in a programme about Vaughan Williams and was as much vexed at her own appearance as she had been by her voice when she first heard it in a broadcast recording in the 1930s. She had by now put on a good deal of weight, her thick black hair was streaked with grey, and she had become very bent so that she appeared even smaller than she had always been. Her beaky nose seemed more prominent and, set between her always bright and penetrating eyes, gave her the appearance of a benevolent witch.

The heart attack she had suffered in 1961 while on a visit to the Rhodeses in the USA, and her retirement from active involvement in planning conferences, had in no way diminished Maud's appetite for foreign travel. She was to attend three biennial IFMC meetings in the last six years of her life. The best of these was that of 1971, which was held in Jamaica, and she flew across the Atlantic to enjoy an enchanted few days at the university just outside of Kingston. She and the other delegates were overwhelmed by the hospitality and the friendliness of the welcome and were particularly delighted at their hosts' idea of sending each member to take Sunday lunch in a separate private home. Edward Seaga, then Minister of Finance and Planning, gave the opening address, and the conference was organized by

Olive Lewin, whose company of Jamaican folk singers entertained them in an open-air theatre high in the mountains, called Little Glyndebourne. Maud felt they had gained real insight into a living folk culture. She specially enjoyed going to two religious revival meetings in which the singing and dancing induced a state of trance in the participants. As usual, once across the Atlantic, Maud managed to fit in a few visits, going first to New York to stay with the Rhodes and then on to Nova Scotia to the Emersons. It was to be her last meeting with one of her best friends, for Fred Emerson died the following year.

In 1973 the conference was a near-disaster and attempts to get it organized had Maud back at the helm and as busy as she had been before her retirement. The IFMC had been invited to San Sebastián by a society for Basque folk music, who said the arrangements would be in the hands of an organization called Cofex-Cat. Maud had an uneasy feeling about it from the start and was not surprised when she heard that local newspapers had announced that the meeting had been cancelled. She then had to spend many hours on the telephone to the new headquarters in Canada, and to Cofex-Cat, trying to persuade them to reverse their decision. When they refused, she found herself involved in frantic telephone calls and cables to and fro across the Atlantic in search of an alternative venue. Claudie Marcel-Dubois eventually persuaded the Musée Basque in Bayonne to act as host, and when this had been agreed there were all the delegates to be notified of the change of plan. Since many were away on their summer holidays, the conference opened with nobody having any idea how many delegates to expect. Professor and Mrs Graham George of Quebec and local dignitaries in Bayonne turned to and performed miracles, according to Maud, but she must have been left wondering whether, in fact, she had retired at all and whether the IFMC was capable of existing without her.

Klaus Wachsmann, who had been associated with the IFMC since its birth in 1947, was now the President. He wrote of Maud's involvement in these later days: 'When one talked to Maud Karpeles one could see that the affairs of the Council were a heavy burden for her and although she readily shared her worries, she rarely followed advice, but she was a good loser if the Executive Board failed to support her view. She had a wonderful sense of humour and a good eye for the ridiculous, and life did provide food for both occasionally.'[4] Not least at Bayonne – but Maud was able to write: 'The conference proved to be an enjoyable affair – even if not exactly what had been planned.'[5]

Germany was to be the host for the 1975 gathering and provided Maud with excuses for two trips abroad, for she was invited to a meeting of the Executive Board in the preceding year to discuss arrangements. Regensburg was the chosen town and here Maud made new friends, Dr Adolf Eichenseer and his wife, Erika. At many conferences in the past Maud had been grateful for the help and advice of representatives from the German Federal Republic, particularly Professor Egon Kraus, who persistently alerted his government to the IFMC's activities. Hence she was expecting good organization and felt confident when she started out that no disasters such as had made Bayonne so memorable would occur this time. On her way to the conference on the train from Munich (a journey of 1½ hours) she began to feel faint and ill. Her travelling companion, Klaus Wachsmann, alerted a guard and the two of them were escorted to a first-class compartment where she was able to lie down. When the train drew up to the Regensburg platform she was amazed to be greeted by a Red Cross team, complete with wheelchair.

Typically, she recovered in time to be present at the opening ceremony and was fully able to appreciate the performances of Bavarian folk music laid on for the entertainment of the delegates. She described the end of one of these performances:

> Adolf Eichenseer . . . suddenly announced at the beginning of the second part of the concert, that he wished to introduce 'a remarkable lady who was about to be 90' and proceeded to make flattering remarks about me. With the assistance of two neighbours I mounted the platform and endeavoured to respond, but I felt very embarrassed and as far as I can remember I said not much more than that it was very improper of Dr Eichenseer to have given my age away. However, I received a standing ovation from a large audience. I think what impressed them most was the way in which unassisted I jumped off the platform.[6]

This was to be Maud's last international conference – twenty-four in all, counting the inaugural meeting of 1947 – but for any other travels she might embark on, the episode at Regensburg had put a splendid idea into her head: at airports and stations from this time on, she contrived to get herself met by a retinue of helpers and a comfortable wheelchair.

Maud's principal preoccupation in her ninetieth and ninety-first years was to get her autobiography completed, which she managed to do, though the last chapters are somewhat sketchy. Towards the end of it, she spared half a page from folk music to reflect on her family, of whom, from her generation, only her brother Arthur remained. She saw him infrequently, as he had retired from the banking firm belonging to the Raphaels and gone to live in Devon. Of her three sisters, Lucy, the eldest, had died in Montreux in 1925, only a few weeks after her second marriage – two years after Cecil Sharp and Maud had visited her there, and one year after Sharp's own death. Florence, who never married, had lived in the Channel Islands until she managed to get the last boat for England before the arrival of the German army. After that she had remained in London where she and Maud met frequently. She was rarely well and died in 1959. Helen Kennedy, the youngest sister, and Maud's constant companion on the folk dance scene, had died in 1976 after seven years of severe and painful illness, during which she was devotedly nursed by her husband, Douglas, in their home in Suffolk. Lucy's daughter, Katie Kacser (who figured as the shopping assistant in Maud's retinue of helpers), and Helen's son Peter had provided her with three great-nephews, a great-niece, and a great-grand-niece by the time she reached ninety.

Maud's heart attack in New York in 1961 had been but a prelude to a number of more or less serious episodes which went on into her nineties. The worst of these had been in 1972, between the splendid Jamaica conference and the debacle preceding the one in Bayonne. She was out of action for many weeks and never regained her full strength, not that such weakness was able to deter her from any project she was anxious to pursue. In 1976 she suffered two heart failures, which saw her being 'bundled' off to hospital in the middle of the night from Cadogan Square. Each time friends of all ages rallied round to comfort, help, and look after the business she had in hand at the moment.

On 12 November 1975 her ninetieth birthday was celebrated with a splendid party given by Ursula Vaughan Williams at her house in Gloucester Crescent, Camden Town. To this, Maud arrived in a taxi carrying three capacious shopping bags – 'For the swag', she explained. She left with them excellently filled. The party was a jubilant occasion and included all her best friends of all ages, from their twenties through to their eighties, though none, apart from Maud, had reached their tenth decade. It was notable that throughout her life, as she herself remarked, disparity of age had never presented a bar to friendship. The week around the party was filled with other celebrations and the Chelsea postmen were kept busy delivering letters, presents, and telegrams from every part of the globe.

The last months of her life were devoted to finishing off her reminiscences, in the last pages of which, far from dwelling on her own affairs, she wrote a long dissertation on the subject of style in the singing of folk songs and the vexed question of allowing them to acquire accompaniments and to be sung by professional singers. This was a subject on which she felt strongly and she had in recent years managed to persuade several singers, notably Thomas Hemsley, to fall in with her views. She wrote: 'To some it may seem that the realm of the concert hall is a far cry from the country cottage, which has been the home of the folk song for so many years. But folk song is not tied to its traditional setting. It is part of the great world of music. And it will retain its essential nature under the most diverse conditions provided that it is treated with artistic integrity.'[7]

On the last day of September 1976, Maud was invited to a dinner party by Martin Kingsbury of Faber & Faber, who had been a friend, and sometimes her publisher, for the twenty years since they had met at the Commonwealth Arts Festival in Liverpool. The company present could all have been her grandchildren or great-grandchildren. Earlier that day she had made two phone calls. One was to Jane van Boschan, since the 1940s her patient dressmaker and mender of worn-out clothes. What she had said was, 'Many Happy Returns. That's all you're getting!' Maud had always kept a birthday book, which she consulted scrupulously. The other call was to Ursula Vaughan Williams, not apparently apropos of any recent occurrence. She had rung up to say how much, over a period of nearly forty years, her friendship had meant to her. The dinner party was an excellent one and she returned happily in a taxi to Cadogan Square. She was taken ill and died in the early hours of the next morning.

In *The Times* of 2 October, Ursula wrote:

She was a true citizen of the world, and time did not blunt or mellow her lively and critical outlook, nor did she lose her delights and treasures of the intellect. Her friends will like to know that she was able to go to a committee meeting at Cecil Sharp House two days before her death, that the last evening of her life was spent enjoying a dinner party with young friends; and that she died peacefully in her home.[8]

On 30 November, in the Church of the Holy Sepulchre, Holborn Viaduct, known as the Musicians' Church, many friends gathered for a memorial service. The rector read a poem about dancing by the seventeenth-century poet John Davies, and a great friend and authority on folk song, the Rev. Kenneth Loveless, read from Ecclesiastes. The choir sang Vaughan Williams's motet *Valiant-for-Truth* from *The Pilgrim's Progress*, and the congregation joined in another Bunyan–Vaughan Williams collaboration, the hymn 'He Who Would Valiant Be', set to a folk tune he had collected, 'Our Captain Called All Hands'. Between the readings, Jean Stewart, an old friend from wartime parties, played on the viola 'She's Like the Swallow', the hauntingly beautiful tune Maud had discovered in Newfoundland, with which her name will always be associated.

Notes

The majority of the sources quoted in this biography are held in the Vaughan Williams Memorial Library, except for some privately held correspondence and typescripts to which the author was granted access.

The following abbreviations are used in the Notes: CJS – Cecil J. Sharp; MK – Maud Karpeles; VWML – London, Vaughan Williams Memorial Library.

Karpeles, *Cecil Sharp*: Maud Karpeles, *Cecil Sharp: His Life and Work* (London: Routlege & Kegan Paul, 1967).
Karpeles Diaries: VWML, Maud Karpeles Manuscript Collection, MK/3/226, Diary for 1916; MK/3/227, Diary for 1917.
MK autobiography: VWML, Maud Karpeles Manuscript Collection, MK/7/185, unpublished autobiography of Maud Karpeles.
MK correspondence: correspondence in private hands.
Sharp Correspondence: VWML, Cecil J. Sharp MSS, Correspondence.
Sharp Diaries: VWML, Cecil J. Sharp MSS, Miscellaneous material, CJS/7/12–15, American Diaries 1915–1918; online at http://library.efdss.org/exhibitions/sharpdiaries/sharpdiaries.html.
Slocombe, IFMC: Marie Slocombe, IFMC: The First Five Years, unpublished typescript.

Chapter 1

[1] MK autobiography, p. 1.
[2] MK autobiography, pp. 1–2.
[3] MK autobiography, p. 2.
[4] MK autobiography, p. 3.
[5] MK autobiography, p. 4.
[6] MK autobiography, p. 7.
[7] MK autobiography, p. 9.
[8] MK autobiography, p. 9.
[9] MK autobiography, p. 4.
[10] MK autobiography, pp. 4–5.
[11] MK autobiography, pp. 9–10.
[12] MK autobiography, p. 10.
[13] MK autobiography, p. 6.
[14] Ralph Vaughan Williams, *Some Thoughts on Beethoven's Choral Symphony, with writings on other musical subjects* (London: Oxford University Press, 1953), p. 133.
[15] MK autobiography, p. 6.
[16] MK autobiography, pp. 11–12.
[17] MK autobiography, p. 7.
[18] MK autobiography, p. 11.

Chapter 2

[1] MK autobiography, p. 13.
[2] MK autobiography, p. 13.
[3] MK autobiography, pp. 12–13.
[4] MK autobiography, p. 3.
[5] MK autobiography, pp. 15–16.
[6] MK autobiography, p. 14.
[7] MK autobiography, p. 16.
[8] MK autobiography, pp. 16–17.
[9] MK autobiography, p. 8.
[10] MK autobiography, p. 18.
[11] MK autobiography, p. 18.
[12] MK autobiography, p. 22.
[13] MK autobiography, pp. 25–27.
[14] MK autobiography, pp. 28–29.
[15] MK autobiography, p. 19.
[16] MK autobiography, p. 31.
[17] MK autobiography, p. 31.
[18] Mrs [Helen] Kennedy, 'Early Days (continued)', *EFDS News*, no. 9 (May 1925), pp. 277–83 (p. 281).
[19] Mrs [Helen] Kennedy, 'Early Days', *EFDS News*, no. 7 (May 1924), pp. 172–77 (p. 175).
[20] MK autobiography, p. 21.

21. VWML, Maud Karpeles Manuscript Collection, MK/3/1, CJS to MK, 19 May 1910.
22. Kennedy, 'Early Days', pp. 174–75.
23. MK autobiography, pp. 22–23.
24. MK autobiography, p. 23.

Chapter 3
1. MK autobiography, p. 24.
2. MK autobiography, p. 24.
3. MK autobiography, p. 34.
4. Karpeles *Cecil Sharp*, p. 51.
5. MK autobiography, p. 34.
6. Karpeles, *Cecil Sharp*, p. 41.
7. Karpeles, *Cecil Sharp*, p. 110.
8. Mrs [Helen] Kennedy, 'Early Days (continued)', *EFDS News*, no. 9 (May 1925), pp. 277–83 (p. 279).
9. W. D. Howells, *The Seen and Unseen at Stratford-on-Avon* (New York and London: Harper and Brothers, 1914), pp. 33–35.
10. Howells, *Seen and Unseen*, p. 79.
11. MK autobiography, p. 37.
12. Karpeles, *Cecil Sharp*, p. 117.
13. Karpeles, *Cecil Sharp*, p. 18.
14. VWML, Maud Karpeles Manuscript Collection, MK/3/33, CJS to MK, 3 September 1913.
15. VWML, Maud Karpeles Manuscript Collection, MK/3/34, CJS to MK, 5 September 1913.

Chapter 4
1. MK autobiography, p. 46.
2. Karpeles, *Cecil Sharp*, p. 121.
3. VWML, Cecil J. Sharp MSS, Correspondence, Box 1, CJS to Harley Granville-Barker, 29 September 1912.
4. VWML, Cecil J. Sharp MSS, Correspondence, Box 1, Harley Granville-Barker to CJS, 9 February 1914.
5. MK autobiography, p. 48.
6. VWML, Cecil J. Sharp MSS, Correspondence, Box 1, telegram Harley Granville-Barker to CJS, 15 December 1914.
7. VWML, Maud Karpeles Manuscript Collection, MK/3/35, CJS to MK, 21 December 1914.
8. MK autobiography, p. 49.
9. VWML, Maud Karpeles Manuscript Collection, MK/3/36, CJS to MK, 25 December 1914.
10. VWML, Maud Karpeles Manuscript Collection, MK/3/38, CJS to MK, 31 December 1914.
11. VWML, Maud Karpeles Manuscript Collection, MK/3/42, CJS to MK, 15 January 1915.
12. VWML, Maud Karpeles Manuscript Collection, MK/3/37, CJS to MK, 27 December 1914.
13. VWML, Maud Karpeles Manuscript Collection, MK/3/39, CJS to MK, 5 January 1915.
14. Sharp Diaries, 2 January 1915.
15. Sharp Diaries, 4 January 1915.
16. VWML, Maud Karpeles Manuscript Collection, MK/3/49, CJS to MK, 5 February 1915.
17. MK autobiography, p. 50.
18. VWML, Maud Karpeles Manuscript Collection, MK/3/53, CJS to MK, 21 February 1915.
19. VWML, Maud Karpeles Manuscript Collection, MK/3/57, CJS to MK, 11 March 1915.

Chapter 5
1. MK autobiography, p. 51.
2. MK autobiography, p. 52.
3. MK autobiography, p. 52.
4. Karpeles, *Cecil Sharp*, p. 130.
5. Karpeles, *Cecil Sharp*, p. 130.
6. Karpeles, *Cecil Sharp*, pp. 130–31.
7. Karpeles, *Cecil Sharp*, p. 131.
8. MK autobiography, p. 53.
9. MK autobiography, p. 54.
10. Karpeles, *Cecil Sharp*, p. 131.
11. Karpeles, *Cecil Sharp*, p. 131.

Chapter 6
1. VWML, Cecil J. Sharp MSS, Correspondence, Box 7, Folder A, Olive Dame Campbell to CJS, 4 September 1915.
2. VWML, Maud Karpeles Manuscript Collection, MK/3/68, CJS to MK, 18–23 February 1916.
3. Karpeles, *Cecil Sharp*, p. 132.
4. VWML, Maud Karpeles Manuscript Collection, MK/3/78, CJS to MK, 18 April 1916.
5. Sharp Diaries, 24 April 1916.
6. VWML, Maud Karpeles Manuscript Collection, MK/3/56, CJS to MK, 4 March 1915.
7. Sharp Diaries, 24 April 1916.

8 Karpeles, *Cecil Sharp*, p. 133.
9 MK autobiography, p. 59
10 Sharp Diaries, 30 June 1916.
11 VWML, Maud Karpeles Manuscript Collection, MK/4/13, Helen Storrow to MK, 13 July [1916].

Chapter 7
1 MK autobiography, p. 72.
2 Cecil J. Sharp, *Ballad Hunting in the Appalachians: Extracts of Letters Written by Cecil J. Sharp* (Boston: Todd [printer], 1916), p. 3.
3 MK autobiography, p. 73.
4 Sharp, *Ballad Hunting in the Appalachians*, p. 4.
5 Sharp Diaries, 28 July 1916.
6 VWML, Cecil J. Sharp MSS, Correspondence, Box 7, Folder A, Olive Dame Campbell to CJS, 4 September 1915.
7 Sharp, *Ballad Hunting in the Appalachians*, p. 4.
8 MK autobiography, p. 78.
9 Sharp Diaries, 4 August 1916.
10 Sharp Diaries, 30 July 1916.
11 MK autobiography, p. 73.
12 MK autobiography, p. 74.
13 MK autobiography, p. 75.
14 Karpeles, *Cecil Sharp*, p. 147.
15 Karpeles, *Cecil Sharp*, p. 150.
16 Sharp Diaries, 8 August 1916.
17 Karpeles, *Cecil Sharp*, p. 152.
18 Sharp Diaries, 7 September 1916.
19 Sharp Diaries, 11 September 1916.
20 Sharp Diaries, 11 September 1916.
21 Sharp Diaries, 13 September 1916.
22 Sharp Diaries, 20 September 1916.

Chapter 8
1 MK autobiography, p. 61.
2 MK autobiography, p. 62.
3 Sharp Diaries, 14 November 1916.
4 Sharp Diaries, 9 December 1916.
5 Sharp Diaries, 9 December 1916.
6 Sharp Diaries, 11 December 1916.
7 Karpeles, *Cecil Sharp*, p. 136.
8 Sharp Diaries, 27 February 1917.
9 Sharp Diaries, 3 March 1917.
10 Karpeles, *Cecil Sharp*, p. 136.
11 Sharp Diaries, 11 April 1917.
12 Karpeles Diaries, 14 April 1917.
13 Sharp Diaries, 14 April 1917.
14 Sharp Diaries, 17 April 1917.
15 Sharp Diaries, 18 April 1917.
16 Sharp Diaries, 16 April 1917.
17 Sharp Diaries, 25 April 1917.
18 Sharp Diaries, 5 May 1917.
19 Sharp Diaries, 6 May 1917.
20 Karpeles Diaries, 6 May 1917.
21 Sharp Diaries, 12 May 1917.
22 Sharp Diaries, 14 May 1917.
23 Sharp Diaries, 15 May 1917.
24 Karpeles, *Cecil Sharp*, pp. 157–58.
25 Sharp Diaries, 24 May 1917.
26 MK autobiography, p. 49.
27 Sharp Diaries, 28 May 1917.
28 Sharp Diaries, 6 June 1917.
29 Sharp Diaries, 10 June 1917.

Chapter 9
1 Karpeles Diaries, 21 June 1917.
2 Sharp Diaries, 26 June 1917.
3 Sharp Diaries, 29 June 1917.
4 Karpeles Diaries, 29 July 1917.
5 Karpeles, *Cecil Sharp*, p. 158,
6 Karpeles Diaries, 31 July 1917.
7 Sharp Diaries, 1 August 1917.
8 Sharp Diaries, 5 August 1917.
9 Karpeles Diaries, 5 August 1917.
10 Sharp Diaries, 7 August 1917.
11 VWML, Cecil J. Sharp MSS, Correspondence, Box 7, Folder B, CJS to Mrs Storrow, 26 August 1917.
12 Sharp Diaries, 12 August 1917.
13 Sharp Diaries, 15 August 1917.
14 Sharp Diaries, 20 August 1917.
15 Sharp Diaries, 24 August 1917.
16 Sharp Diaries, 29 August 1917.
17 Karpeles, *Cecil Sharp*, p. 161.
18 Karpeles, *Cecil Sharp*, p. 162.
19 Karpeles, *Cecil Sharp*, pp. 161–62.
20 Sharp Diaries, 31 August 1917.
21 Karpeles, *Cecil Sharp*, pp. 163–64.
22 Sharp Diaries, 10 September 1917.
23 Sharp Diaries, 12 September 1917.
24 Sharp Diaries, 15 September 1917.
25 Karpeles Diaries, 13 September 1917.
26 Karpeles Diaries, 18 September 1917.
27 Sharp Diaries, 18 September 1917.
28 Karpeles Diaries, 23 September 1917.
29 Karpeles Diaries, 28 September 1917.
30 Sharp Diaries, 1 October 1917.
31 Sharp Diaries, 1 October 1917.
32 Karpeles Diaries, 6 October 1917.
33 Sharp Diaries, 8 October 1917.
34 Karpeles Diaries, 17 October 1917.
35 Sharp Diaries, 20 October 1917.

36 Sharp Diaries, 22 November 1917.
37 Sharp Diaries, 23 November 1917.
38 Sharp Diaries, 1 December 1917.
39 Karpeles Diaries, 5 December 1917.
40 Sharp Diaries, 20 December 1917.
41 Sharp Diaries, 25 December 1917.
42 Sharp Diaries, 31 December 1917.

Chapter 10
1 Sharp Diaries, 1 January 1918.
2 Sharp Diaries, 9 January 1918.
3 Sharp Diaries, 21 January 1918.
4 Sharp Diaries, 19 January 1918.
5 Sharp Diaries, 8 February 1918.
6 Sharp Diaries, 10 March 1918.
7 Sharp Diaries, 15 March 1918.
8 Sharp Diaries, 19 March 1918.
9 Sharp Diaries, 20 March 1918.
10 Sharp Diaries, 24 March 1918.
11 Sharp Diaries, 13 April 1918.
12 Sharp Diaries, 13 April 1918.
13 Sharp Diaries, 16 April 1918.
14 Karpeles Diaries, 15 April 1918.
15 Sharp Diaries, 1 May 1918.
16 Sharp Diaries, 4 May 1918.
17 Sharp Diaries, 6 May 1918.
18 Karpeles Diaries, 6 May 1918.
19 Karpeles Diaries, 9 May 1918.
20 Sharp Diaries, 9 May 1918.
21 Sharp Diaries, 10 May 1918.
22 Karpeles Diaries, 10 May 1918.
23 Sharp Diaries, 27 May 1918.
24 Sharp Diaries, 31 May 1918.
25 Sharp Diaries, 1 June 1918.
26 Sharp Diaries, 2 June 1918.
27 Sharp Diaries, 9 June 1918.
28 Sharp Diaries, 11 June 1918.
29 Karpeles Diaries, 12 June 1918.

Chapter 11
1 Karpeles Diaries, 26 June 1918.
2 Sharp Diaries, 26 June 1918.
3 Karpeles Diaries, 26 June 1918.
4 Karpeles Diaries, 5 July 1918.
5 MK autobiography, p. 69.
6 Sharp Diaries, 23 July 1918.
7 Sharp Diaries, 28 July 1918.
8 Karpeles Diaries, 5 August 1918.
9 Sharp Diaries, 9 August 1918.
10 Sharp Diaries, 12 August 1918.
11 Sharp Diaries, 16 August 1918.
12 Sharp Diaries, 16 August 1918.
13 Sharp Diaries, 19 August 1918.
14 Karpeles Diaries, 27 August 1918.
15 Sharp Diaries, 22 August 1918
16 Karpeles Diaries, 12 September 1918.
17 Sharp Diaries, 15 October 1918.
18 Sharp Diaries, 18 October 1918.
19 Sharp Diaries, 13 October 1918.
20 Sharp Diaries, 18 October 1918.
21 MK autobiography, p. 67.
22 Sharp Diaries, 30 October 1918.
23 Sharp Diaries, 28 October 1918.
24 Sharp Diaries, 3 November 1918.
25 Sharp Diaries, 7 November 1918.
26 Karpeles Diaries, 11 November 1918.
27 Karpeles Diaries, 11 November 1918.
28 Sharp Diaries, 11 November 1918.
29 Sharp Diaries, 13 November 1918.
30 Karpeles Diaries, 16 November 1918.
31 Sharp Diaries, 27 November 1918.
32 Karpeles Diaries, 27 November 1918.
33 Sharp Diaries, 28 November 1918.
34 Sharp Diaries, 5 December 1918.
35 Sharp Diaries, 21 December 1918.

Chapter 12
1 Karpeles, *Cecil Sharp*, p. 172.
2 Karpeles, *Cecil Sharp*, p. 172.
3 Karpeles, *Cecil Sharp*, p. 172.
4 Karpeles, *Cecil Sharp*, p. 173.
5 MK autobiography, p. 100.
6 Karpeles, *Cecil Sharp*, p. 176.
7 Karpeles, *Cecil Sharp*, p. 174.
8 Karpeles, *Cecil Sharp*, p. 174.
9 VWML, Maud Karpeles Manuscript Collection, MK/4/12, Arthur Somervell to MK, 9 October 1926.
10 A. H. Fox Strangways, 'Our Folk Dances', *Music & Letters*, 4 (1923), 321–33 (p. 321).
11 Fox Strangways, 'Our Folk Dances', p. 328.
12 MK autobiography, p. 105.
13 MK autobiography, p. 105.
14 MK autobiography, pp. 106–07.
15 MK autobiography, p. 107.
16 MK autobiography, p. 108.
17 Karpeles, *Cecil Sharp*, p. 177.
18 MK autobiography, p. 108–09.
19 MK autobiography, p. 108.
20 MK autobiography, p. 109.
21 MK autobiography, p. 113–14.
22 A. H. Fox Strangways, *Cecil Sharp* (London: Oxford University Press, 1933), p. 189.
23 MK autobiography, p. 112.
24 Fox Strangways, *Cecil Sharp*, p. 190.
25 Karpeles, *Cecil Sharp*, p. 189.

[26] Karpeles *Cecil Sharp*, p. 191.
[27] MK autobiography, p. 115.

Chapter 13
[1] MK autobiography, p. 117.
[2] MK autobiography, p. 117.
[3] VWML, Jane Schofield Diaries, 23 June 1924.
[4] Schofield Diaries, 4 August 1924.
[5] Schofield Diaries, 5 August 1924.
[6] Schofield Diaries, 8 August 1924.
[7] MK autobiography, p. 119.
[8] MK autobiography, p. 131.
[9] MK autobiography, pp. 125–26.
[10] MK autobiography, p. 133.
[11] MK autobiography, p. 127.
[12] Schofield Diaries, 9 August 1927.
[13] MK autobiography, p. 146.
[14] MK autobiography, p. 146.
[15] MK autobiography, p. 147.
[16] MK autobiography, p. 147.
[17] Maud Karpeles, 'The Abram Morris Dance', *Journal of the English Folk Dance and Song Society*, 1 (1932), 55–59.
[18] MK autobiography, p. 153.
[19] MK autobiography, p. 148.
[20] Schofield Diaries, 7 [6] August 1927.
[21] *Cecil Sharp House: A Souvenir* (London: EFDSS, 1980), [p. 1].
[22] *Cecil Sharp House: A Souvenir*, [p. 2].
[23] 'The Cecil Sharp Memorial', *EFDS News*, no. 21 (September 1929), 193–97 (p. 194).
[24] MK autobiography, pp. 142–43.
[25] Karpeles, *Cecil Sharp*, p. 25.

Chapter 14
[1] MK autobiography, p. 157.
[2] MK autobiography, p. 157.
[3] MK autobiography, p. 157.
[4] MK autobiography, pp. 158–59.
[5] MK correspondence, MK to Helen Kennedy.
[6] MK correspondence, MK to Helen Kennedy.
[7] MK autobiography, pp. 160–61.
[8] MK correspondence, MK to Helen Kennedy.
[9] MK correspondence, MK to Helen Kennedy.
[10] MK autobiography, p. 162.
[11] MK correspondence, MK to Helen Kennedy.
[12] MK correspondence, MK to Helen Kennedy.
[13] MK correspondence, MK to Helen Kennedy.
[14] MK correspondence, MK to Helen Kennedy.
[15] MK autobiography, pp. 164–66.
[16] MK autobiography, p. 169.
[17] MK autobiography, p. 170.
[18] MK autobiography, p. 170.
[19] MK autobiography, p. 171.
[20] MK autobiography, p. 137a.
[21] Karpeles, *Cecil Sharp*, p. 193.
[22] 'Opening of Cecil Sharp House', *EFDS News*, no. 24 (September 1930), 297–99 (p. 298).

Chapter 15
[1] Henry W. Nevinson, *Last Changes, Last Chances* (London: Nisbet & Co., 1928) pp. 162-63.
[2] MK autobiography, p. 123.
[3] MK autobiography, p. 136.
[4] MK autobiography, p. 139.
[5] MK autobiography, pp. 171–72.
[6] MK autobiography, p. 174.
[7] MK autobiography, p. 175.
[8] MK autobiography, p. 176.
[9] MK autobiography, p. 177.
[10] MK autobiography, pp. 180–81.
[11] MK autobiography, pp. 181–82.
[12] MK autobiography, p. 182.
[13] MK autobiography, p. 182–83.
[14] MK autobiography, p. 183.
[15] MK autobiography, p. 186.
[16] MK autobiography, p. 188.
[17] MK autobiography, p. 191.
[18] MK autobiography, p. 190.
[19] Arthur Batchelor, 'A Concept of Europe', *EFDSS News*, no. 42 (September 1935), 245–52 (p. 246).
[20] MK autobiography, p. 189. In fact, a silent film was made by Doris Plaister for the EFDSS, showing the arrival of the teams in London, Thames river trip, procession through Hyde Park, and Open Air Theatre performances (film deposited with British Film Institute; DVD copy available in VWML).
[21] MK autobiography, pp. 190–91.
[22] MK autobiography, p. 191.
[23] Batchelor, 'A Concept of Europe', p. 245.

Chapter 16
[1] MK autobiography, p. 194.
[2] MK autobiography, pp. 194–96.

3. MK autobiography, p. 197.
4. MK autobiography, p. 197.
5. MK autobiography, pp. 197–98.
6. MK autobiography, p. 203.
7. MK autobiography, p. 203.
8. MK autobiography, p. 204.
9. MK autobiography, p. 8.
10. MK correspondence, MK to Ursula Wood (Vaughan Williams).
11. MK autobiography, p. 207.
12. MK autobiography, p. 206.
13. MK autobiography, p. 208.
14. MK correspondence, MK to Ursula Wood (Vaughan Williams).
15. MK autobiography, pp. 208–09.
16. MK correspondence, MK to Ursula Wood (Vaughan Williams).
17. MK correspondence, MK to Ursula Wood (Vaughan Williams).
18. MK correspondence, MK to Ursula Wood (Vaughan Williams).
19. MK autobiography, p. 210.
20. MK autobiography, p. 211.
21. MK correspondence, MK to Ursula Wood (Vaughan Williams).
22. MK autobiography, p. 212.

Chapter 17
1. MK autobiography, p. 213.
2. MK autobiography, p. 213.
3. MK autobiography, p. 214.
4. MK autobiography, p. 218.
5. Slocombe, IFMC.
6. MK autobiography, pp. 220–21.
7. MK autobiography, p. 225.
8. Tola Korian, 'The Venice Festival: Some Impressions of a Visitor', *Journal of the International Folk Music Council*, 2 (1950), 3–5 (p. 4).
9. Douglas Kennedy, ' England's Ritual Dances', *Journal of the International Folk Music Council*, 2 (1950), 8–10 (p. 9).
10. Slocombe, IFMC.
11. MK autobiography, p. 227.
12. Slocombe, IFMC.
13. Slocombe, IFMC.
14. Karpeles, *Cecil Sharp*, p. 170.
15. Karpeles, *Cecil Sharp*, p. 170.
16. 'Mrs Storrow', *English Dance and Song*, 9.2 (December 1944), 16.
17. MK autobiography, p. 232.
18. MK autobiography, p. 229.
19. MK autobiography, p. 229.
20. Slocombe, IFMC.
21. Slocombe, IFMC.
22. MK correspondence, MK to Ralph Vaughan Williams.
23. MK autobiography, p. 223.
24. MK autobiography, pp. 223–24.
25. Slocombe, IFMC.
26. Slocombe, IFMC.
27. MK autobiography, p. 247.
28. MK autobiography, p. 231.
29. MK autobiography, p. 156.
30. MK autobiography, p. 240.
31. 'Editorial', *Journal of the International Folk Music Council*, 8 (1956), 1–2 (p. 1).
32. [Frank Howes], 'Swan Song of Folk Music', *The Times*, 23 July 1956, p. 11.
33. MK autobiography, p. 244.
34. MK autobiography, p. 244.
35. MK autobiography, pp. 245–46.

Chapter 18
1. MK autobiography, pp. 246–47.
2. MK autobiography, p. 248.
3. MK autobiography, p. 252.
4. MK autobiography, p. 253.
5. MK autobiography, p. 253.
6. MK autobiography, p. 256.
7. MK autobiography, p. 261.
8. MK autobiography, p. 262.
9. MK autobiography, p. 262.
10. MK autobiography, p. 263.
11. G. M. Story, 'A Folksong Collector', in *Selected University Orations* (St John's: Harry Cuff Publications, 1984), pp. 73–74.

Chapter 19
1. MK autobiography, p. 276.
2. MK autobiography, pp. 277–78.
3. MK autobiography, p. 278.
4. Klaus Wachsmann, 'In Memoriam: Maud Karpeles (1885–1976)', *Yearbook of the International Folk Music Council*, 8 (1976), 9–11 (p. 10).
5. MK autobiography, p. 271.
6. MK autobiography, p. 272.
7. MK autobiography, p. 282.
8. 'Dr Maud Karpeles: Folk Music and Dance Revival', *The Times*, 2 October 1976.

Select Bibliography

Selected works by, and edited by, Maud Karpeles:

Fox Strangways, A. H., with Maud Karpeles, *Cecil Sharp* (London: Oxford University Press, 1933).
——, and Maud Karpeles, *Cecil Sharp*, 2nd edn (London: Oxford University Press, 1955).
Karpeles, Maud, *Twelve Traditional Country Dances*, pianoforte arrangements by R. Vaughan Williams (London: Novello for the English Folk Dance Society, 1931).
——, 'English Folk Dances: Their Survival and Revival', *Folklore*, 43 (1932), 123–41.
——, 'The Abram Morris Dance', *Journal of the English Folk Dance and Song Society*, 1 (1932), 55–59.
——, 'A Return Visit to the Appalachian Mountains', *Journal of the English Folk Dance and Song Society*, 6 (1951), 77–82.
——, 'Some Reflections on Authenticity in Folk Music', *Journal of the International Folk Music Council*, 3 (1951), 10–14.
——, 'Definition of Folk Music', *Journal of the International Folk Music Council*, 7 (1955), 6–7.
——, ed., *Folk Songs of Europe*, International Folk Song Anthologies (UNESCO) (London: Novello, 1956).
——, ed., *The Collecting of Folk Music and Other Ethnomusicological Material: A Manual for Field Workers* (London: International Folk Music Council and Royal Anthropological Institute, 1958).
——, *Cecil Sharp: His Life and Work* (London: Routledge & Kegan Paul, 1967).
——, ed., *Folk Songs from Newfoundland* (London: Faber and Faber, 1971).
——, *An Introduction to English Folk Song* (London: Oxford University Press, 1973).
——, ed., *Cecil Sharp's Collection of English Folk Songs*, 2 vols (London: Oxford University Press, 1974).
——, ed., *The Crystal Spring: English Folk Songs Collected by Cecil Sharp* (London: Oxford University Press, 1975).
Sharp, Cecil J., *English Folk Songs from the Southern Appalachians*, ed. by Maud Karpeles, 2 vols (London: Oxford University Press, 1932).
——, *The Country Dance Book, Part 1, Containing a Description of Eighteen Traditional Dances Collected in Country Villages*, rev. and ed. by Maud Karpeles, 2nd edn (London: Novello, 1934).
——, *English Folk-Song: Some Conclusions*, 2nd edn with Preface by Maud Karpeles (London: Novello, 1936); 3rd edn rev. by Maud Karpeles (London: Methuen, 1954); 4th edn rev. by Maud Karpeles (London: Mercury Books, 1965).
——, *The Sword Dances of Northern England*, Part III, rev. by Maud Karpeles, 2nd edn (London: Novello, 1951).
Sharp, Cecil J., and Maud Karpeles, *The Country Dance Book, Part V, Containing the Running Set Collected in Kentucky, U.S.A.* (London: Novello, 1918).
——, ——, *Nine English Folk Songs from the Southern Appalachian Mountains* (London: Oxford University Press, 1967).
——, ——, *Eighty English Folk Songs from the Southern Appalachians*, (London: Faber, 1968).

Selected secondary sources:

Atkinson, David, 'Resources in the Vaughan Williams Memorial Library: The Maud Karpeles Manuscript Collection', *Folk Music Journal*, 8 (2001), 90–101.
Boyes, Georgina. '"The lady that is with you": Maud Pauline Karpeles (1885–1976) and the Folk Revival', in *Step Change: New Views on Traditional Dance*, ed. Georgina Boyes (London: Francis Boutle, 2001).
Carpenter, Carole Henderson, 'Forty Years Later: Maud Karpeles in Newfoundland', in *Folklore Studies in Honour of Herbert Halpert: A Festschrift*, ed. Kenneth S.

Goldstein and Neil V. Rosenberg (St John's: Memorial University of Newfoundland, 1980), pp. 111–24.

Gregory, David, 'Maud Karpeles, Newfoundland, and the Crisis of the Folksong Revival, 1924–1935', *Newfoundland Studies*, 16 (2000), 151–65.

Lovelace, Martin, 'Unnatural Selection: Maud Karpeles's Newfoundland Field Diaries', in *Folk Song, Tradition, Revival, and Re-Creation*, ed. by Ian Russell and David Atkinson (Aberdeen: Elphinstone Institute, University of Aberdeen, 2004), pp. 284–98.

Story, G. M., 'A Folksong Collector: Maud Karpeles, 22 May 1970', in *Selected University Orations* (St John's: Harry Cuff Publications, 1984), pp. 73–74.

Select Discography

Maud Karpeles on her collecting trips in the 1950s made a number of recordings for the BBC (some in collaboration with Peter Kennedy or Patrick Shuldham-Shaw), which are listed here, along with the names of the performers.

BBC 17141 (1950): Dol Small, Nellysford, VA; Mrs Puckett, Afton, VA.

BBC 17142 (1950): Mrs Victoria Morris, Mt Fair, VA; Mrs Oscar Allen, Lynchburg, VA.

BBC 17143 (1950): Mrs Oscar Allen, Lynchburg, VA; C. B. Wohlford, Marion VA.

BBC 17144 (1950): Horton Barker, Chilhowie, VA.

BBC 17145 (1950): Horton Barker, Chilhowie, VA; Mrs Donald Shelton, Flag Pond, TN; Mrs Maud Long, Hot Springs, NC; Mrs Charlie Noel, Hot Springs, NC.

BBC 17146 (1950): W. H. Stockton, Flag Pond, TN; Mrs Long, Hot Springs, NC; Mrs Shelton, Flag Pond, TN; Miss Landers, Jonesboro, TN.

BBC 17147 (1950): Miss Landers, Jonesboro, TN; Mrs Long, Hot Springs, NC; Andy J. Edwards, Coffey Ridge, TN.

BBC 17778 (1952): William Squires, Holford, Somerset; George Bunston, Hambridge Green, Somerset; Edwin Thomas, Allerford, Somerset.

BBC 17779 (1952): Sidney Richards, Curry Rivel, Somerset.

BBC 17780 (1952): Sidney Richards, Curry Rivel, Somerset.

BBC 17781 (1952): Sidney Richards, Curry Rivel, Somerset; Frederick Crossman, Huish Episcopi, Somerset.

BBC 17782 (1952): Edwin Thomas, Allerford, Somerset.

BBC 18618 (1952): John William Partridge, Cinderford, Gloucestershire; William Payne, Gloucester, Gloucestershire.

BBC 18619 (1952): Peter Jones, Bromsash, Herefordshire.

BBC 18620 (1952): Peter Jones, Bromsash, Herefordshire.

BBC 23792 (1955): Mrs Corrie Grover, Berwyn, PA.

BBC 23793 (1955): Mrs J. (Florence) Puckett, Afton, VA; Mrs J. L. Leila Yowell, Charlottesville, VA; Mrs Emma Shelton, Alleghany, NC.

BBC 23794 (1955): Mrs Donald (Emma) Shelton, Alleghany, NC.

BBC 23799 (1955): Mrs Matty S. Dameron, Stuarts Draft, VA; Mrs Donald (Emma) Shelton, Alleghany, NC.

BBC 23800 (1955): Mrs Donald (Emma) Shelton, Alleghany, NC.

BBC 23801 (1955): The Sugarloaf Sheltons, Alleghany, NC.

BBC 23802 (1955): Mrs Oscar Allen, Lynchburg, VA; Mrs Martha Wiseman Aldridge, Three Mile, NC.

The Headington (Oxfordshire) morris dancer and concertina player William Kimber was recorded talking to Maud Karpeles by Peter Kennedy in 1963: EFDSS LP 1001 (1963).

A copy of a BBC recording of an interview with Maud Karpeles, of uncertain provenance but thought to have been used in a radio broadcast called *60 Years of Folk*, is held in the Vaughan Williams Memorial Library: 400 CDA BBC.

Note on the author

Simona Pakenham
25 September 1916 – 17 November 2010

Simona Pakenham studied at the Central School of Speech and Drama and at the Old Vic Theatre School. Between 1936 and 1955 she acted, chiefly in repertory, often directed by her husband, Noel Iliff, and worked as a radio announcer at the BBC during the Second World War.

Her first book, *Ralph Vaughan Williams: A Discovery of his Music* was inspired as a result of her hearing the composer's Fourth Symphony for the first time. She wrote the libretto for the nativity play *The First Nowell* with music by Vaughan Williams; this was first performed in 1958 at the Drury Lane Theatre with her husband directing.

She also wrote *Pigtails and Pernod* (an account of her childhood spent in Dieppe), *60 Miles from England* (1967, describing the English 'colony' in Dieppe), *In the Absence of the Emperor* (1968, a history of events during Napoleon's exile on Elba), and *Cheltenham, a Biography* (1971).

Acknowledgements

We wish to thank the following people for their help and support with this project, and for their permission to publish:

    Nicolas Bell (British Library)
    Georgina Boyes
    Hugh Cobbe (RVW Trust)
    Tony Engle (Topic Records)
    Roland Goodbody (University of New Hampshire)
    Ju Gosling
    Reg Hall
    David Iliff
    Bryan Ledgard
    Roger Marriott
    Barry Ould (Percy Grainger Estate)
    Simona Pakenham
    Judy Savage (Pinewoods Camp)
    Derek Schofield
    Stephanie Smith (Smithsonian Institution, Washington, DC)
    Katy Spicer (EFDSS)
    Danny Walkowitz
    Mike Yates.

Photo credits

Except as indicated below, all images are from the EFDSS Photograph Collection.

p. 12:   G. T. Kimmins, *The Guild of Play Book of Festival and Dance* (London: Curwen, 1907)

pp. 26–7, 133, 139, 140, 143, 146–7, 177, 188–9, 191, 192, 200, 228: VWML, Peter Kennedy Collection, Maud Karpeles Materials

p. 58:   University of New Hampshire Library, Milne Special Collections, CDSS Archives (MC 140)

pp. 63–4: VWML, Cecil J. Sharp MSS, Miscellaneous Materials

p. 118: VWML, Cecil J. Sharp MSS, Field Notebooks

pp. 66–7, 69, 80, 81, 85, 93, 96, 103, 106, 115, 117, 120, 126: VWML, Cecil Sharp Photograph Collection

p. 78:   John C. Campbell Folk School

p. 128: Percy Grainger Estate

p. 231: Topic Records / British Library

p. 232: British Library (all rights reserved)

p. 271: David Iliff Collection.

Every effort has been made to source the owners of images and we welcome communication with anybody who would claim ownership of any of the images contained in this book.

Index

Abbot's Bromley Horn Dance, 143
Abingdon morris dance, 148
Abram Circle Dance, 165–6
Aldrich, Richard, 71, 90, 113, 116, 121, 151
Allen, Sir Hugh, 158, 212
Algonquin Hotel, 56, 60, 74, 81, 86, 90, 99, 109, 112
Amherst College, 75, 98, 159, 172, 175, 190, 193
Ampthill, Lady, 171, 199
Andral, Maguy, 208, 224
Anglo-Basque festival, 187–90
Appalachian Mountains, 77–85, 90–7, 99–107, 114–21, 123–7, 226–7, 235
    black population, 99, 125
    diet, 82, 99, 125
    'grippe' infections, 92, 94
    missionaries and religion, 80, 84, 91. 95, 101, 106, 124–5
    modernization, 227
    mountain people, 79–80, 164
    picture palaces, 114
    sanitation, 90, 100
    sulphur springs, 119, 121
    suspicions of spying, 95, 116, 118
    travel, 81–2, 106, 125
Aran Islands, 208
Arbeau, Thoinot, 149
Archive internationale de la danse, 208
Australia, 17, 44, 198
Avril, Elsie, 30, 143–4, 158–60, 164

Bach, J. S., 8
    St Matthew Passion, 210
Bach Choir, 210, 247
Baldwin, Stanley, 158
Bampton morris dance, 25
Band, Robin, 244
Barbeau, Marius, 241
Baring-Gould, Rev. Sabine, 32–3
Barnett, Marjorie, 159
Bartók, Béla, 236, 245
Batchelor, Arthur, 204
Battle of the Somme, 81
Bayonne, 187, 253–5
BBC, 158–9, 227, 230, 240, 246, 252
Beaumont, Cyril W., 149
Beethoven, Ludwig van, 8
Belgrade, 205

Belstead House School, 142
Bennett, Arnold, 89
Benson, Frank R., 14, 42, 50
Berea College, 94–5
Berlin, 10–12
Biarritz, 232–3
Blato, 208
Bloomsbury House, 210–12, 217
Board of Education, 138, 145
Bondfield, Margaret, 158
Boughton, Rutland, 144
Boult, Adrian, 161
Bowyer, Molly, 119
Brackley morris dance, 148
Bronson, Professor Bertrand, 235
Bryan, Rev. Dr, 124
Bucharest, 244
Budapest, 236–7, 245
Bunyan, John, 257
Burford, 148
Busoni, Ferruccio, 10
Butterworth, George, 21, 41, 45, 54, 59, 71, 83–4, 130
Buxbaum, Friedrich, 213–14
Buxton, 161, 167
Byrd, William, 182

Callery, Mrs Dawson, 59, 62, 73–4, 90, 131
Cambridge University, 145, 153, 156
Campbell, John, 76–80, 83, 90, 94–5, 97, 100, 104, 107–8, 129
Campbell, Olive Dame, 76–9, 83–4, 95, 100, 107–8, 129, 142
    and Appalachian collections, 62–3, 70, 72, 108, 193
Carey, Clive, 144, 179, 195
Carnegie Trust, 158, 166, 183
Caruso, Enrico, 109
Cecil Sharp House, 158, 175, 184, 190, 193, 195–7, 227, 237, 256
    building and opening, 167–71, 182–3
    and dance festival (1935), 199, 204
    and IFMC, 224, 229–30, 245
    war damage, 217, 219
Cecil Sharp's Collection of English Folk Songs, 251
Chelsea Physical Training College, 19, 23–5, 151
Chelsea Polytechnic, 139–40, 144, 149, 151,

Index

156
Chopin, Frédéric, 8, 89
Christian Council for Refugees, 212, 219
Clare College, Cambridge, 156
Coffey family, 116
Cohen, Harriet, 212
Commission internationale des arts populaires (CIAP), 221, 223
Commonwealth Arts Festival, 236, 256
Conant, Lily (née Roberts), 61–3, 75, 90, 98, 108–9, 113, 123, 129, 175
Conant, Richard, 109, 113, 123, 175
Corelli, Marie, 137
Corfield, Frederick, 219
Cossart, Ernest, 57
Country Dance and Song Society of America, 59
Cowell, Sidney Robertson, 226
Craig, Gordon, 10
Crossman, Fred, 240
Crystal Spring, The, 214, 251
Czech Trio, 212

Daking, D. C., 137
d'Arányi, Jelly, 212
Davies, John, 257
Davis, Miss, 124
de Long, Miss, 104
Dearmer, Rev. Percy, 129, 151
Denman, Hercy, 150
Dhiagilev ballet, 21
Dimmock family, 174
Donald, Laura, 119
Dorking Festival, 230
Duncan, Isadora, 10, 59–60
Dyson, George, 212

Eban, Abba, 244
Eichenseer, Adolf, 254
Eighty English Folk Songs, 251
Eisenhower, General Dwight D., 220
Eliot, Maine, 64–5, 68, 75
Emerson, Fred and Isabel, 175, 179, 249, 253
England, John, 17, 240
English Folk Dance and Song Society (EFDSS)
    award to MK, 246
    and dance festival (1935), 199–204
    formation, 195
    and IFMC, 223, 229–30
    and royalties dispute, 208–9, 229
    Sharp centenary concerts, 239–40
    and standards in folk dancing, 228–9
English Folk Dance Society (EFDS)

American branches, 59, 74–5, 86, 90, 108, 159
    formation, 25, 29–32, 34–43
    and international dances, 187–90
    memorial fund, 152–3, 156, 158–60, 166–7, 170, 175, 186
    merger with Folk-Song Society, 195
    North American tour, 179, 184
    post-war activities, 133–50, 152–64, 166–7
    wartime activities, 133, 137
English Singers, 144, 160, 182
Esperance Girls' Club, 19
Etherington, Rev. Francis, 33, 161, 198, 209–10, 215, 241, 247
Etherington, Gordon, 210

Fabian Society, 13, 160
Fairbanks, Douglas, 114
Ferguson, Howard, 216
Ffrangcon-Davies, Gwen, 144–5, 195
Finzi, Gerald, 216
First World War, 24, 51, 54, 71, 83, 112–14, 123
    armistice, 125, 127, 129
    troops and folk dancing, 137
Fish, Edith, 79–81
Fisher, H. A. L., 138, 152–3, 170, 183
Fiske, Roger, 252
Fitzgerald, Betty, 116
Fitzgerald, Philander, 116
Flaherty, Robert, 208
Fletcher, Henry Markham, 167
Florrie (MK's maid), 213–14
Flower, Sir Archibald, 29, 70
folk clubs, 196
folk dances
    Călușari, 201–4, 207
    cushion dance, 175–6
    Kola, 206
    Kumpanija, 207–8, 244
    Moresco, 207
    'Running Set', 104–5, 107–8, 114, 136, 155, 160, 184
    Russalija, 207
    'Square Eight', 114
    see also morris dances
Folk Music and Education conference, 236
Folk-Song Society, 195
Folk Songs from Newfoundland, 251
Forest of Dean, 234
Foss, Charlotte, 108
Fox Strangways, A. H., 61, 142, 150, 193–5, 198
France, Anatole, *The Dumb Wife*, 56–8

Frank (bathing-machine attendant), 4–5, 184
Freiburg, 224, 236
Fry, C. B., 28

Gadd, May, 159
Gentry, Jane, 84
George, Graham, 248, 253
Ghana, 246–7
Gilchrist, Anne, 193
Gilman, Susan, 59, 62, 75, 90, 98, 108, 122–3, 131
Gilmour, T. Lennox, 29
Gomme, Lady, 29
Goossens, Leon, 160
Grainger, Percy, 122–3
Granville-Barker, Harley, 30, 50–1, 56–8, 60, 158, 161, 183
Green Mountains, 159
Greene, Plunkett, 160, 167, 195
Grove Park Inn, 95, 107, 125
Guild of Play, 12
gypsies, 234

Hake, Miss, 7–8, 10
Halifax, Lord, 199
Hambridge, 17, 198, 240
Hamilton House School, 7–8, 10, 13, 21
Harvard University, 235
Headington morris dance, 17, 30, 171
Heffer, Marjorie, 222
Heffer, Mary, 155
Heilbut, Emil, 11
Heilbut, Katie (Katie Kacser), 148–9, 216, 255
Heirn, Emmy, 214
Helston Furry Dance, 32
Hemsley, Thomas, 256
Hensley, Emma (Emma Shelton), 82–3, 108, 129, 227
Henson, Ben, 100
Herbage, Julian, 252
Hervey, Mrs Dudley, 142
Hess, Myra, 212, 216
Hindman Settlement School, 104–5
HMS *Glowworm*, 219
Holst, Gustav, 57, 61, 71, 153, 158, 160–1
Holst, Imogen, 153, 161, 204, 213
Howells, W. D., 35, 40
Howes, Frank, 229, 246
Hughes, Dom Anselm, 221
Hyde Park, 143, 152, 199

Iden Payne, Ben, 74, 88, 122
Ileana, Princess, 199
Incorporated Society of Musicians, 212

Indiana University, 225–6, 235
Instone, Anna, 252
International Folk Dance Council, 204, 222
International Folk Dance Festival (1935), 199–204, 222
International Folk Music Council (IFMC), 222–54
   authenticity debates, 224–6
   Basle conference, 223–4
   Bayonne conference, 253–5
   Biarritz conference, 232–3
   Cecil Sharp House conference, 229–30
   definition debates, 229–30, 235, 248
   Ghana conference, 246–7
   Indiana conference, 225–6
   Jamaica conference, 252–3, 255
   and politics, 233, 239
   radio committee, 227–8, 230, 246, 248
   São Paulo conference, 235
   Venice conference, 224–5
   Yugoslavia conference, 227–8
International Music Council, 224, 241
Introduction to English Folk Song, An, 252
Invalid Children's Aid Association, 11

Jacques, Reginald, 161
Jamaica, 252–3, 255
Jenkins, Alec, 222
Jenkins, Sir Gilmour, 222, 240
Jerusalem, 244
Jesuits, 215
Johnson, Dr, 90–1
Jusserand, M., 118

Karpeles, Arthur, 1–2, 12, 33, 56, 88, 95, 255
Karpeles, Emily, 1–2, 4, 24
Karpeles, Florence, 1–2, 7, 131, 255
Karpeles, Helen, *see* Kennedy, Helen
Karpeles, Joseph Nicolaus, 1, 24, 54, 88, 131
Karpeles, Lucy, 1–2, 7, 11, 148, 255
Karpeles, Maud
   appearance, 10, 184, 252
   her autobiography, 252, 254–6
   awarded OBE, 240
   awarded Freedom of EFDSS, 246
   awarded honorary degrees, 241, 245, 248
   and broadcasting, 159, 252
   'busman's holiday', 205–8
   and Cecil Sharp House, 170–1, 182–4
   childhood, 1–9
   and cooking, 214
   her death, 256–7
   her diaries, 88–90, 131
   dispute with EFDSS, 208–9, 229

education, 6–9
enmities, 216, 229
expressions of pleasure, 230, 232
and formation of EFDS, 25, 29–32, 34–43
and formation of IFMC, 222–4
friendship with Ursula Vaughan Williams, 210–11, 255–6
and German language, 8, 10
and hats, 131, 184
health, 98, 101–2, 104, 111–13, 127, 210, 215, 233, 241, 245, 252, 254–5
and Henry Nevinson, 184–6
independent collecting, 164–6, 230, 233–4
and international dance and song, 187–90
and International Folk Dance Festival, 199–204
introduction to folk dance, 19–28
and lecturing, 161, 164
and literature, 8–9, 89
meeting with Sharp, 14–15, 19–21, 43
and *A Midsummer Night's Dream*, 51
and music, 6–8, 10–11
Newfoundland trips, 172, 175–9, 190–3
and politics, 13, 152
publications, 166, 214, 251–2
and refugees, 210–14, 219
and religion, 5, 8, 13, 152, 198, 210, 215
and Sharp biography, 193–5, 227
and Sharp household, 43–5, 48–9, 88, 132–3, 145, 156, 245
Sharp's 'adopted daughter', 45, 94
and Sharp's death, 150–2, 156, 184
and standards in folk dancing, 228–9
and Stratford festivals, 13–14
and theatrical folk performances, 145
in USA (1915), 62–8
in USA (1916), 73–88
in USA (1917–18), 88–131
USA return visits, 159, 225–7, 236
war work, 73, 212
Kay, Mattie, 24, 42, 48, 57, 59, 144
Kendall, Nellie, 8
Kennedy, Douglas, 70–1, 132, 210, 213–14
and Cecil Sharp House, 167, 170, 219, 229
and EFDS, 32, 41, 150, 152–3, 158–60, 164, 167, 179, 190
and Helen's death, 255
and IFMC, 225, 229, 235
marriage, 49–50, 54, 61
and wartime, 54, 71, 213–15, 219
Kennedy, Helen, 42, 70
Kennedy, Helen (née Karpeles)
and Cecil Sharp House, 175, 182, 229
childhood, 1–2

her death, 255
and EFDS, 25, 29–32, 34–43, 70, 133, 138, 160–1, 167
introduction to folk dance, 20–8
marriage, 49–50, 54, 61
and Stratford festivals, 13–14
and wartime, 214–15, 219
Kennedy, John, 133, 205–8, 219, 222, 244
Kennedy, Peter, 230, 234, 255
Kennedy-Fraser, Marjory, 32, 152, 167, 190
Kennedy Scott, Charles, 144
Kershaw, Lees, 165
Kettlewell, Peggy (née Walsh), 29–30, 45, 148, 159
Kimber, William, 17, 19, 30, 170–1
King's Theatre festival, 144–5, 152, 156
Kingsbury, Martin, 236, 256
Kipling, Rudyard, 89
Kiver, Ernest, 8
Knuckles, Delie, 94, 100
Kodály, Sarolta, 244
Kodály, Zoltán, 236–7, 240, 244–5, 247
Korčula, 207–8, 244
Korian Terlicka, Tola, 221, 225
Kraus, Egon, 254
Kunst, Jaap, 239

Lakefield, Ontario, 172–4
Lambeth Palace, 200, 208
Langstaff, Esther and Meredith, 225
Laval University, 241
Leslie, Shane, 118
Lewin, Olive, 253
Library of Congress, 227
Lincoln, Massachusetts, 57, 62, 113, 129, 131, 151, 227
Liszt, Franz, 123
Liverpool, 61, 70, 131, 151, 236, 256
Lock, John, 219
London Chamber Orchestra, 160
London University, 160
Longman, Margaret, 144
Loveless, Rev. Kenneth, 257
Lowestoft, 4–5, 8, 184
Lucas, Perceval, 29, 41, 81, 83, 130
Ludgrove School, 41, 43–4, 118
Lund, Engel, 195, 212, 216

MacDonald, Ramsay, 158, 199
McInnes, Campbell, 195
Maisky, M., 201, 204
Mansfield House Settlement, 11–12, 20, 28, 30, 32
Marcel-Dubois, Claudie, 208, 224, 253

Marlborough House School, 183
Marson, Rev. Charles, 198, 209, 240
Masque of Caliban, The, 74–5
Maud, Sir John, 222, 229
Maurice, Mary, 222
Meir, Golda, 244
Memorial College (University), Newfoundland, 175, 179, 248–9
Mendelssohn, Felix, 50–1
Menges Quartet, 216
Menuhin, Yehudi, 236
Mercury training ship, 28
Milkina, Nina, 212
Minehead, 32, 161, 197–8, 234, 241
Minnich, Dr, 148–50
Mitchell family, 125
Montreux, 148–9, 255
morris dances, 23–5, 133, 148, 164–6, 187, 226
    Sharp and, 17, 171
    women and, 23–4
Mount Holyoke College, 87
Mozart, Wolfgang Amadeus, 11
Mukle, May, 214

Nash, Virginia, 116
National Gallery concerts, 216
Neal, Mary, 14, 19
Nevinson, Evelyn (née Sharp), 151, 184, 186, 214, 217
Nevinson, Henry, 151, 161, 179, 184–6, 214, 217
New Oxford History of Music, 221
New Scala Theatre, 160
Newcastle-upon-Tyne, 149–50
Newfoundland, 98, 122–3, 127, 172, 175–9, 190–3, 248–9, 257
Nijinsky, Vaslav, 21
Nolan, Willie, 102
Novello & Co., 208–9

Oliver, Michael, 252
Oneida mountain school, 101
Oppé, Paul, 73, 150
Oppenheim, E. Phillips, 89
Oriana Madrigal Society, 144

Pace, Eliza, 106
Pachmann, Vladimir de, 8
Packhard, Dr, 77, 79, 81, 83, 94
Paderewski, Jan, 90
Padstow Hobby Horse, 32
Pamplona, 232
Parry, Hubert, 8

Paterson, A. J., 41
Paton, Dr, 175, 179
Peak of Otter, 123–4
Performing Right Society, 209
Perrey, Harry, 68–70
Pettit, Katharine, 102, 104–5
Pine Mountain School, 101–2, 104–5, 107, 142, 159, 226
Playfair, Nigel, 57
Playford, John, 23, 70, 148
Poel, William, 74
Porter, Richard, 166
Pospíšil, František, 187
Powell, Talithah, 95
Price, Walter, 213
Purcell, Henry, 238

Queen Mary Hall concerts, 212
Queen's Hall, 219

Rabold, Charles, 59, 61, 74, 77, 88, 90, 98, 108, 111, 131
Raff, Joseph, 7–8
Raglan, Lord, 161
Raphael, Henry Lewis, 1
Raphael, Sir Herbert, 12
Raphael, Rosalie, 13
Rauter, Ferdinand, 195, 212, 214, 216
Rea, Sir Walter, 167
Reading, Lady, 118
Red Cross, 219, 254
Reed, W. H., 8
Refugee Musicians' Committee, 212
Rennel, Lord, 199
Rhodes, Willard and Lillie, 241, 247, 250, 252–3
Roberts, Lily, *see* Conant, Lily
Robertson, Alec, 252
Rosé, Arnold, 212–14
Rostal, Max, 212
Royal Albert Hall, 160, 165–6, 200
Royal College of Music, 151
Royden, Maud, 158
Royton morris dance, 165
Rumney, Violet, 234
Ruskin, John, 9
Russell Sage Foundation, 62, 104, 108

St Denis, Ruth, 21
St Paul's Cathedral, 213–14
St Paul's Girls' School, 153, 161
Schofield, Jane, 153, 161, 167
Schofield, Kenworthy, 153, 155
Scottish Country Dance Society, 199

Scovill, Peggy, 108, 113, 123, 131
Seaga, Edward, 252
Second World War, 212–20
Seeger, Charles, 226–7
Shakespeare, William
    As You Like It, 142
    A Midsummer Night's Dream, 50–1, 56–7, 59
    Twelfth Night, 30
    The Winter's Tale, 50, 74
Shalom, Mordecai, 244
Shap moors, 156
Sharp, Cecil
    and aesthetic dancing, 21, 98
    anti-American sentiments, 109–12
    appearance, 15
    awarded honorary degree, 145
    his biography, 193–5
    Civil List pension, 45
    his death, 150–2
    domestic arrangements, 43–5, 48–9
    early career, 15–28
    and education, 138
    English Folk-Song: Some Conclusions, 251–2
    and formation of EFDS, 25, 29–32, 34–43
    friendliness and charm, 15, 79–80
    friendship with Etherington, 33–4
    health, 45, 62–3, 83, 87, 91–2, 94–5, 97, 100–2, 104, 106–8, 119, 144–5, 148–50
    and international music, 187
    and Mary Neal, 19, 25
    meeting with Helen Storrow, 57
    meeting with MK, 14–15, 19–21, 43
    meeting with Olive Campbell, 62–3
    and morris dance, 17, 171
    and post-war EFDS activities, 136–50
    and theatre productions, 50–1, 56–9
    vegetarianism, 48, 68, 82, 107, 133
    in USA (1914–15), 56–68
    in USA (1916), 72–88
    in USA (1917–18), 88–131
Sharp, Charles, 43, 54, 85, 87–8, 133
Sharp, Constance, 43–4, 61, 72–3, 111, 129, 151, 156
    and Charles's injury, 85, 87–8
    and cooking, 48, 133
    health, 70, 148
Sharp, Dorothea, 43, 45, 133
Sharp, Evelyn, *see* Nevinson, Evelyn
Sharp, Joan, 25, 43, 70, 74, 133, 156
Sharp, Susannah, 25, 43, 133, 156, 165
Shaw, George Bernard, 13, 160
    Androcles and the Lion, 56–7
    The Doctor's Dilemma, 56

Mrs Warren's Profession, 113
Shaw, Martin, 151
Shelton, Mrs Donald, *see* Hensley, Emma
Short, Mary Ann, 102
Shuldham-Shaw, Patrick, 167, 223, 234, 251
Shuldham-Shaw, Winifred ('Holly'), 152, 166–7, 173, 183, 223
Sinclair, Marjorie, 153
singing games, 25, 167
Skopje, 206
Sloan family, 92, 100
Slocombe, Marie, 230, 233, 239–40
Smith, Professor Alphonso, 84–5
Smith, Charles, 164–5
Somervell, Sir Arthur, 139, 158, 161
Spanish flu, 127, 129
square dancing, 229
Stanford, C.V., 238
steam heating, 57, 111, 136
Sterling Mackinlay, Jean, 160, 167
Stern, Uncle Julius and Aunt Gonni, 10, 12
Stevenson, Robert Louis, 89
Stewart, Jean, 216, 257
Storey family, 91
Storrow, Helen, 59, 62, 68, 75, 90, 98, 108, 113, 129, 131
    and Appalachian collecting, 71, 76–7, 99–100
    and EFDS memorial fund, 159–60, 166, 175, 183, 227
    first meeting with Sharp, 57
    and MK's return visits, 159, 174–5, 227
Story, G. M., 248
Stratford-upon-Avon, 211
    EFDS schools, 25–30, 34–43, 51, 68, 70, 131, 136–9, 142
    Shakespeare Festival, 13–15, 20, 61
Strauss, Richard, 11
Strindberg, August, 98
Sullivan, Michael, 174
Susskind, Walter, 212

Terry, Ellen, 10
Thorndike, Sybil,1 58
Three Choirs Festivals, 8, 211
Tiddy, Reginald, 41, 56, 71, 83, 130
Tombs, Aunt Maria, 118
Tomlinson, Ernest, 213
Tracey, Hugh, 236, 238
Trefusis, Lady Mary, 143, 145, 152–3, 155, 166, 171, 183
Twelve Traditional Country Dances, 166

UNESCO, 222–4

University of Minnesota, 112
University of Virginia, 84–5
Upton-upon-Severn morris dance, 164

Vachell, H. A., 89
van Boschan, Jane, 216, 230, 256
van Wyck, Arnold, 216
Vassar College, 175, 178
Vaughan Williams, Adeline, 121, 138
Vaughan Williams, Ralph, 25, 151, 172, 184, 221, 247, 252
    Bunyan settings, 257
    and Cecil Sharp House, 167, 183
    his death, 238, 240
    and EFDS, 29, 42, 152–3, 155, 158, 160–1
    and IFMC, 223–4, 229–30
    and international music, 187
    and Kodály, 236–7
    marriage, 232
    meeting with Ursula, 210–11
    and MK's dancing, 23
    and Newfoundland songs, 190, 193
    and Raff's *Cavatina*, 7–8
    and refugees, 212–13
    6th Symphony, 230
    and *Twelve Traditional Country Dances*, 166
    war service, 54, 71, 83, 111
Vaughan Williams, Ursula (Ursula Wood), 213–16, 219, 222, 232, 240, 245, 251
    friendship with MK, 210–11, 255–6

Victoria, Queen, 199

Wachsmann, Klaus, 253–4
Wagner, Richard, 11, 216
Wagner, Winifred, 216
Wallis, Roger and Hazel, 240
Walter, Arnold, 213
Washington Irving High School, 109
Weingartner, Felix, 11
Wellesley College, 61–2
Wells, Evelyn, 102, 142, 226, 235
Wells, H. G., 13
Wheeler, Laurel, 114
White, Henry, 116
Wick, Jean, 58
Wilberforce, Archdeacon, 13
Wilkinson, George, 41, 71, 83
Wilkinson, Norman, 30, 50
Williamson, Stanley, 252
Wilson, Steuart, 30, 160–1, 195, 221, 223, 229, 245
Wilson, President Woodrow, 127
Withypool, 198, 210, 217, 219, 241
Women's Land Army, 73
Wood, Michael, 210, 216
Wood, Ursula, *see* Vaughan Williams, Ursula
Wright, Claude, 41

Yankovitch sisters, 205
York, 132–3, 142
Yugoslavia, 205–8, 224, 227–8